Researching in the Class

The Anglophone world is gripped by a moral panic centred on child abuse in general and fear of the paedophile in particular. Evidence suggests an alarming rise in the number of false allegations of sexual abuse being made against teachers, and demonstrates that the fallout from being falsely accused is far-reaching and sometimes tragic. Many people in this position cannot sustain family relationships, have breakdowns and are often unable to return to the classroom when their ordeal is over.

Researching Sex and Lies in the Classroom draws on in-depth qualitative research exploring the experiences and perceptions of, and the consequences for, those who have been falsely accused of sexual misconduct with pupils, and for the family members, friends and colleagues affected by or involved in the accusation process. The book also highlights the dilemmas and difficulties the authors themselves have faced researching this field, such as:

- ethical and methodological concerns over whether or not the teachers had indeed been falsely accused, or were guilty and taking advantage of this project to construct an alternative, innocent identity;
- the difficulty of obtaining institutional ethical clearance to undertake and publish research that challenges master narratives concerning children and their protection;
- the reluctance of funders to support research in controversial and sensitive areas.

Researching Sex and Lies in the Classroom reveals findings that are both informative and shocking. It interrogates the appropriateness of current investigative and judicial procedures and practices, and it raises general questions about the surveillance and control of research and academic voice. It will be of great benefit to academics and researchers interested in this field, as well as postgraduate students, teachers and other professionals working with the fear of allegations of abuse.

Pat Sikes is Professor of Qualitative Inquiry in the School of Education at the University of Sheffield.

Heather Piper is a Professorial Research Fellow in the Education and Social Research Institute at Manchester Metropolitan University.

Contents

Acknowledgements

We want to thank all those people who spoke with and helped us in the course of our research. We are particularly grateful to the teachers, their family members, friends and colleagues who, for us and in the service of our project, shared current difficult and painful experiences or revisited the acuity of past times. The effects of being accused of sexual misconduct never entirely go away. Many people have a constant reminder in that their day-to-day life is quite other from what it would have been: they may be in a different or no job; their relationships may have broken down or be unequivocally altered; their health, physical, mental and emotional, may have been damaged. It is important that this is recognised.

The members and executive of F.A.C.T. have been extremely supportive to us. We recognise the risk we take in thanking them publicly since, as we will explain within the text, having any contact with that organisation was said to be compromising. We, and F.A.C.T., know that it wasn't.

We received critical feedback from a number of colleagues, friends and members of our families who read numerous drafts and gave constructive advice. Thank you Lesley Atkinson-Baldwin, Yvonne Downs, Jennifer Lavia, John Piper, Robyn and Joby Sikes-Sheard, Mark Vicars.

Abbreviations

CRB	Criminal Records Bureau
ESRC	Economic and Social Research Council
F.A.C.T.	Falsely Accused Carers and Teachers
FASO	False Allegations Support Organisation
IRB	Independent Review Board
IRSC	Investigation and Referral Support Co-ordinator
LEA	Local Education Authority
PAFAA	People Against False Accusations of Abuse
POVA	Protection Of Vulnerable Adults
SOFAP	Support Organisation for Falsely Accused People

Foreword

Judge Judy is an American court TV show that has consistently received the highest rating of its genre since it first aired in 1996. It features Judith Sheindlin, a brassy, no-nonsense, incisive jurist who doesn't suffer fools gladly. Close to 30 years' prior experience in family court, not to mention parenting and grandparenting, has given her keen insight into human nature and made her an astute judge of character. When adolescents are involved as defendants, she commonly quips to parents, 'How do you know when a teenager is lying?' A pregnant pause follows while said parents who apparently don't watch the show much puzzle over her singular ability to differentiate truth from falsehood; then she continues drily, 'When their lips are moving.'

I thought of *Judge Judy* while reading Pat Sikes' and Heather Piper's accounts of teachers accused of sexual misconduct and wondered where the disconnect occurs between her understanding – children lie; indeed, it is their nature to do so – and the children-as-innocent master narrative that Sikes and Piper critique – that children do not lie about abuse. It is acceptable to doubt a student's excuse for not getting her homework done or to applaud her fanciful rendering of her encounter with Santa Claus. That is, unless either story contains a hint of something sexual; then we better alert the authorities because nowadays the litigable net has broadened: individual school personnel, not just school districts as a whole, can be sued for deliberate indifference regarding abuse as a result of the Supreme Court's ruling on Fitzgerald versus Barnstable (see Gatto, 2009). So what is it about sexuality that has Anglophone societies in such a state of panic, and – the corollary – why are we so attached to the notion that children are innocent and asexual? Sikes and Piper theorize it brilliantly: we are living in a moment that is a perfect storm for pedophilic paranoia. First, they follow Beck's (1992) characterization of the pre- and post-millennial years as a 'risk society,' one in which the central sentiment is 'I am afraid!' Then they provide an explanation and historical overview of how moral panics form and function to set the context for the contemporary moral panic around child abuse and pedophilia.

I thought of *Judge Judy* again while reading the concluding chapter of this book when Sikes and Piper suggest that allegations of misconduct might be better handled through a process akin to that which occurs in family court until the need for a full criminal prosecution is confirmed. It does seem to me that such a venue would be less combative and traumatic for all involved, and so I hope that people who are in a position to make changes to the travesty of natural justice that characterized the cases in this book will pay attention. But they, like Sikes and Piper, will have to be brave to propose a counter-narrative to the current one in play, which necessarily demonizes teachers through holding childhood innocence sacrosanct.

The element of a moral panic's development that resonated with me most strongly was the coalescence of the media and politics in inciting public fear. I have a personal story that is more along the lines of the swine flu panic in that it lacks a moral dimension or 'folk devil' component – though arguably, as in the mad cow disease panic, farmers became the scapegoats. In the summer of 1973, a chemical company in Michigan accidentally mixed several thousand pounds of polybrominated biphenyl (PBB), a fire retardant, into the feed supply serving farms in the area. My family's dairy farm, then operated by my parents Blaine and Adela Johnson, was contaminated as a result. Although my dad knew something was up with the feed because the cows were apathetic about eating it, he initially attributed it to a possible mold in the grain, as the previous harvest had been a pretty wet one. He accordingly changed feed companies, but the damage had already been done; after the source of the problem had been discovered several months later, tests showed our farm to be among the highest levels of contamination in the state at 22 parts per million. Nobody knew what the health effects on humans consuming milk or meat might be, so a statewide panic ensued in which all animals on farms containing trace amounts of the chemical – initially 1 ppm, later reduced to 0.3 ppm – were slaughtered, regardless of whether the animals themselves were contaminated. The media fanned the flames by airing footage of dying animals, and indeed, during the time of contamination we did have some sick cows – but that was because they weren't eating the feed, not because the PBB was killing them.

Contaminated farms such as ours who were forced to slaughter their animals were compensated for their loss, which then led to opportunistic co-optation from farmers whose contamination levels were lower than the 0.3 ppm limit. One such farmer, a neighbour of ours, approached my dad for a sample of our quarantined milk that he could then pass off as his own so that he, too, could cash in on the tragedy. When he was unsuccessful, he joined others in claiming all manner of herd and personal health problems and found lawyers who were delighted to litigate on their behalf. In the subsequent Senate hearings (here is where politics enters the arena), Dad tried to be a voice of reason in his testimony, calling these complaints into question;

he and I had been biopsied to test our levels, and we were among the highest in the state at 338 and 619 ppm respectively (our levels were higher than other family members because Dad drinks a lot of milk and I was a toddler at the time. PBB is stored in fat, so once it's ingested via the fat in milk, it stays in the body). If anyone was going to be sickened by PPB contamination, surely it would be us; had we had the misfortune to be one of our cows, we'd have been slaughtered 1,000 times over. But we were healthy – and continue to be, although when journalists periodically interview us at anniversaries, they're not interested in hearing it. Once, after several hours of taping my family, the only sound byte that made it into the final copy was Dad's joking response to whether the family had suffered any health problems: 'Well, our daughter Tara has PBB hair.' That's what they called my bed-head from wild sleeping. But the perpetrators of panic provide something for people to blame their problems on, and logic interferes with their narrative. I'm thinking of the story Dad tells of a woman, carrying an obviously ill child in her arms, who came up to him after his testimony at a Senate hearing and screamed, 'Murderer! Look what you've done to my daughter!'

This all-too-human tendency to capitalize on calamity – we see it, too, in looting after natural disasters – is one element that Sikes and Piper do not directly address in this book, but I do think it is a factor in some misconduct cases. Recently Mother Jones commentator Kevin Drum (2009) critiqued a Los Angeles Times article in which Jason Song (2009) deplored the L.A. Unified School District's apparent failure to follow up on complaints of sexual abuse once police or prosecutors dropped criminal actions, 'leaving students vulnerable to molesters.' But Drum troubles several of Song's assumptions (e.g., that allegations should follow teachers even if they're cleared of wrongdoing), not to mention his bad writing, and invites readers to respond. Several responses mirror Sikes and Piper's concerns; I'll note a couple of them here:

- 'Kids, particularly teens, are very savvy. They know they can lie about a teacher and get the teacher in trouble. I have seen girls lie about a male teacher touching or flirting or just looking at them "weird" only to later recant and say they were trying to get out of being in trouble or get even with the teacher for getting them in trouble.'
- 'What are the levels of acceptable negative outcomes in cases like these? … I am certain that we as a society could lower the incidents of molestation (by whatever definition) by employing more assertive pre-employment (and continuous) background checks and increased supervision, but at what intellectual, civil liberties, and economic costs?'

Sikes and Piper would also likely criticize Song's belief that LAUSD should have continued to pursue charges that had been dropped by authorities because, as they note in this book, the criminal justice system has more resources and trained personnel at their disposal to investigate such matters than schools do. Additionally, the 'where there's smoke there's fire' mantra that figures so prominently in their study appears, expressed in Song's article by the district's superintendent: 'If there's smoke there, then we should err on the side of the security and safety of students.' I heard this same sentiment recently at an AERA session in which the possibility that teachers might be wrongfully accused – that children might lie – was dismissed as such a rare occurrence that it was worth the occasional sacrifice in order to stamp out what was characterized as rampant misconduct. But this pervasive and unquestioned narrative of children-as-innocent affects real people, as Sikes and Piper's data chapters masterfully illustrate. Not just the accused teachers, but their families and colleagues – and yes, even the children. Teresa, the teenage narrator in Chapter 9, fits the first response to Drum's article above, except she didn't recant her story. She will forever be known now as either a liar or a victim – a label that will likely have consequences at the very least in her relationships with future teachers.

The part of the *Times* article that brought the PBB incident to mind was the financial figures associated with three of the five cases mentioned: The families of the victims sued the district and settled for $1.6 million, $90,000, and $1.2 million. I'm not saying that victims of abuse are not entitled to some form of compensation; however, given that the majority of sexual abuse is perpetrated by family members, friends, or neighbours (Wachter & Lee, 2009), these particular victims were dubiously fortunate that their attacker was one of the relative few who work at school, thus giving them access to the district's (or rather, the insurer's) deep pockets. Educator sexual misconduct is good business for lawyers, and so I think there is also a financial dimension to the current moral panic that makes me doubt it'll subside as long as it is lucrative as well as morally satisfying to point pedophilic fingers at accused teachers.

A final thought on PBB, research and this book: the other day I received a newsletter from The Michigan Department of Community Health, who, in cooperation with Emory University in Atlanta, has conducted ongoing studies of people contaminated by PBB and their children. As I read the colourless vignettes about whether and to what extent girls menstruated earlier or if children born to contaminated mothers had higher or lower birth weights (two studies had conflicting reports), the only one that piqued my interest was one demonstrating no increased risk of death – that 'in fact, deaths due to cancer and other chronic diseases are lower than expected.' This struck me partly because it suggests a counter-narrative to that which operates in the medical field – that PBB must be carcinogenic – but mostly because I know there is a story behind these data, one that disappears when qualitative research isn't brought to bear on an investigation. Here is where Sikes and

Piper shine: they use their data to tell a story, achieving a degree of verisimilitude that makes their participants live and breathe. I am mindful of the careful ethical considerations that were a part of the decision making about this book's execution and I am looking forward to implementing it in my classes – both my teacher education students, who (particularly the men) are fearful of the very kind of situations portrayed here, and my graduate students, who are hungry for exemplary nontraditional representations of data. Pat and Heather, thank you for a job well done.

Tara Star Johnson, Ph.D.
Purdue University
West Lafayette, Indiana, USA

Chapter 1

Why we have done this research and written this book

A cautionary and introductory tale

It was late in the evening, around 11, when Rebecca[1] rang. From her first words and by the catch in her voice it was patently clear that something was very wrong. She hadn't got far into her 'how are you alls' and 'sorry to be phoning at this time' before she burst into tears and the reason why she was ringing began to spill out. The long and the short of it was that the mother of a four-year-old boy in her reception class had apparently alleged that Rebecca had behaved in a sexually inappropriate way with the youngster. The situation was complicated because the mother had no English and ever since her son had joined the school, she'd been making repeated complaints, via her husband, about how other members of staff and also classmates treated and interacted with the boy.

Immediately after the allegation was reported to the head, Rebecca had been sent home, told not to talk to any of her colleagues and advised to contact her professional association. Having done this and when she'd given her account, the union rep had told her not to worry and that he was sure that it would all, eventually, be sorted out. In what was obviously an attempt to ease her mind he'd also remarked there were currently approximately 25 cases of alleged teacher abuse going on within the region he was responsible for and that 'this sort of thing was par for the course these days'.

Early the following afternoon Rebecca was informed that she could go back to school in the morning. The head told her that the nursery nurse and the three teaching assistants who worked with her in the same classroom had all attested that she'd never ever even been alone with the boy in question, had definitely not been seen to do what had been suggested, and that, after further enquiry, it had also transpired that there'd been a mix-up in translation and that the mother hadn't meant what she'd initially been reported to have said.

Background

What happened to Rebecca serves as a salutary introduction to this book. Here, our primary concern is with the perceptions and experiences of male teachers (and of members of their families, their friends and colleagues) who have been accused of sexual misconduct with female students which they say they did not commit and of which they have eventually been cleared or the case has been dismissed due to insufficient evidence. However, that Rebecca, a young woman who worked in the foundation stage, could also find herself in a comparable sort of position, highlights the way in which being accused of sexual abuse can happen to any teacher who may then experience similar consequences in terms of distress and anxiety with regard to the fact that they have had an allegation made against them, albeit one which is later found to be false or unproven.

It does seem to be the case that, as Rebecca's union representative noted, allegations against teachers are not unusual these days and that, furthermore, the incidence of false accusations is rising (Lepkowska *et al.*, 2003; NASUWT, 2003; Myers *et al.*, 2005; Revell, 2007). Within the UK, figures compiled by the NASUWT (Williams, 2004), show that, while in 1991, 44 such allegations were made against their members, in 2003 there were 183.

In a move which seems to acknowledge a growing problem, a network of Investigation and Referral Support Co-ordinators (IRSCs) was formed in 2001 to help Local Education Authorities (LEAs), police and social services deal with allegations of child abuse by teachers, school staff and carers. IRSC data on 1,629 allegations recorded by 122 LEAs between September 2003 and August 2004 showed that 30 per cent concerned sexual abuse and inappropriate behaviour, the majority being made against men (DfES,[2] 2004a, 1.8. and 1.9).

We became interested in investigating teachers' perceptions and experiences of having allegations of sexual misconduct made against them as a result both of hearing a number of stories concerning individuals so accused and because of our previous, respective work on topics which linked teachers and sex. Thus: Pat had investigated consensual sexual relationships between male teachers and female students over the legal age of consent (see Sikes, 2006a and 2008), while Heather had researched the problematics of touch between professionals – teachers and carers – and children of all ages (see Piper and Smith, 2003; Piper *et al.*, 2005; Piper and Stronach, 2008). Our reading around the area had made us aware that teachers in other countries were also becoming increasingly fearful of being accused of sexual abuse (see for example, Jones, 2001, 2004; Shakeshaft, 2004; Cavanagh, 2007; Johnson, 2008a) and that this fear was negatively affecting pedagogy and recruitment (particularly of men) to the profession (e.g. Skelton, 2003; Mills *et al.*, 2004; Murray, 2009; Simpson, 2009). However, it was the stories that we heard about the accused men that really led to our decision to look into this issue further because it did seem that they and their families were often going through horrendous, and even *Kafkaesque*, experiences which did not end even when there was found to be no substance to the allegations.

The official line is that 'fortunately, cases of malicious allegations or false allegations that are wholly invented are very rare' (DfES, 2004b, 2.9). However such confidence fails to match the reality that, at the time when this assertion was first made, a professional association, the NASUWT, recorded that fewer than four per cent of cases of alleged (physical and sexual) abuse involving 1,907 of their members over 'recent years' had resulted in a conviction (NASUWT, 2004). While these figures do not necessarily mean that 96 per cent of allegations were untrue they do reveal something of the scope and nature of the problem. More recent, but less precisely dated, figures suggest a similar rate of proven guilt. Thus, 'over the last few years there have been 2,316 allegations against NASUWT members alone. Of the 2,231 [*cases which have been*] concluded, in a staggering 2,116 either no grounds were discovered for prosecution or the allegation was not proven at court' (NASUWT, 2009).

This is a complex area, and while findings from our research lead us to question the DfES view that 'almost invariably there is a real incident or event that is the basis for an allegation', we can agree that 'in many cases the allegation is based on different perceptions of an incident by different people, or a misunderstanding, or misrepresentation, or exaggeration' (DfES, 2004a, 2.9). (Of course, our work only allows us to speak about allegations of a sexual nature. The situation may be different with respect to reports of physical abuse.)

Clearly, understandings, perceptions, meanings and definitions are of prime importance. In an attempt to provide an 'objective' baseline the IRSC explained:

> Words such as false, unfounded, unsubstantiated and malicious are often used in the same context when describing an allegation. The meanings are very different and it is important for staff to understand the distinction between them and use them correctly. The term false can be broken down into two categories:
>
> * <u>Malicious</u> This implies a deliberate act to deceive. A malicious allegation may be made by a pupil following an altercation with a teacher or a parent who is in dispute with a school. For an allegation to be classified as malicious, it will be necessary to have evidence, which proves this intention.
> * <u>Unfounded</u> This indicates that the person making the allegation misinterpreted the incident or was mistaken about what they saw. Alternatively they may not have been aware of all the circumstances. For an allegation to be classified as unfounded, it will be necessary to have evidence to disprove the allegation (. . .)
>
> An unsubstantiated allegation is not the same as a false allegation. It simply means that there is insufficient identifiable evidence to prove or disprove the allegation. The term, therefore, does not imply guilt or innocence.
>
> (DfES, 2004b: 7–8)

Regardless of all this definitional gymnastics though, as successive Secretaries of State for Education have said (in remarkably similar words),

> once the allegations have been made, whether they are true or not, a life may be ruined.
>
> (Estelle Morris, 2001, quoted in Revell, 2007: 20)

> I am very much aware of the devastating effect that false or unfounded, allegations can have on a teacher's health, family and career.
>
> (Charles Clark, Secretary of State for Education quoted in DfES, 2004c)

> I am very much aware of the devastating effect that being wrongly or unfairly accused can have on an individual, their family and their career.
>
> (Ruth Kelly, 2006, quoted in Revell, 2007: 22)

Indeed the fallout is far-reaching and sometimes tragic. Many facing false allegations cannot sustain family relationships, have breakdowns, and cannot return to the classroom when their ordeal is over. Suicide, too, is not unheard of (NASUWT, 2004; Teacher Support Network, 2008). Statistics show that a 'significant number of people resign after an allegation is made against them' regardless of the veracity of the accusation (DfES, 2004a, 2.11). Careers and lives are ruined, and experienced professionals are lost.

Procedures for dealing with allegations are, to a considerable extent, to blame for these consequences. A major problem has been that investigations have tended to be protracted, stretching out over months and even, in some instances, taking longer than a year (see Hansard, 2009 for a case which took nearly four years). Thus, Rebecca's 24 hours really does make her experience the exception. This time-lag issue is recognised both by teachers' associations which have campaigned for swifter, more effective, efficient and equitable investigations and by the Secretary of State for Education who stated that:

> The length of time it takes to investigate an allegation and the surrounding publicity can make its impact so much more severe. I am committed to tackling those issues, rapidly, fairly and consistently to better protect teachers from false allegations while at the same time continuing to maintain effective protection for children.
>
> (Charles Clark, Secretary of State for Education quoted in DfES, 2004c)

Unfortunately, attempts to speed up the process as described in DfES guidelines (DfES, 2004a, 2004b, 2004c) and which came into force in 2005 have not worked as effectively as was hoped. Although they may have sometimes led to events progressing at a faster pace, there is concern that this has been at the cost of thorough investigation leading to greater risk of miscarriages of injustice (Revell, 2007: 7).

Suspension of teachers against whom an allegation has been made is another seriously problematic area, partly because both the assessment of the risk of the person remaining in school and the decision to suspend are the responsibility of each individual headteacher and school's governing body (DfES, 2004c: 3). Research undertaken for a *BBC Radio 5 live* programme revealed how variable practice can be. Thus, over the five years between 2003 and 2008, national suspensions of teachers rose by 86 per cent from 168 to 314. However, whilst one local authority suspended 40 teachers in the period, in another authority there were no suspensions whatsoever (Donald MacIntyre Show, 14/9/08). Although alternatives, such as swopping classes or assignment to a non-contact task, are often possible, it seems that frequently, once an allegation has been made, teachers are suspended. Some will only learn that they have been accused as they are escorted from the premises having been forbidden to return until the matter is resolved. Even though, according to the guidelines, 'in employee relations terms, suspension is deemed a neutral act' (DfES, 2004c: 2), that 'is in itself not a disciplinary measure' (Myers *et al.*, 2005: 95), the rhetoric does not usually match the perceptions or experiences of anyone who is in any way involved (and in fact the notion of neutrality of suspension is now contentious following a challenge in the Court of Appeal[3]).

The fact that allegations have been made often produces a presumption of guilt and 'once reported, the staff involved are forbidden to discuss the case with anyone' (Myers *et al.*, 2005: 117). It is not surprising that 'whether the person is guilty or not, suspension is always traumatic, even life changing' (Myers *et al.*, 2005: 94). As Barry Sheerman, Chair (in 2009) of the Commons Select Committee for Children, Schools and Families said on a *File on 4* programme, 'you cannot suspend a teacher without damaging their career' (File on Four, 2009). Indeed you can't and furthermore, it is well recognised that the anxiety caused by suspension is such that 'frequently [*investigatory*] proceedings will be interrupted by the stress and ill health of the teacher concerned', and 'capability procedures relating to ill health may, in some circumstances, supersede the disciplinary process' (Myers, *et al.*, 2005: 99).

Then there is the whole issue of anonymity. Once again teachers' associations have been active (but at the time of writing, unsuccessful) in campaigning for a change to the current situation whereby the names of teachers against whom allegations have been made can be revealed to the media whilst investigations are still underway and before any judgement is passed. This practice can be particularly damaging to the families and friends of the teachers and, apart from the psychological and emotional harm it can cause, it also puts people at risk of physical attack from the 'vigilantes' who take it upon themselves to punish those they believe to be paedophiles.[4]

Of course, children do need to be protected and this means that when they make an allegation of abuse they must be listened to seriously and investigations have to be undertaken. This is not at issue. However it does seem that the practices, policies and procedures around child protection that we currently have in the UK do put innocent teachers at serious risk of being publicly identified as suspected, if not actual, abusers. For instance, the introduction of the Independent Safeguarding Authority's *Vetting and Barring Scheme* (see Independent Safeguarding Authority, 2009) in October 2009, makes it a duty to share information about any accusations, proven or not.[5] To return to Rebecca's case, this means that in any reference for a job at another school, her headteacher would be required to mention the discounted and dismissed allegation made against her. The old adages that 'mud sticks' and that 'there's no smoke without fire' are, we would suggest, particularly pertinent and persistent when it comes to accusations of child abuse.

In 2005 in a measured and reasonable manner which provides a clear contrast to some of the hysterical pronouncements that are made on the topic, Kathleen Marshall, the Scottish Commissioner for Children, said,

> We have lost our innocence about the abuse of children by those who are supposed to care for them. We cannot reclaim that. However there is currently panic and paranoia about child abuse. We need to move through that to a state of wisdom, in which we accept the realities of child abuse, but acknowledge that we cannot completely stop it. We must develop the maturity to create a system that gives children the maximum possible protection while supporting loving and caring relationships and an environment that encourages healthy development.
>
> In order to do this we must take steps to reduce unreasonable and disproportionate fear in innocent adults and we must, after listening to children, take steps to shape our systems in a way that they can trust not to harm them even more.
>
> (Marshall, 2005)

Our aim here is to give some insight into what the consequences of this panic and paranoia can be like for those innocent adults, however many or few of them there really are, who are falsely accused and whose fears have proven to be neither unreasonable nor disproportionate. To date, and for understandable reasons which we will be exploring later, these people's voices have rarely been heard outside of newspaper reports which may, in themselves, have contributed to upping the ante and increasing the fears. We believe that it is important to examine critically the current system of child protection and to acknowledge that serious injustices have been done. Hearing people's stories is an important step on the way towards greater equity. Our research and this book are a beginning.

How the book is organised

In putting the book together we have followed a relatively traditional research report format, setting the scene and discussing the context for our investigation, then describing our research experiences and approaches before presenting and discussing our data. Thus, Chapter 2, *Immoral panics*, focuses on the contemporary moral panic around child abuse and paedophilia, which we consider to be at least partly responsible for the growing number of false allegations against teachers and other professionals working with children and young people. Here, we outline what is entailed in the idea of a moral panic, particularly within the context of the sort of 'risk society' that currently seems to prevail. After establishing this background we elaborate some examples of child abuse panics to help provide a backdrop to our overall thesis. In addition we consider underpinning notions of childhood innocence and vulnerability, and the consequent professional child protection frameworks, including the Children Act (HM Government, 1989). Finally we consider the idea that, given this context, an increase in false accusations could perhaps have been anticipated, and suggest that a move towards a less risk averse and more considered professional practice would be beneficial for all.

In Chapter 3, *'A courageous proposal, but . . . this would be a high risk study': ethics review procedures, risk and censorship*, we consider the problems we encountered in getting our research off the ground. Thus we describe our attempts to gain ethical clearance for our project; our failure to obtain funding; and our experience of censorship of our writing about these difficulties. We believe that the evidence suggests that these problems had more to do with the way in which our research raised questions around what Sheila Cavanagh calls the 'master narrative of childhood sexual abuse' (2007: 9) which asserts that children are sexually innocent and do not lie about abuse, than with the strength and soundness of our proposals. Our account raises questions around the role of ethics review procedures and the scope and extent of academic freedom as well as discussing the emotional and professional impact our experiences had upon us as individuals, academics and researchers.

In Chapter 4, *Truths and stories*, we talk about the methodology, methods and style of re-presentation that we decided to use and the dilemmas that our choices entailed. Given that we were interested in knowing how accusations of sexual abuse were perceived and experienced by everybody touched by them, we opted for an auto/biographical (Stanley, 1992) life history, narrative approach. This approach raised questions about potentially giving voice to people who actually were guilty of what they had been accused of and who were using the chance to participate in our research as an opportunity to create a story and identity of innocence. Protection of informants assumes particular significance given the nature of our enquiry and so we also talk about our chosen strategy of creating composite, fictionalised stories for reporting and re-presenting our findings. Chapters 5, 6, 7, 8 and 9 contain those stories under the titles of *Confused, angry and actually betrayed: It was time to get out*; *Timpson versus Regina*; *How do you tell teenage children their father's been accused of sexual assault?*; *It didn't take long for the rumour mill to start grinding*; and *Nobody can prove anything for definite*. Chapter 10 concludes the book with a discussion and summing up.

As is always the case, we have had to leave out at least as much as we have included but we stand by our decisions and selections on the grounds that our intention was, primarily, to give an evocative, evidence-based impression of what it can be like when a male teacher is accused of sexually assaulting a female student. This time round we chose not to investigate female teacher, male pupil, or lesbian or gay abuse allegations or, for that matter, incidents of cyber accusations, where pupils use internet sites or texting. However, in the course of our research we did come across these sorts of cases and we anticipate that, in the future, we may well turn our attention to them.

We expect that the primary audience for this book will be academics and postgraduate students interested both in aspects of teachers' lives and careers and in issues associated with research in this field. As we also deal with problems faced by researchers attempting to investigate sensitive and difficult areas and topics, we think that we have something to say to the wider social science community too. Finally though, and given that all teachers potentially face allegations, we see the stories we have to tell as being relevant to those on initial and in-service teacher education courses, as well as to teachers and other professionals working with the fear of such allegation. We hope that these readers do not ever have cause to identify too closely with the people who took part in our research and who so generously shared their stories with us.

Finally: the whole area of child protection is one that seems to be continually being updated (as a glance at the Safeguarding Children section of the Every Child Matters website will confirm). What we have written is current at the time of going to press. We cannot vouch for accuracy in the future.

Chapter 2

Immoral panics

Moral panics

In our opinion there does seem to be a contemporary moral panic around child abuse and paedophilia which is at least partly to blame for a rise in unproven accusations against teachers and other professionals working with children and young people. Others (e.g. Furedi, 1994) have suggested that moral panics tend to occur during times of rapid social change, when society is not able to adapt to dramatic upheaval and when many are experiencing a loss of control. From this, we could perhaps anticipate a rapid increase in the propensity for moral panic in the current uncertain economic times. Moral panics have traditionally been understood to be a pattern of mass behaviour based on the false or exaggerated perception that some cultural behaviour or group of people (frequently a minority group or subculture) is dangerously deviant, or is considered to constitute some form of menace to society.

Historically the media has tended to be blamed for fuelling moral panics, directly as a side effect of the way in which they cover social issues, whereas more recently it has been suggested that others should carry some of this responsibility. While mass hysteria shares some characteristics, moral panics are distinct and are identifiable in that they are specifically framed in terms of *morality*: the witch-hunts in Europe and North America of the fifteenth, sixteenth and seventeenth centuries are a prime example of the phenomenon. Moral panics often revolve around issues of sex or violence and are frequently accompanied by some widely circulated folklore or legend. The term was coined in 1972 by Stanley Cohen when he described the effects of the media coverage of the Mods and Rockers in the UK during the 1960s (although Michael Young used the words a little earlier in 1971 in relation to drug takers). However, it has been claimed that the classic Middletown Studies in the US in 1925 (Lynd and Lynd, 1929; 1937) contained the first in-depth study of such a phenomenon. Whatever the origin of the term and the idea, it would appear that every generation has the potential to generate and experience unfounded bouts of moral panic.

In his seminal exposition, Cohen (1972) wrote that moral panics need a number of actors in order to reach their potential: the *media* who over-report, distort, and create false stories that result in news coverage that follows a stereotypical pattern; the *public* who then react; *law enforcement agencies* that must be seen to be doing something, as these situations demand new remedies; and *politicians* and *legislators* who are additionally required to suggest possible solutions. Meanwhile the creation of *folk devils* or deviants (i.e. those whose actions are considered harmful to society), along with the development of a *disaster mentality*, ensures the consolidation of the panic via predictions of impending doom, overreaction, rumour and mass delusion. Cohen's analysis has been extended by others who suggest that a number of indicators are also required to confirm when a moral panic is in play: *concern,* which must be at a heightened level; *hostility* towards those involved in the behaviour; substantial *consensus* that the threat exists; and a *disproportionality and volatility* in relation to the problem that is posed, usually via exaggerations of the 'claim makers' (Goode and Ben-Yehuda, 1994). More recently, counterbalancing action groups have been generated in response to particular moral panics, who in turn seek to use the media and other means to cope with any identified new threat (McRobbie, 1995: 199). A key such group in this respect for those accused of abuse is F.A.C.T. (Falsely Accused Carers and Teachers).

Academic debate around moral panics is rather like feminist studies, in that a number of 'waves' can be identified. Cohen, writing in the early 1970s, is clearly identifiable with the first wave, along with the contributions of Hall and Jefferson (1976), and Hall *et al.* (1978), for example. The second wave can be identified in the early to mid 1990s as part of the response to the satanic abuse panic and other child abuse panics (see later), and includes writers such as Ann Bradley (1994) and Frank Furedi (1994). More recently writers have begun discussing moral panics alongside or in opposition to the idea of the 'risk society' (Beck, 1992) and as such can perhaps be identified as the third wave.[1] Sheldon Ungar (2001) for example has pointed out that moral panics don't always need a folk devil, as suggested by Cohen. Thus the panic around swine flu is an example of a moral panic lacking an identified or personified folk devil, and the short-lived bird flu panic operated in the same way (although such medical panics lack the particular moral dimension and so might be excluded from any 'purist' definition). Sean Hier (2003) draws on a range of writers so as to forecast a proliferation of moral panics as exaggerated symptoms of a heightened sense of uncertainty in risk society – which can end up with people being afraid but not even sure what they are afraid of, perhaps providing substance to the inaugural injunction of Franklin D. Roosevelt (and picked up by Barack Obama) that 'the only thing we have to fear is fear itself' (1933).

Previous references to 'risk society' (and from here on inverted commas are dispensed with) should be elaborated at this stage, as ideas concerning risk society are easily conflated with discussions of moral panic. In social science, contributions by such as Anthony Giddens (1991) and Ulrich Beck (1992) have fixed the status of risk society as an unavoidable and significant analytic concept during the years on either side of the millennium. However, the social trend was also identified by the critic and commentator Susan Sontag in the late 1980s in discussing responses to the spread of HIV/AIDS. She noted the widespread 'sense of cultural distress or failure', encouraging 'fantasies of doom'; a modern social pessimism premised not on 'Apocalypse Now', but 'Apocalypse from Now On'; creating a perpetual state of fear which could only damage 'our sense of reality, our humanity' (cited in Feldman and Marks, 2005: xxvii). The prevalence of risk-based discourse in contemporary society and governmental practice has diverse ramifications. It involves 'the effort to exterminate ambivalence . . . and . . . to define precisely – and to suppress or eliminate – everything that could not or would not be precisely defined' (Bauman, 1991: 7, 8), as well as the assumption or illusion that life's contingencies are susceptible to human calculation and control in order to avoid risk (Giddens, 1991). This characteristic represents a significant social change, as Beck illustrates:

> The driving force in the class society can be summarised in the phrase *'I am hungry!'* The . . . risk society . . . is expressed in the statement: *'I am afraid!'* The commonality of anxiety takes the place of the commonality of need. The . . . risk society marks . . . a social epoch in which solidarity from anxiety arises and becomes a political force.
>
> (Beck, 1992: 49)

In this situation, the role of authorities and government is less about shaping and imposing the moral order, and more about avoiding risk and passing on the hot potato of blame (Ungar, 2001: 276), and 'public trust is the ultimate victim' (ibid: 284). In such circumstances, the idea that a proliferation of moral panics is a symptom of the exaggerated sense of uncertainty in risk society appears reasonable enough (Hier, 2003).

For all this concern, it could perhaps be argued that the term 'moral panic' has been overused and, through incorporation into everyday parlance, has lost some of its theoretical and rhetorical impact. We are also reminded that: 'there is no [single] moral panic "theory" as such, proponents can be identified with many theoretical positions' [broadly speaking: Cohen with symbolic interactionism, Hall with Marxism, and McRobbie with a more poststructural stance]. 'The moral panic is a sociological phenomenon, an analytical concept much like stratification, interaction, deviance . . . Among students of the moral panic, there are advocates of a diversity of "theories" . . .' (Goode, 2000: 551).

However analysed, current moral panics appear to have characteristics that were less obviously evident in earlier ones. For example, recent moral panics would seem to have been fuelled as much by professionals as by the media, and consequently appear more significant and operationally focused in their impact. In addition earlier panics tended to result in quite different responses from the lay public and the professionals; crudely put, a panic about 'yobs' could result in angry residents demanding punishment, and youth workers initiating outward bound weekends. Nowadays though, it is more likely to be the professionals who are deemed to be in need of punishment: and their colleagues who are the ones demanding this. Contemporary moral panics also have a tendency to cluster or 'stick' to other panics sharing overarching concerns, which makes it much more difficult to identify them at an early stage or to argue against them coherently. The 'paedophile panic' (arguably enshrined with the Sex Offenders Register in 1997), and 'child killer' panic (Bradley, 1994) fit all too easily alongside the satanic panic and panics around claimed geographic clusters of high density child sexual abuse (exemplified in the UK by the Cleveland affair – see below) of an earlier era, and arguably to the broader panic around child abuse which forms the backdrop to this book.

We now spend a little time revisiting and describing earlier panics in order to give readers an informed sense of the ways in which, in the grip of panic, events can spiral and escalate and individuals can come to be demonised and scapegoated. The panics we discuss all involve children, although not all have a sexual component.

Satanic panic

> It is this institutionalised suspicion that means the apparently irrational satanic ritual abuse panic can be explained, and also that it has never completely disappeared. It is still important to challenge the myth wherever it flares up, but more than that to question the more mainstream misanthropy that feeds it.
>
> (Cummings, 2006)

The idea of a highly organised cult of satanists intent on the sexual abuse and murder of children originally appeared in the United States in the early 1980s.[2] The satanic panic was based on the belief that children were being subjected to ritualised sexual abuse.[3] Child sexual abuse had become an obvious candidate for contemporary moral panics, being defined not merely as a social ill, but as evil. Social workers, therapists and other professionals appear to have helped fuel the satanic panic, the source of which was a particular nursery in California. A mother, described as both religious and mentally disturbed, decided (apparently with no real evidence) that her two-year-old son had been anally abused at his nursery. Her anxieties were infectious and soon other parents echoed her concerns. Children were taken to counsellors who elicited 'disclosures' and in a short time it was claimed that the school was providing cover for a sex ring. At a similar time a psychiatrist – Lawrence Pazder – published a book with a female patient (who later became his wife) which tells the story of her life and her abuse by a satanic cult that was reported to have occurred earlier in her life (Pazder and Smith, 1980).[4] It is claimed the book particularly appealed to some therapists and social workers who accepted the idea of repressed memories and who gradually coalesced their anxieties around cults and sexual abuse, and notions of large-scale abuse of children. The story of the nursery was reported in newspapers and on television, which eventually led to a reporter bringing in the 'expert' – Pazder – to investigate. He claimed that the accused nursery worker was central to an international satanic conspiracy and the satanic panic was launched. It is important to note that the nursery worker was later cleared of all accusations; in other words the accusations were formally and authoritatively deemed to be false (see Victor, 1993 for detail).

As the waves from this heavily reported case washed across Western societies, some professionals accepted quite easily that an organised network of satanists was engaged in brainwashing and abusing victims. Others who dealt with such cases in a professional context judged it wise to downplay Satan's role, but nevertheless still thought it possible that networks of ritualised abuse were commonplace. Such beliefs, although perhaps now appearing quite bizarre (involving sharks and dragons that kill children, drinking of human blood, babies being stabbed in a balloon and cooked in an oven etc.) were accepted by many at the time, and their effects were not benign. They led to social workers on both sides of the Atlantic taking relatively large numbers of children 'into care' (or to be 'looked after' according to the current UK euphemism). In-service training courses sensitised workers to the newly identified risks and alerted them to the warning signs that they needed to watch out for. The first (but for the most part unreported) allegation and investigation in the UK was in Congleton in Cheshire (1987), rapidly followed by widely and sensationally publicised cases in Broxtowe in Nottingham, and Middleton in Rochdale (1987–88).

An investigation on BBC TV (2006) of the Rochdale case served to remind us of the phenomena. The case began when a young boy was referred to the local Social Services Department for apparently hiding under tables while at school. It was claimed on the programme that the social worker who had been allocated to the family in order to investigate the situation had read about the satanic panic and found the case satisfied the 'promiscuous indicators of abuse' (Cummings, 2006) which included a fascination with urine and faeces, a fear of ghosts, and a preference for not being left with babysitters. Following a sequence of events which bear comparison with those surrounding the nursery in California, 12 children were subsequently taken from their homes. The BBC reporters, through access to the tapes of contemporaneous interviews with the children, demonstrated how those children were led and encouraged to talk about 'ghosts'. One of the children who was denying that anything untoward had occurred is heard saying: 'why don't you listen to us like it says on the [NSPCC] posters?' Professor Elizabeth Newson was brought in as an expert witness and she noted how 'there was an unhealthy excitement about it, which we also saw in Cleveland [see below] . . . they had begun to believe that they were expert', adding later that 'the social workers were adding to the children's powerlessness' (Midgely, 2006). Yet such sentiments carried little weight and within a relatively short space of time many groups of social workers and other professionals (cases in 80–90 areas were reported and investigated across the UK) were convinced that children were victims of a conspiracy involving members of the establishment including Freemasons and some of the police officers who were supposed to be carrying out these investigations. In retrospect it is perhaps not surprising that the term moral panic has been applied to this phenomenon. As with the initial case in the US, many experts were brought in, most supported the claims, and the media reported the phenomenon. Stories were accepted at the time by those keen to believe them (read Nathan and Snedeker, 1995 for a detailed account), in spite of there being in most cases 'no bodies, no bones, no bloodstains, nothing' (Waterhouse, 1990).

The Cleveland affair

At a similar time the panic in Cleveland, focusing on diagnosed anal abuse, was taking place, based on the belief by some that many children were victims. Children at a local hospital were subjected to a test which attempted to identify 'anal dilation' which, it was claimed, only happened in sexually abused children. Why the children were at the hospital in the first place is not clear. Campbell (1988), for example, has stated they were already the focus of suspicion. The tests were instigated by Doctors Higgs and Wyatt, following a paper written by Doctors Hobbs and Wynne, which had appeared in *The Lancet* (1986). While this scandal was dissimilar in some ways to the satanic panic, especially in the way it remained confined to just one area in the UK (Cleveland), it nevertheless mapped onto other concerns related to children at that time. The prevailing discourse took for granted that children were being abused in their thousands and it appears to be no accident that it occurred at a similar historical moment. Again an expert was required to endorse the situation and on this occasion the anthropologist Jean La Fontaine provided this service (La Fontaine, 1994). Following an investigation she supported the claims and concluded that more than a hundred children had been anally abused, adding that 'children do not often make false allegations of sexual abuse'. We return to this point elsewhere in the book as these sentiments reappear and have been reiterated and have arguably led directly to the professional truism or working hypothesis or mantra that 'children never lie about abuse'. However, while La Fontaine accepted many of the claims in the Cleveland example, elsewhere (1998) she made it clear that she distanced herself from the satanic claims. Rather, she considered the satanic stories were usually elicited by therapists eager to hear more. Why she was convinced by one scenario rather than another is not clear, although the fact that the Cleveland cases were backed by the high level *medical* 'expertise' of clinicians, rather than *social* 'expertise', may have been influential.

Campbell (1988) also wrote sympathetically in support of social workers and paediatricians making diagnoses of anal abuse and it has been suggested that, in a Channel 4 *Dispatches* programme, she promoted the myth 'more enthusiastically than any American evangelist group or salacious tabloid' (Cummings, 2006). Campbell reported doctors as being 'confident of the diagnosis because it was affirmed in the *only* available academic research' (1988: 44), in other words the paper by Doctors Wynne and Hobbs, which it could be claimed prompted the panic in the first place. These allegations once voiced were 'generally impossible to refute', reported Lewis (1987), quoting a judge involved in the enquiry.

Eventually both the relatively isolated anal abuse scandal in Cleveland and the 80–90 satanic or ritual abuse scandals proliferating across the UK died away; few today consider them to have the credibility they were once granted, and as far as we are aware the anal dilation test has been abandoned as a determining indicator of sexual abuse. This is of course not to undermine or ignore the fact, which we recognise fully, that some children are abused, that some elements of abuse in some cases are ritualistic, and that in some of the cases discussed here a small number of children remained in care for perfectly good reasons, as a result of appropriate professional intervention.

Although the anal and satanic panics appear to have begun and ended in a relatively short period of time they involved a significant amount of hostility within and between particular professional groups, and were not without casualties. The Nottingham case for example initially resulted in praise for the efforts of the police and social workers from the media, local councillors, and even the Prime Minister, following initial prosecutions. However, relationships soured when the police set up their own investigation and reported they did not consider satanic abuse or witchcraft to be occurring. In response, the local Social Services Department claimed the police did not have sufficient knowledge of this type of abuse, and were not prepared to acquire it. More than 20 years later, a number of children are beginning to speak out about their experiences, claiming that the only abuse perpetrated on them was solely the responsibility of the agencies. In some cases they had been removed and cut off from their families (usually during what came to be referred to as 'dawn raids' where social workers and police would arrive in the early hours of the morning, and physically remove children from their beds), in some cases for up to ten years (BBC 1, 2006).

Baby P

Twenty years on, significant changes can be identified: various pieces of legislation have intervened (e.g. HM Government's The Children Act, 1989, *Every*

Child Matters, 2003; and *Working Together to Safeguard Children,* 2006); the imperatives of children's rights and children's voice have gained prominence and, although the same moral panic around child abuse can still be identified, the pendulum has swung in the opposite direction. Social workers and other professionals who may once have been involved in over-interventionist practices resulting in the kind of situations described above (and in some cases influenced by budgetary and/or staffing constraints), are now responding to the tenet that children are best left with their natural families in all but the most severe of circumstances. Obviously such generalisations risk simplification and stereotyping, and we stress that it is the *trend* that we are keen to identify here, rather than specific individuals (beyond those particularly implicated).

In late 2008 and early 2009, the UK saw considerable excited and judgemental media coverage of what has come to be referred to as the 'Baby P' case (see Butler, 2009 for a more reasoned account). While this case involved the appalling death of a young child in the care of his natural mother and two men who periodically lived with her (one her boyfriend), and claimed public imagination in much of the media the baby's death was considered to be the fault of social workers (with health workers following up behind), resulting in a media and political campaign to remove the Head of Children's Services from her post in Haringey, the London Borough where the child lived. The same borough had also been the focus of similar attention following the high profile death of a little girl, Victoria Climbié, in 2000: the subsequent enquiry was primarily responsible for the introduction of the *Every Child Matters* legislation in 2003.

A consideration of the 'Baby P' case is informative in relation to the moral panic which surrounds child abuse. Unlike the satanic abuse panic described above, where professionals were involved in 'dawn raids' etc., in this case professionals (social workers, police, clinicians) waited too long, appeared to do or were perceived to have done very little, and were subsequently blamed for the death of the child. Apart from the obvious 'damned if they do and damned if they don't' attacks on social workers and other professionals who are involved in difficult decision making, this case demonstrates the role of many others without whom the panic could not have been sustained, and it helps explain how one single case can take on a life of its own and in turn determine the public perception of many others.

In brief, Baby P (who was named as Peter, many months on) died on 3rd August 2007, but little was heard of him, or known about him at that time. He had been visited by social workers, seen by a range of health care professionals, and had even been taken to a doctor one or two days before he died, but the doctor missed the fact that he had broken ribs and most likely a broken spine, and reportedly failed to examine him properly because he was 'miserable and cranky'. He died soon afterwards following another blow which knocked out a tooth that was later found in his stomach. Post-mortem investigation provided evidence of many other abuses. However, the case only became high profile around November 2008, more than a year after his death, when the various adults involved in directly caring for the young boy were found guilty of allowing his death (although his mother had pleaded guilty a little earlier). The prosecution was unable to prove 'murder', and the names of his mother and her boyfriend initially remained *sub judice*, presumably because there were other children in the family whose identity was being protected. Such secrecy undoubtedly contributed to the events which followed.

Very quickly the case became party political, with David Cameron, leader of the Conservative Party, attacking what he described as a 'raft of excuses' by Gordon Brown the Labour Prime Minister. With urgency, the Secretary of State, Ed Balls, ordered an independent enquiry and many national and local newspapers were leading with inflammatory headlines. *The Sun* newspaper began a campaign against the head of Haringey Children's Services (e.g. 'Blood on their Hands' – *The Sun,* and 'Baby P Chief at Ascot' – *London Evening Standard* – this headline was accompanied by a picture of Sharon Shoesmith, the Head of Haringey Children's Services, at Ascot horse races a few weeks after the child had died). This campaign continued with pictures of Baby P appearing in *The Sun* newspaper on 15th November ('Beautiful Baby P: Campaign For Justice'), soon to be accompanied by a dossier of the numerous contacts made by health and social workers and a catalogue of his many injuries (e.g. 'The Damning Baby P Dossier' – *Daily Mail*). By the 26th November *The Sun's* campaign had attracted more than a million signatures 'demanding justice' as well as the sacking of Sharon Shoesmith: 'the smug Haringey director of children's services [who] must be fired'. By 1st December, Ed Balls ordered the removal of Sharon Shoesmith ('Baby P Victory: At last after 26 days and 1.4m voices, council boss Shoesmith axed' – *The Sun*) and on 8th December she lost her job, approximately one month since the start of the press involvement and 16 months after Baby P's death. (Ms Shoesmith was unsuccessful in an appeal against dismissal another month on, but at the time of writing it is understood that further legal action is to follow.) During the spring of 2009, four more social workers from Haringey were sacked, having had direct or line-management responsibility for Baby P. Later, the various health trusts admitted failings (hard to plead otherwise when their staff saw the child on more than 30 occasions), and disciplinary enquiries began in relation to the doctors concerned. But the relative calm and anonymity of these procedures, with professionals who actually met and held the child, are in stark contrast with the experience of Sharon Shoesmith, who never did.

A couple of months following her dismissal, Sharon Shoesmith was interviewed by *The Guardian* newspaper and some extracts are included here because of the similarities to the experiences of many teachers accused of abusing their pupils. Sharon Shoesmith first heard of Baby P when her deputy informed her that he had died: 'but when you get a child who's died is "known" to us, is on our "at risk" register [actually this term is historic as it was renamed the 'child protection' register some time following the implementation of *The Children Act*] that's the biggest horror that could have been . . .' (Edemariam, 2009: 4). She decided not to resign even though friends suggested she should, because 'that was the weakest thing I could do' (*ibid*: 4). After outlining a number of factual inaccuracies or points of clarification in regard to the case and how it was reported, she commented that it is impossible for someone in her position to claim that it wouldn't happen again, as 'you can't stop people who are determined to kill their children' (*ibid*: 6). She emphasised that 'none of the agencies involved with the family are responsible for the death. Those responsible for this tragedy have been prosecuted' (*ibid*: 6). She also reminded the readers that in the UK a child dies at the hands of their parents every ten days, and that if you 'sack every director of every children's service where there is a child death, you're going to turn them over at the rate of a third a year' (*ibid*: 6), and clearly this would be an unrealistic proposition.

Whatever the calculus of responsibility and blame that should be applied to Baby P's case, some features are indicative of how such cases are played out in risk society. During the campaign by *The Sun* newspaper, Sharon Shoesmith's 89-year-old mother was informed by reporters that her daughter was responsible for the death of a child, which obviously caused her considerable distress; Sharon Shoesmith and her youngest daughter received death threats which led her daughter to move out of London; her emails and voice messages included many calling her a child killer; one man apparently rang her at 5 a.m. every morning with different suggestions of how she could kill herself; and police officers advised her to avoid taking the Tube as it would be easy for someone to push her off the edge of a platform. Such events led her to consider suicide, but fortunately she had a supportive family and her daughters moved in and supervised her day and night. In early 2009 she was without a job, had no redundancy pay, no savings or a pension, and was being financially supported (as well as emotionally) by friends and family. Meanwhile, similar to the aftermath of the Victoria Climbié case (apparently referred to as the Climbié bulge), there was an anecdotal increase across the country in the number of children being taken into care. Haringey saw many social workers leave the borough which further increased the workloads of those remaining. The numbers registering on social work courses nationwide reportedly reduced, potentially therefore having a negative effect on the future protection of vulnerable children.

Reflections

Through the Baby P case, the cost, both personal and professional, of 'failing' to prevent child abuse has been demonstrated in a highly visible way, but the substantive conditions in which such work takes place arguably worsen.

In such an environment it is unsurprising if teachers, social workers, care staff and their managers tend to operate in a self-protective way, in order to be able to show that at all times they have followed rules and procedures designed to prevent or avoid abuse. Informal contacts with middle and very senior managers in social work elicit the suggestion that a primary component in a long and successful career is luck. That is, the luck not to find oneself in a position where there is formal (even distant and indirect) responsibility for a situation in which a child has been seriously harmed, or a child dies. Like being involved in a car crash, such events can come out of the blue yet have the capacity to change careers, not to mention lives, taking on a momentum of their own in the glare of media attention. All the scenarios discussed above occurred over the last 20 years, and examples are also evident in other anglophone societies where similar concerns and processes can be identified. For all this commitment and energy and the apparent concern with child abuse, the consequent attempt to make all places that are occupied by children 'risk-free' appears not to be working, and many negative unintended consequences may be noted. Our interest here is to query what the cases and context discussed previously tell us about society's attitudes to children and to child abuse more generally. In order to do this we ask three questions, which we do not answer in a definitive way, but which we hope help to provide some context for the rest of the book.

How do we think about children?

As Catherine Scott (2006)[5] has argued, the image of an abused child, which has recently come to be almost universally understood to be a sexually abused child, is an integral element of the iconography of our society today. Estimates of the actual occurrence of child abuse vary from one in four to one in ten, for instance (Gilbert et al., 2009). A substantial network of statutory agencies and high profile charities exists to detect and prevent abuse by an apparent army of paedophiles, and in most anglophone countries anyone who works with children in a paid or voluntary capacity is required to obtain police clearance – in the UK these are referred to as CRB checks (Criminal Record Bureau checks). Although it does not extend to simply being a parent, or an aunt or uncle, the scope of this requirement is defined in a very inclusive way, and as a result it has been possible for commentators to query its logic and effectiveness. 'According to the Government, the total number of potentially dangerous perverts and other 'unsuitable individuals' in need of vetting is up to 9.5 million people . . .' (Hume, 2006).

Various measures are also proposed to track and identify sex offenders, so that the communities in which they live know that they have a paedophile among them. Children are 'taught' at school to defend themselves against abuse, via 'educational' programmes, with messages such as: 'If it doesn't feel right, you can say no' (Scott, 2006). The belief in the existence of numerous sexual predators has shaped legislation and social attitudes, even to the extent of changing the attitudes of adults to their own motivation and probity, so that self-doubt and self-regulation becomes the norm (Piper and Smith, 2003). The apparent assumptions on which such mechanisms and approaches are based are hard to reconcile with the authoritative statement that 80 per cent of child abusers are biological parents (Van Hasselt and Hersen, 1999), and if we add step-parents to this figure, this leaves a relatively small percentage of abuse that can be attributed either to the 'stranger' or to professionals. A heightened awareness of abusive behaviour can easily switch into an operational *expectation* of abusive behaviour which, while appropriate in some critical situations, fails to address the hidden and domestic nature of most abuse, while actually placing at risk many who work with children. The key problem of how to balance the claims of 'children's rights', 'parent's rights' and, indeed, 'worker's rights' remains unresolved, except on a case by case basis, with damaging consequences for many.

The sexually abused child is presented as the ultimate innocent victim, and any contact between an adult and a child is perceived as a potential act of exploitation. The abused child and the abuser have become models of how persons now relate to each other. It could be inferred from the plot lines of much popular UK TV crime drama that child abuse or incest is involved in a very high proportion of the cases which the police investigate, apparently as common as burglary or assault. The paradox of the obsession with children as actual or potential victims of sexual predation is that they become sexualised in a way they previously were not. Endless public iterations of anxiety over the sexual harm supposedly inflicted on many minors, and the florid reporting of 'international rings' trading in child sexual pornography, have turned children into objects of forbidden sexual desire. The repeated pairing of the image of the child with the image of the sexual victim has made many adults anxious about their own feelings and impulses, how others will perceive their actions, and even whether their own children or those in their care will 'turn them in' for fictional offences. Repeated stories about children as objects of lust can create mental associations that set in train a whole range of fears and unease that would not otherwise have existed:

> I can feel though, with . . . my step daughter of 12, a definite hesitation and suspicion of myself that's very much an implanted awareness . . . Potentially more serious though is a feeling that this implanted awareness alerts any proclivity I have towards 'the taboo'; that it might awaken otherwise nonexistent desires. It feels like this awareness acts like a carrier of an 'infection' to abuse . . .
>
> (email correspondent cited in Piper *et al.*, 2006)

In this sexualised environment, only the naive or unobservant can continue to insist that children will never lie about sexual abuse. It is one thing to say this about three-year-olds, but entirely another to think it about a 14-year-old who watches UK television and reads teenage-oriented magazines featuring guides on 'position of the month'. The furore in the UK in February 2009 provoked by the birth of a child to parents aged 13 (in the case of the first mentioned putative dad) and 15, has again demonstrated the confused and contradictory public attitudes to youthful sexuality, and also that many members of the population do not live according to the rules (formal and otherwise) that are presented as defining what is right and normal. The dominant image of the child as victim can induce a blindness to the real level of awareness of many young people, and their ability to be an active agent in many situations, whether they fully understand them or not. This has significant consequences for teachers and other professionals.

What should we understand about professionals in their working environment?

Perhaps the first thing to note is that professionals, similar to parents, and members of government, cross boundaries and roles. Many professionals are parents, many parents are professionals and some are government ministers. As such, few are immune from society's fears, which permeate all our lives in different ways. In the case of the satanic abuse panic, professionals fiercely supported one another within their own professional group (e.g. most social workers stuck together, and at the time there were few critical voices) but often opposed those from a different group (e.g. the police). The scapegoats in this scenario were many of the parents, believed at worst to be in league with the devil and at best to be involved in ritualised or random abuse. In the Cleveland affair, within a very small part of UK society (essentially one particular hospital) most professionals (regardless of their group) stuck together, against the many attacks from the public, the media and politicians, as the enemy was perceived to be anyone who disputed the anal dilation test. Again, the scapegoats were the parents, although fortunately this case was fairly shortlived. With the Baby P case, beyond the trial and imprisonment of the three guilty adults, and with reporting restrictions in place, the scapegoat was Sharon Shoesmith, the Head of Children's Services, who as far as anyone was aware (and there was considerable delving by some reporters into her private life) had never personally harmed any child. Because of the legal requirements that kept the baby's name and that of his mother and her boyfriend secret, another person had to be found and blamed. The furore which was witnessed in Parliament, in the newspapers and elsewhere eventually resulted in her sacking by her employers in the hierarchy of the London Borough of Haringey (who were being leant on very strongly), who clearly would not have considered this action themselves, or else they would have taken it a year earlier. 'Society' feels it has a right to demand sackings (with or without supportive legislation) and professionals cannot rely on those with whom they work to protect them, or on normal notions of employee's rights, as justice is decided upon elsewhere.

It is relevant that the medical practitioner who failed to spot the fractured spine shortly before Baby P's death received far less publicity or abuse than the Children's Services manager who would not reasonably be expected to know the detail of every child protection case in a large borough, and had of course never seen the child in question. At the time of writing disciplinary action in respect of the doctor was ongoing through the slower and more discrete channels of the General Medical Council and, while her career was obviously likely to be seriously affected, it was not put under the same sort of harsh public gaze experienced by Sharon Shoesmith and many of the teachers and their families who we have had contact with. It appears that, while society is anxious about the parenting skills of some parents, for a professional, adopting the status of *in loco parentis* is a dangerous thing to do. A diversion at this stage is to wonder about the variability of the imperative to sack or resign when public servants fail or oversee failure might be interesting. Apparently an epidemic of fatal teenage stabbing in cities does not constitute grounds for sacking very senior police officers (even though one responsibility of the police is to keep public spaces safe and another is to protect lives). Similarly the near collapse of the financial system appears not to require the sacking of the Governor of the Bank of England or the Head of the Financial Services Authority (let alone their political Master). Beyond registering that these obvious imbalances are indicative of the particular assumptions and environment within which all those working with children and young people have to operate, we have no space in which to develop such issues further.

What might we learn about society and its responses to child abuse?

By 'society' we necessarily include everyone, but especially the government, policy makers, the media, colleagues, parents and the lay 'public' etc. The context of heightened awareness, confusion and panic around child abuse, and the patterns of response that result in the type of scenarios outlined above and described throughout the rest of this book, seem set to continue. Individuals and groups are caricatured; those in an 'out-group' (which can just mean a different profession) are 'othered', and rational responses are not always apparent from government ministers, our law courts, and in many of the formal enquiries that follow these high profile cases. All are affected by the high media profile that such cases attract. What makes a particular case high profile is also worthy of consideration in itself, but is again beyond the remit of this book.

However, we return to the idea that current practice does not protect children. We have argued this elsewhere (see Piper *et al.*, 2006, for example). As professionals (including ourselves) watch their own backs, and watch all other adults for some sign of deviation, and seek to find a scapegoat on which to project our anger, a situation is created that neither protects children nor the professionals who work closely with them. Cowburn and Dominelli (2001; see also Hatty, 2000) have argued this point and have demonstrated how the use of particular social constructions, such as those relating to the 'paedophile', do not serve community safety in ways that were intended. For example, they noted that describing some men (sic) in such negative terms merely serves to differentiate them from other men. Effectively this allows for the construction of two groups of men, the 'good' (the protectors) and the 'bad' (the predators). However, as they observe, those considered 'good' sometimes become vigilantes when 'protecting' the vulnerable (children and women). We might wonder about the motives of the man who reportedly rang Sharon Shoesmith every morning to tell her of different ways she could kill herself, and the many others who send her (and some of the teachers we refer to throughout) death threats, even though in many of these cases abuse has not been proved.

Finally it seems timely to wonder why it is that 'the same voices who are so keen to diagnose gaping wounds in society are often also the most given to attack the profession[s] that administer the social bandages' (*The Guardian*, 2009: 40). The contradictory and damaging discourses and moral panics that surround child abuse show no sign of abating. Professionals responsible for child protection will continue to be pilloried when their efforts and systems are unequal to the task of preventing others perpetrating abuse and causing harm or death. At the same time, while many adults are pointing the finger and seeking out scapegoats, a context has been created in which some young people (for a variety of reasons, as we discuss elsewhere) are able to make false allegations. In the long run this harms everyone involved, including the young people themselves, but also the adults who are falsely accused and who face both legal process and public humiliation.

In the foregoing discussion we have sought to delineate the characteristics of an environment in which teachers and other professionals working with children and young people are placed at risk. We have also developed some ideas about how this damaging environment has developed and how it can be interpreted and understood. However, such diagnosis does not in itself constitute a remedy, and in the meantime individual teachers will find themselves in extremely distressing and career changing situations. In the rest of the book we explore some of these, and also reflect on the task of researching in an area of such contestation and sensitivity.

Chapter 3

'A courageous proposal, but . . . this would be a high risk study': ethics review procedures, risk and censorship

Getting started – easier said than done

In our experience, very few research projects run through from conception to conclusion without any hiccups whatsoever. We weren't expecting an entirely smooth passage for our proposed work but the difficulties we encountered right from the start were such that there were times when it seemed highly unlikely that we would ever be able to even begin. In the first place, our initial application for ethical clearance was turned down and it took the best part of six months and three attempts to be given the go-ahead to proceed. Then, having spent a long time on preparing submissions, we failed to obtain funding from any of the various bodies we approached. Finally, we ran into trouble when, prior to its publication, a paper we had written about these experiences was felt to be problematic and we were encouraged and advised to make changes.

We have compelling evidence to suggest that all of the difficulties we have encountered are to do with the topic we were addressing rather than with the strength and soundness of our applications, proposals and writings. Thus, this chapter presents and discusses that evidence and focuses on our quest to do the research. We should note that another version of the following story appeared under the title of *'Risky Research or Researching Risk? The Real Role of Ethics Review'* (Sikes and Piper, 2008 in Satterthwaite *et al.*, 2008) and we present the account given here with the full agreement of the original editors and publisher. We believe that this is 'one of those times when the same content needs either to be presented in different ways or in different places in order to make it accessible to different audiences' (Sikes, 2009: 19) since, in this case, the tale we have to repeat constitutes an integral part of our story — and of this book.

Seeking ethical clearance OR Becoming ethical?

Our starting point

For reasons that will become clear, we feel that we need to state that we unequivocally take the line that, in accordance with universal and local and cultural notions of what constitutes right and proper relationships, research and researchers should not do any harm, or wrong others. We believe that research and researchers should seek to be respectful and fair and should promote the good. In other words, our unwavering position is that research and researchers should be ethical. Our view on what constitutes ethical research practice draws from deontological concerns with the duties and rights of researchers and research participants; from consequentialist concerns about the likely effects of being involved in, or in any way touched by, a particular research project; from virtue ethics where the concern is with advancing the general good; and from an awareness that different situations and cultural settings generate their own research related ethical questions and issues that demand unique and contextual answers and treatment.

Ethical research and ethical review committees

When we started our careers as educational researchers (back in the late 1970s and mid 1990s respectively) the research related literature that we were reading made little or no mention of research ethics and ethical practice. Concern with ethics seemed to be something that was more in the purview of psychological- and medical-related research. Indeed, on the jacket cover of Bob Burgess' 1989 edited collection, *The Ethics of Educational Research*, it says that

> much of the literature on social and educational research is concerned with the design, collection and analysis of research data. While many works focus on technical procedures, they avoid ethical questions about the conduct of social investigation. It is this gap in the literature that *The Ethics of Educational Research* is intended to fill.
>
> (1989, jacket cover)

Undoubtedly there was a gap and while we don't think the absence can be taken to mean that social and educational researchers were necessarily behaving unethically, it probably is fair to say that, notorious cases such as Laud Humphries' (1970) *Tearoom Trade* and Maurice Punch's (1986) account of his difficulties in publishing his research about Dartington Hall aside, the almost total silence about ethical issues and practices does beg some questions. And it's worth noting too that while there are now a number of publications dealing with ethics and the social sciences (e.g. Homan, 1991; Mertens and Ginsberg, 2008), the Burgess book is still one of the very few full length texts that deals exclusively with ethics and educational research (Simons and Usher, 2000 and Nind *et al.*, 2005 are exceptions).

It's probably fair to say that it was partly because of feminist researchers, such as Ann Oakley (see Oakley, 1981), raising questions about research relationships, and partly as a result of the growing awareness, sparked by postmodernism, of what multiple perspectives and different social realities

meant in practice for researchers, that the need for attention to ethics gradually began to be recognised as being as important as it is. At a time when, as
Maggie MacLure has put it, 'othering' is 'the pervasive concern in contemporary research' (2003: 3), how people are treated takes on a central position.

Professional organisations such as the British Educational Research
Association (BERA, 2004), the British Sociological Association (BSA,
2002) and the British Psychological Association (BPS, 2006) and their
counterparts in other countries have responded to this increased awareness
and all now have ethical codes and guidelines for their members to follow.
Similarly, in a move which Saville Kushner has described as a 'step change
in the politics of social research' (2006: 9), since 2006 the Economic and
Social Research Council (ESRC) has required its grant holders to abide by
its ethics framework (ESRC, 2005). BERA, the BSA and the ESRC are all,
obviously, keen to uphold standards and to protect the reputation of the
professions and disciplines that they represent and it seems that they no
longer consider it sufficient to trust simply to individual researchers' own
integrity. As Martyn Hammersley points out though, there is no evidence
to suggest that there is or has been 'substantial unethical behaviour
on the part of social scientists' that would justify such a lack of trust
(Hammersley, 2008: np).

A significant consequence of these philosophical and zeitgeist shifts in
thinking about people, power and social relationships is a greater propensity
to seek redress for injuries and this too has had an impact on the conceptuali-
sation and conduct of research. Scandals such as the *Tuskegee Study of Untreated
Syphilis in the Negro Male* (Jones, 1981: although see also Shweder, 2004) and
the *Alder Hey Organ Retention* case (Redfern, 2001) have played their part in
prompting universities to reconsider their approach to research ethics, partly
to protect themselves against litigation as well as out of a concern for good,
ethical practice. Therefore it's now usual for staff and students of universities
to have to seek ethical clearance and follow specific protocols for all research
involving human participants and/or their tissue. In many cases these clearance procedures and protocols do seem to be tailored to biomedical work and
this has caused social and educational researchers frustrations, if not down-
right difficulties (see Hammersley, 2008).

Some commentators (e.g. Lincoln, 2005; Canella and Lincoln, 2007;
Tierney and Blumberg Corwin, 2007 and Johnson, 2008b) have questioned
the role of ethical review bodies, suggesting that, sometimes, they work as
mechanisms of surveillance, control, discipline maintenance and censorship. It's argued that, rather than having the well-being of research
participants and researchers as their main aim, these bodies also work to
promote methodological conservatism and, in addition, prohibit investigation of what are deemed to be 'risky' topics and/or sites. Furthermore, what
Christine Halse and Anne Honey have described as an 'institutional
discourse of ethical research' has strongly influenced notions of 'what

ethical research is taken to be and how ethical researchers are configured' (2007: 336).

Ethical review committees (known as Institutional Review Boards [IRBs] in the USA) do appear to have taken on the role of ethical regulators and in so doing claim both considerable authority and 'the ability to determine what is and is not, would and would not be, ethical in any particular research project, and to make *better* judgments about this than the researcher(s) involved in the project being regulated' (Hammersley, 2008: np). In some cases, regulation of this kind does seem to be based on the assumption that 'the researcher is a moron' (Tierney and Blumberg Corwin, 2007: 396) who, left to her/his own devices, is likely to make wild and dangerous judgements (see Dawson, 1994). This positioning and scripting of the researcher, along with the technologisation, institutionalisation and formalisation of research ethics (Halse and Honey, 2007) which is inherent to the ethics review committee and IRB systems, can result in unethical practice as researchers adopt a strategic approach to filling in the required forms (Canella and Lincoln, 2007; Hammersley, 2008). But there are other problems too, such as the way in which receiving approval at the start of a project 'create(s) the illusion that ethical concerns have been addressed and that no further concern is necessary' (Canella and Lincoln, 2007: 327; see also Allen *et al.*, 2009). Following on from this are the dangers of a one size fits all type perception that fails to recognise that each research situation generates its own ethical questions and issues that demand unique and contextual answers (see Pring, 2000). Taking this point even further, formalised ethical review systems have been criticised for their lack of sensitivity to different cultural contexts and hence for their colonising potential (Tuhiwai Smith, 1999; Canella and Viruru, 2004; Allen *et al.*, 2009). And then there is the way in which ethics review committees generally, and informed consent forms in particular, could be used to absolve researchers of any responsibility for possible ill effects suffered by research participants (Fine *et al.*, 2000; Scott, 2003).

The point is that formalised ethical review procedures are not guarantors of ethical research and members of research committees are not always best placed to make decisions about any particular research project. Indeed, the procedures can work to the detriment of ethical practice: although our belief is that the vast majority of researchers are concerned to behave ethically. Ethical research committees can also curtail academic freedom and hinder, if not prevent, research into sensitive, difficult, controversial areas (see Redwood, 2008). In the more specific context of stories told under the heading of 'research', it seems to us that ethical review committees are playing an increasingly significant role in 'validating' the kinds of stories and accounts that are to be accorded some status as 'truths' (see Lincoln, 2005). Our own experiences, which we now share, are, we feel, an example of the problem.

Our experiences with ethics committees

In accordance with institutional requirements, before we began to approach anybody to be involved in our research we submitted the necessary ethical review applications. The forms that have to be filled in ask for information regarding the background to and basis for the project; its aims and objectives; methodology and methods; how participants are to be identified and contacted; what measures will be taken to ensure confidentiality of personal data; whether informed consent will be sought; if there is potential for any physical or psychological harm to participants; whether payment will be made, and if there are any issues relating to the safety of researchers.

Applicants usually receive a reply within ten days so when a fortnight had elapsed we began to wonder what was going on. Queries elicited vague comments about one or other of the three statutory reviewers being off sick or attending conferences and eventually a month went by before we received notification that our proposal had not been approved. It turned out that one reviewer, who we will (pseudonymously) call Sue, had, in effect, questioned the fundamental basis of our research by expressing the view that the vast majority of accusations made against teachers have at least some foundation in fact. This position is similar to that taken by the DfES who, as we noted in Chapter 1, assert that 'fortunately, cases of malicious allegations or false allegations that are wholly invented are very rare' (DfES, 2004b, 2.9). We were, of course, acutely aware of the difficulties around truth that our proposed research raised and had addressed this seriously problematic area in our application (and in the next chapter will discuss in some detail how we have dealt with it). However, since Sue didn't cite any research evidence to support the claim that false allegations are very rare (and nor do the DfES for that matter), we were left wondering how best we could proceed. After all, our project focused on perceptions and experiences of teachers who said such accusations had been made against them and who had, eventually, been exonerated or received a verdict that there was insufficient evidence to take the case further. What is more, and like the teachers' associations, we were saying that this is by no means a very rare state of affairs for a teacher to find themselves in. Sue's objections could be read as suggesting that we were addressing a non-existent and impossible (or inadmissible) phenomenon.

In Chapter 2 we described the way in which the idea that children always tell the truth about abuse appears to have emerged some 20 or more years ago in the UK and USA (and elsewhere), when a number of cases of ritual and/or satanic abuse came to trial. As we have indicated, most of these cases were eventually dismissed (Webster, 2005: 88–94). Over the years, the entirely proper notion that children who make an accusation must in the first instance be believed appears to have been rescripted as children never lie about abuse (see Chapter 2). Even the language of children making 'disclosures' could be seen as a form of words which presupposes the guilt of the person whose activities are the subject of the 'disclosure' (see Butler-Sloss, 1988). Unfortunately, generalisations that lump all children and young people together are almost inevitably bound to be problematic when applied to specific and actual examples of paedophilic accusation, although this is what has tended to have happened (see Kincaid, 1992 and 1998). For instance and as we have suggested, while it is highly unlikely that a four-year-old could describe sexual intercourse in detail if they had not experienced or observed it, the idea that a 15-year-old who is angry with one of their teachers is incapable of falsehood concerning sexual behaviour is far less plausible. It was the latter type of scenario that we were interested in but Sue was saying that the only valid argument for allowing us to continue with the research was for us to present a body of research evidence to categorically demonstrate that adolescents do make fallacious sexual allegations against their teachers. As far as we can find out, and not surprisingly given the difficulties undertaking it would involve, no such research exists.

Sue also found difficulty with our usage of quotation marks around the word 'false' in our project title which, at the time was *Guilty Until Proved Innocent? Teachers' perceptions and experience of 'false' accusations of sexual misconduct against pupils*. Her reservations were based on the grounds that any future publicity for, or publication of, our research which referred to 'false' allegations could be upsetting to any youngsters reading about the work who had made accusations resulting in convictions, and particularly distressing to those who had witnessed actual abusers being acquitted. As we explain in the next chapter we did eventually remove both the quotation marks and the word false, although our reasons for doing this were primarily founded in quite a different argument.

Sue made clear her commitment to taking an entirely child-centred approach in which the overriding and paramount concern always has to be with the welfare of 'the child' or 'the young person': with 'child' and 'young person' being in the abstract and general. While such a stance is in line with a literal interpretation of the Children Act (1989) it is contentious because it raises questions as to the paramountcy of other vulnerable groups (the elderly, severely disabled etc.), not to mention other members of society presumed to be less important in such an analysis. We consider people who have been falsely accused to belong to just such a vulnerable group who are, we believe, deserving of attention to their well-being. However, taking the paramountcy of the child view with regard to our project, meant that damage caused to anyone as a result of being falsely accused had to be regarded as secondary, if not irrelevant, in the light of any possible (and theoretical) distress to a (generalised) young person. Here it's worth pointing out that the primary purpose of the ethics review procedure that we were subject to is stated to be the protection of potential research participants (and researchers). In our case those participants were specific teachers who had been accused of sexual abuse, members of their families, their colleagues, and people associated with their schools. However, we were being taken to task for failing to protect unknown and, most significantly, hypothetical children who were to play no part in the research process. While we appreciate and accept the need to attempt to anticipate unforeseen consequences arising in the course of, or subsequently to, an actual project, we feel that it is quite another matter to have to try to predict future damage to people who are entirely unconnected to and uninvolved in, that research. Such forecasting and pre-empting of problems is, we would suggest, beyond the scope of most mortals. Also, seeking to obviate all possible risk could lead to a situation where only the most anodyne of projects would receive clearance. Thus, and for instance, research with any sort of social justice agenda would be likely to be prohibited because of the risks those with minimal social power might be exposed to as a result.

We have no doubt that Sue undertook her responsibilities as an ethics reviewer with seriousness and with the intention to be fair and just, both to potential informants and to us as fellow researchers. However, in our opinion and on the basis of the evidence available to us it seems that the way in which the procedure operates resulted in Sue adopting a regulatory role which cast her as a protector of the young and innocent, and her actions, if not her intentions, led us to the conclusion that she considered us as researchers to be at best naïve and at worst dangerous. In effect, she was positioning us as unethical, irresponsible researchers (Halse and Honey, 2007: 346). This impression was further strengthened by her negative comments relating to our plan to seek advice from F.A.C.T. – a national association for 'Falsely Accused Carers and Teachers' (of which, more in the next chapter). Apart from anything else, these comments, in our view, implied that we were considered likely to be overly influenced by the group and incapable of acting independently of them.

Sue concluded her feedback by describing how difficult she had found the task of commenting on a proposal that was so closely related to, and intimately bound up with, her work and with her strongly held beliefs, values and commitments and she speculated on whether or not this might constitute a conflict of interest. (And it is perhaps relevant to note here that, like Sue, one of us has a similar background in child protection work, and is experienced in interviewing abused children and their abusers.) Had this conflict been taken into account and had Sue withdrawn from the process at the start and another person been put in her place, we might well have been able to proceed with the research, as the other two reviewers had granted clearance. As it was though, our resubmission, which acknowledged Sue's concerns, also failed to satisfy a fresh batch of reviewers. However, this committee's concerns and demands were entirely different. Thus we were advised that: 'the [researchers] need to state clearly and in sufficient detail how confidentiality and/or anonymity will be protected' (although we believed we had done this and from their comments, the original reviewers did too); there was said to be a 'lack of detail regarding how informed consent will be obtained' (although this was clearly and unequivocally stated); and 'more detail is needed on what procedures will be followed to ensure that the researchers' personal safety won't be put at risk' (since we had outlined standard procedures about alerting family and colleagues about where we were going and when, we felt that this comment suggested the reviewer had decided that the teachers we would be speaking to definitely were sex offenders – and indiscriminate ones at that).

Our third submission, which was the same as the second albeit with sentences drawing the reviewers' attention specifically to the sections which they had said were absent, was successful and we were able to start contacting potential participants.

What happened to us does support the charge that ethics committees do regulate and prevent any research that could be described in any way as sensitive or, perhaps more importantly, as risky. The experiences we went through also suggest a degree of arbitrariness and subjectivity, which is in our view inevitable but is at the same time contrary to the rationale for a procedure that, it is claimed, seeks to ensure best ethical practice.

Our experiences with potential funders

In many respects the problems we faced in trying to obtain funding were very similar to those encountered with the ethics review process. We applied to three sources: the ESRC, a teachers' union, and a general research fund competitively available to staff in the institution where one of us works. On each occasion we were unsuccessful. Of course, it could simply be that our proposals were weak. However, the limited feedback we received together with our experiences around obtaining ethical clearance have led us to believe that it is not that simple and that our rejections are worthy of further consideration. We should note that we never expected that we would easily obtain financial support for our work because competition is always intensive and because our work was exclusively qualitative (see Lather, 2004; Sikes, 2006b on governmental and funding agencies' preferences for quantitative projects). Nevertheless, because the government had expressed concern about the rising incidence of false allegations (DfES, 2004d), and since the teachers' associations were actively seeking to find ways of protecting their members (e.g. NASUWT, 2004; Revell, 2007), we felt this was an area with funding potential.

Comments about our theoretical approach and proposed methodology and our capability to undertake the project were all positive and all reviewers agreed that this was an important area to investigate. One reviewer did raise questions about 'issues with reliability and validity with respect to the account elicited' and suggested that, 'it might be valuable to consider in what ways the analysis might be deficient should the accounts and perspectives of accusers themselves not be included in the study'. Another wrote, 'one area of concern is the limited consideration to be given to the motives of accusers, and the way in which they construct their accusations'. The suggestion here seems to be that we should have been seeking to establish 'truth', in a judicial sort of a way, and also that we ought to have interviewed children whose allegations were found to be false. While we had considered the possibility of doing this, we eventually decided against it because of the potential distress it could cause. In the light of Sue's anxieties lest some anonymous child be upset should they come across our work, this seems ironic. However, as we describe in the next chapter, we did eventually come into possession of some data concerning accusers' motivations which we have included in our analysis and in this book.

But returning to our failure to secure funding, we consider the following comments, each of which comes from a different, anonymous reviewer, to be particularly interesting and illuminating in the context of our earlier discussion about the regulation of research:

- The researchers should perhaps not underestimate the strength of likely negative media comment.
- This is seen as a courageous proposal, but . . . this would be a high risk study.
- This is a promising project but it does raise issues.
- . . . the researchers may find that they collude with both the university and the alleged abuser into keeping quiet about the issues raised by research such as this, or alternatively, they may not be able to control the media through a sympathetic journalist . . .

These reviewers were concerned about the difficulties associated with the area and what the media might make of it. So were we. Neither of us is a stranger to the sort of controversy that can be engendered by research linking school students, teachers and sex (see Sikes, 2006c and 2008) or to managing controversy resulting from research more broadly (Piper, 2003). Accordingly we had talked about how to address potential problems in our proposal. Indeed, one reviewer acknowledged this: 'The researchers are aware of the difficulties of dissemination in this sensitive area including possible media interpretations or "sensationalising". These are genuine concerns but they should not prevent research in this area.' However, this is exactly what they might have done had we not decided to go ahead without funding!

Censorship

Having taken the decision to do the research at our own expense and with ethical clearance and institutional permissions to proceed, we found ourselves in difficulties once again. This time our problems stemmed from a paper we had initially presented at the 2007 *Discourse, Power, Resistance* conference. The theme of this conference had been 'Talking Truth to Power' (DPR, 2007) and we had decided to tell the story of our problems around ethics review under the title of 'Not (yet) speaking Truth to Power: not (yet) researching "false" accusations of sexual abuse against school teachers' (Sikes and Piper, 2008).

After the conference, our paper was one of those selected to be included in the edited collection of the proceedings (Satterthwaite *et al.*, 2008), this time with the title 'Risky Research or Researching Risk? The Real Role of Ethics Review' (Sikes and Piper, 2008). A fortnight before the final version of the book was due to go to press and after it had been made available to a small number of people interested in the workings of ethics review committees, we were informed it had aroused some institutional disquiet. The concern focused on our recounting of the events and unease lest Sue be identifiable. Since we had taken steps to anonymise her and had tested this disguise out with a couple of colleagues who were unable to fathom out who she was, we were relatively confident that there wasn't a problem in this respect. Nevertheless, there then followed what we, and no doubt Sue and others involved, experienced as an extremely unpleasant and distressing period, the outcome of which was that we made a number of changes which were 'approved' and the piece was then put forward for publication. In a footnote to our chapter we wrote:

> The wording and detail of this and related sections is significantly different from the version that we originally wrote. Prior to the final submission of the text, we were put under extreme pressure (applied by individuals and institutional sources) to make radical changes which, in our view, softened our critique. The difficulties we experienced add further weight to the arguments we advance here – indeed they deserve to become a story in its own right.
>
> (Sikes and Piper, 2008: 63, note 2)

We have to note here that this is not an easy story to tell, not least because at the time it was hinted that litigation could be a possible outcome if we didn't make required amendments (and this chapter, too, is in line with them). We had no desire to gratuitously offend anyone but our interpretation was that we were being prevented from giving our account of our experiences because this version challenged the authority of the institutional review procedure and the hegemony of the view that children never lie. Like Carol Rambo (2007) who was ordered to withdraw an autoethnographic paper from the journal that had accepted it for publication, we were made vulnerable both in terms of our institutional positions and because, like her, we were told that the censorship was out of concern for our well-being: 'we were worried for you . . . We did it to protect you' (Rambo, 2007: 360). Thus we were, once again, put in the role of naïve researchers.

***

Tara Star Johnson (2008b) has written a narrative concerning her dealings with an Institutional Review Board (IRB) when she was seeking to investigate sexual relationships between female teachers and male pupils. She describes how, like us, she almost didn't get to do her research because of the concerns the committee members had about qualitative approaches and, more pertinent to our experience, because she was looking at children, teachers and sex. We believe that, as academics, we have a responsibility to act as public intellectuals (Goodson, 1997), and to raise difficult questions, to investigate areas that are sensitive and difficult, and to expose areas of injustice. Such a contribution appears to be increasingly problematic.

Chapter 4

Truths and stories

'But how will you know if they're telling the truth?'

We were never under any illusions about the various difficulties our research was likely to involve. For a start, sexual matters of any kind are notoriously tricky to investigate because people aren't always honest or comfortable talking about what they do in this area of their lives (see Lee, 1993; Frith, 2000; Saunders, 2008). Also, because sexual activity usually takes place in private places, out of sight of any observers, it is generally hard, if not impossible, to establish what has actually happened in any (purported) sexual encounter, in terms of who has done what to whom.

Further, when, as in our case, it is claimed that the activity in question is not consensual, let alone that one person implicated says it didn't happen at all, there is the whole area of intention and interpretation. Confirming that somebody looked at or touched someone with sexual intent isn't always easy, especially when erogenous zones or breasts or genitals aren't involved. Setting aside the issue of a looker's or toucher's purpose, and their understanding of what they have done, the way in which a recipient interprets a touch or look can't be unequivocally demonstrated either (see Piper and Stronach, 2008). There is considerable scope for genuine misunderstanding, which is quite separate from the influence of the complex feelings and emotions that can lead to particular and personal conclusions being drawn about the motivations behind any actions, words or behaviours. All of this complicates matters for researchers, particularly in the contemporary climate where there is moral panic around paedophilia. When children and young people, as well as doubt around the veracity of what is said to have happened, are added into the picture, the problems and difficulties are compounded and multiplied.

Truth is at the heart of the issue here, as it so often is in any consideration of the pros and cons of various research methodologies and methods, when the questions that tend to be raised are around what constitutes valid and reliable, that is truthful, evidence. This is largely because, as John Smith and Phil Hodkinson note, the point of research as traditionally, and thus conventionally understood has long been thought of as a matter of discovering the truth. Within the empiricist epistemological perspective that has dominated our understanding of research, truth is defined as the accurate representation of an independently existing reality.

(2005: 916)

Even researchers, like us, who have made it clear that they are interested in subjective perceptions, are 'attached to poststructural and/or postmodern sensibilities' (Denzin and Lincoln, 2005: 11) and recognise multiple realities and ways of seeing and making sense of the world, are still likely to face criticism on the grounds that their work challenges the ontological notion of the existence of one true truth and state of affairs. This is the case for people researching anything, be it pedagogical approaches, curriculum content, management styles, widening participation in higher education or whatever. For us, with our particularly sensitive focus, the issue of truth assumes gigantic proportions. Think about it. We were looking at a potent cocktail made up of sex, children and paedophilia, with the lethal ingredient being whether or not something illegal and abusive, that is claimed to have happened, actually did occur. Thus, questions around truth were absolutely central to all aspects of our work, to the substantive phenomenon we were looking at as well as to our research design, approach and practice.

It is worth repeating that our focus was on the consequences of instances where Person A said Person B had done something to them and Person B denied it. We were not setting out to investigate or prove whether or not the something really had been done, or even if someone had made a misinterpretation. However, due to the sensitivities around child abuse and as a result of the ways in which laws around, and procedures consequent upon, allegations of abuse are framed and enacted, we couldn't avoid colliding with and having to confront the question of whether an offence had indeed been committed.

When we first began thinking about the possibility of doing this work and during our initial attempts to define and describe what it was that we wanted to look at, we made a lot of use of inverted commas and qualifying adverbs. Thus we wrote about 'false' allegations, and about 'truth' and 'lies'. We did this both in order to reflect and emphasise that our concern was with subjective perceptions and experiences and to make it clear that we recognised the problems around assuming or indisputably proving that the allegations were indeed false. Nevertheless, when sharing our thoughts and plans with critical friends we were continually asked, 'how will you know if they're telling the truth?' with the 'they' in this context referring to the teachers. And this was a question we kept asking ourselves. How would we know? The answer mattered because we didn't want anyone to be able to use our research as an opportunity to construct an identity as a wronged innocent (cf Ricoeur, 1990; Plummer, 1995; Sikes, 2000). Apart from simply perpetrating a falsehood, such an identity could actually provide cover and, thereby, scope for further offences to be committed and we clearly did not want to be party to such a possibility. Of course, and somewhat ironically, the accused teachers were in their position precisely because, they claimed, their accusers were themselves taking advantage of the opportunity (made possible by the way that schools and the law work) to construct fallacious identities as abused innocents. These identities were also dangerous, causing serious damage to the accused and to people close to them. Either way, someone involved, whether the teacher or the child, was putting forward an account and self-re-presentation that at least one other person affirmed as untrue and inaccurate. This was the bottom line and on reflection we came to see that the scare quotes were not helping and nor, indeed, was the use of the word false. In fact, such devices were complicating matters even further, adding yet another layer of uncertainty. In addition their use could be read and understood to be suggesting that we (as researchers) had privileged and definite knowledge of the truth since writing 'false' could be seen as implying that we didn't believe the allegations really were fictitious. Thus we began to say simply and precisely that we were investigating perceptions and experiences of allegations of sexual abuse.

Of course, taking this position did not help with regard to the difficulties around whether or not people were telling the truth. But, even if it had been our intention to try to establish what the true state of affairs was, what could we, as academic researchers, rather than as police officers, child protection workers or lawyers, realistically and ethically have done? Or rather, what more could we do than had already been done? After all, each of the cases that became part of our study had been formally investigated with a view to establishing truth; because once an accusation is made it has to be followed up. And in all of these cases, there had, at least eventually, been a declaration that, on the basis of the available evidence, there were insufficient grounds to support the allegation. In the case of one of the men we spoke with, the 'eventually' took some time coming since he served a sentence of almost a decade and then went through half as many more years of appeals before he was finally cleared of any wrongdoing. Another man was initially found guilty and spent over three months in prison before his conviction was ruled unsafe. These time lags came about despite (or maybe as a result of) all of the resources of the child protection services and the criminal justice system. For us to have gone down the track of seeking to establish the truth would have meant doing quite a different sort of project, with different aims and using different approaches and methods. Indeed, it is highly unlikely that we would have achieved ethical clearance to undertake such an investigation, not least because it would probably have required us to interrogate personal information that we, as academics, simply could not expect to be given access to under existing data protection legislation. Nor were we in a position to interview everyone involved in any allegation situation as we would not be able to force anyone to talk with us in the way that the police can.

In many ways, our research dilemma mirrors both the situation that we were investigating and the operation of the law. It can be very difficult to categorically establish that something has happened, especially if there is no one there to see it happen. The high profile prosecution and later exoneration of Colin Stagg for the murder of Rachel Nickell is a much reported and sensational example of the problem of innocent people being wrongly named and accused, in spite of what is reputed to have been strenuous and exhaustive investigation. If such a near miscarriage of justice can occur in a murder case where the full panoply of forensic investigation can be brought into operation, it should not be surprising that mistakes can happen when it is more of a case of one person's word against another.

Given this background, if we were to proceed we had to accept that there were dangers inherent in our project. We had to make it explicit that we recognised that these dangers coalesced around truth, or more specifically, around the possibility that people would lie to us or that we would inadvertently propagate or facilitate lies that could harm vulnerable youngsters. Obviously we would do all that we could to guard against this happening but, having acknowledged the potential problems, our position continued to be that we did believe it was important to research and, more especially, to re-present perceptions and experiences of allegations of sexual abuse made against school teachers. One, albeit slight, safeguard was that, as we have noted, our interest was only in those cases where, after formal investigation, the allegations were unproven, disconfirmed or had been recanted and said to be untrue by the person who had initially made the accusation. This does not necessarily mean that the allegations were definitely false since, as we have seen, the law and other systems can get it wrong, but it offers additional support for the likelihood that they were untrue or mistaken.

Our belief continues to be that our work is justifiable and important because the incidence of allegations does appear to be rising and affecting growing numbers of teachers, their families, colleagues and schools. Given this increase in cases, and given the lack of previous research on the topic it seemed to be time to grasp the nettle and show what the consequences of being accused of sexual abuse can be. We were quite clear that if, at any time, we should come into possession of any evidence that supported any allegation we would pass it on to the relevant authorities. However, beyond our habitual and continual commitment to child protection, we were not going to be actively seeking such evidence. What we were after, in the first instance, were narrative accounts, subjective stories of what it was like for all those touched by an allegation of teacher–pupil sexual abuse.

Why we sought stories

In our view, personal and auto/biographical (see Stanley, 1992) stories offered the only ethically and methodologically acceptable, and indeed the only possible, way of getting any sense of the lived experiences that we wanted to investigate and re-present. We share Jean Clandinin and Michael Connelly's opinion that

> stories are the closest we can come to experience as we and others tell our experience. A story has a sense of being full, a sense of coming out of a personal and social history . . . Experience . . . is the stories people live. People live stories and in the telling of them reaffirm them, modify them, and create new ones.
>
> (Clandinin and Connelly, 1994: 415)

We also agree with David Silverman when he points out that

> all we sociologists have are stories. Some come from other people, some from us. What matters is to understand how and where the stories are produced, which sort of stories they are, and how we can put them to intelligent use in theorizing about social life.
>
> (1998: 111)

But it's not just sociologists who, in the end, have only stories. From the 1960s onwards, it is possible to track an explicit and acknowledged narrative turn within literary studies, historiography, and the humanities and law as well as within the social sciences generally (Plummer, 2000; Hyvarinen, 2007). This is not really surprising given that human beings are storying beings: 'there does not exist, and has never existed, a people without narratives' (Barthes, 1966: 14). We make sense of the world and the things that happen to us by constructing narratives to explain and interpret our perceptions and experiences both to ourselves and to other people, and as Barthes states, it has ever been thus.

Essentially, 'narrative meaning is created by noting that something is a "part" of a whole, and that something is a "cause" of something else' (Polkinghorne, 1988: 6). Narratives provide links, connections, coherence, meaning, sense and so on, and they can become particularly important at times when events become overwhelming, confusing and difficult. Margaret Atwood graphically illustrates how this can be when she has a character in one of her novels say,

> when you are in the middle of a story it isn't a story at all, but only a confusion; a dark roaring, a blindness, a wreckage of shattered glass and splintered wood; like a house in a whirlwind, or else a boat crushed by the icebergs or swept over the rapids, and all aboard powerless to stop it.

It's only afterwards that it becomes a story at all. When you are telling it
to yourself or someone else.

(1996: 298)

When someone is accused of sexual abuse, and particularly when they say that
they didn't do what is alleged, the world can become incomprehensible and
confusing. Certainties and beliefs that people may hold about what is right
and what makes sense can crumble, and events can proceed on what feels like
an unstoppable trajectory. Attempts to story what is said to have happened
and what is happening can provide individuals with what may seem to be the
only control they personally have over what is going on.

Of course, stories are and can only ever be interpretations and re-presentations;
they are not the unequivocal truth but rather are versions of what transpired.
These versions are almost infinitely revisable and retellable, depending on a
whole range of factors and motivations, including the discourses and registers
used, the sorts of storylines, scripts and genre they follow, who the story is
being told to, the particular purpose of its telling on any specific occasion, the
acquisition of new knowledge, and also the benefit of hindsight and maturity.
But stories used in a research context, whether as methodology, data, or the
accounts researchers give of their work, are not alone in their inability to
completely and entirely mimic, reproduce and correspond to events and experiences and feelings. This is because no techniques exist for totally accurately
and truthfully capturing and relating perceived and experienced aspects of life.
All attempts to tell it how it was, whether they come in words or numbers or
visual images, can only be re-presentations, and thus interpretations.
Following on from Polkinghorne's (1988) definition, they are all narratives
too. As Patricia Clough notes, 'all factual representations of reality, even statis-
tical representations, are narratively constructed' (1992: 2). With regard to the
sort of auto/biographical accounts that we were interested in obtaining,
Jerome Bruner emphasises the narrativity when he writes:

> an autobiography is not and cannot be a way of simply signifying or refer-
> ring to a 'life as lived'. I take the view that there is no such thing as a 'life
> as lived' to be referred to. On this view, a life is created or constructed by
> the act of autobiography. It is a way of construing experience – and of
> reconstructing and reconstructing it until our breath and our pen fails us.
> Construal and reconstrual are interpretive . . . Obviously, then, there is no
> such thing as a 'uniquely' true, correct or even faithful autobiography.
>
> (1993: 38–39)

There is much discussion and debate around the nature and definition of
narrative and narrative enquiry (see for example, Barthes, 1966, 1977;
Bruner, 1985; Polkinghorne, 1988; Van Maanen, 1988; Riessman, 1993;
Porter Abbott, 2002, 2005; Rudrum, 2005; Chase, 2005). Adopting a

narrative, storied approach is clearly no less problematic than using any other methodology or form of re-presentation (and note that we follow Riessman, 2008, in using narrative and story interchangeably). Nevertheless, accepting all of the difficulties and the limitations and the dangers associated with our particular focus, we still felt they were the best way of eliciting what it is like to be, or to be a family member, friend or colleague of, someone accused of sexual abuse. We wanted insight into subjective experience and we reasoned that accounts, stories told by the people who had had the experience in question were the only source. Taking this line does not mean that we were blind to the way in which stories are, as Norman Denzin puts it, contextually grounded, dialogic 'performative accomplishments' (1997: xiii). Nor were we so naïve as to believe that we couldn't be hoodwinked. However, we did take the decision that, in the first instance we would treat the stories we were told with the same degree of respect and scepticism with which we treat anything anyone tells us in the day-to-day relating/narrating of life and experience that is social communication (see Sikes, 2000: 265). This, to us, was a matter of ethical practice with regard to research relationships since we felt that it would be unacceptable to approach the people we wanted to talk to from an obvious position of disbelief.

Of course, our seeking of stories had a particular purpose and was bounded within the understanding – on our part and on the part of the people we spoke with – that we were engaged in research. This understanding obviously influenced the language and discourse people used. It influenced their decisions to talk to us and what they chose to tell us and, as we have already acknowledged, it is possible that some people may have accepted our invitation to talk with a view to disguising guilt. This risk was one that we had no choice but to accept.

Catherine Riessman (2008) categorises approaches to the analysis of narrative, as 'thematic' (what they tell), 'structural' (how they tell it) and 'dialogic/performance' (why they tell it). In our own listening to and making sense of the stories we were told, we were primarily interested in the content of what people said. How they told their stories, in terms of the forms, structures and emphases they used, and their reasons for speaking to us, were of less significance. Again, this was because our fundamental concern was with what the experiences of accusations of sexual abuse were said to be like.

We chose to take a broadly grounded constructionist approach to analysis (see Corbin and Holt, 2005), looking to the narratives themselves to provide clues to the ways in which allegations of sexual abuse are contemporaneously perceived, experienced, treated and lived out. Our starting point was that while we expected that each individual we talked to would have their own unique and personal story, there would be patterns and similarities due to the shared general context and culture in which those stories are set and constructed. Thus we anticipated collective stories (see Richardson, 1990: 26), affected by key influences including official definitions, policies, procedures and legislation pertaining to allegations of sexual abuse made in schools, moral panic around children and sex, and fear of the paedophile in particular, shaping both experience and storylines and scripts (see Goodson and Sikes, 2001: 75–88).

Like Laurel Richardson we take the view that writing is, in itself, a method of enquiry, 'a way of "knowing" – a method of discovery and analysis' (1994: 51). It was either Graham Wallas or EM Forster who first coined the phrase, 'how can I know what I think till I see what I say?' but, regardless of the question's originator, for us too it is in the process of writing, of finding the words that best express what we are trying to say and convey, that we gain further insight into whatever it is we are writing about. Richardson suggests, and we agree, that the search for words moves one beyond 'prefabricated narratives' (2003: 190) into analysis. Thus it was that in writing about and seeking to re-present the stories we were told through composite fictionalised stories, we were also consciously and explicitly, involved in analysis. Later on in this chapter we will say a little more about our writing process and how we wrote, but essentially we were analysing as we heard the stories and as we compared, contrasted and contextualised the experiences they described. We were analysing, too, when we characterised and constructed plots and storylines.

Re-presenting the stories we were told

When we first began thinking about doing this work, before we had begun to talk with anyone or collected any stories, we decided that we would adopt a fictionalised approach to re-presentation and writing up. This choice was made for analytical reasons and also because it seemed to us that such an approach offered the best way of addressing the particular ethical, methodological and epistemological challenges that our project entailed. It is worth elaborating these issues more fully.

Minimising risk of identification

In the first place we thought that fictionalising people's stories would provide the greatest chance of maintaining anonymity, thereby yielding some protection against any potential harm that might ensue from taking part in the research. Ensuring the well-being of research participants and guarding against negative consequences of being involved in any project is always a priority for researchers but it was crucially important for us because we were dealing with an especially vulnerable group of people whose identities really needed to be concealed. All of the accused teachers that we were going to be speaking with had been the object of negative attention, experiencing gossip, innuendo and suspicion within their immediate workplace and often in their wider communities too. Several had been subjected to the full force of media hostility. Having personal knowledge of what this could be like (see Sikes,

2008) made us particularly sensitive and concerned to avoid being responsible for further unpleasant public exposure. We therefore wanted to do all that we could to minimise the possibility of anyone, be they the teachers, members of their families, their friends, colleagues, pupils or schools, being identifiable from what we wrote. Thus we couldn't give specific biographical details such as age, subject taught, geographical location, marital status, duration of any prison sentence served, or how long appeals took. Such information could be followed up, and could lead anyone who really wanted to find them straight to names and addresses.

Our own experiences had alerted us to the extraordinary lengths that the media will go to in order to 'out' people as paedophiles and we knew that the publication of any book or academic article which referred to or even touched on paedophilia could well come within the purview of a journalist looking for a story. Such stories have tragically led to the harassment and even murder of mistakenly identified and innocent people (see, for instance the case of Daniel Gorman reported in the *St Albans Review* in 2008 [Lewis, 2008]).

But the media is not uniquely problematic in this regard. It is the fear of incorrectly identifying someone as a child abuser, and unleashing persecution and worse, which lies behind opposition to legislation like Megan's Law (enacted in the USA) and pilot schemes (put into operation in the UK in 2008) which are intended to alert communities or parents to possible sex offenders. Furthermore, on the internet there are a number of sites that seek to name and shame (if not to incite violence against) paedophiles and they too sometimes get it wrong (see Goodchild and Barrett, 2004). The dangers are very real. Fictionalising and creating composite stories (see Clough, 2002; Sparkes, 1995 and 2007) from individual accounts does, we believe, minimise risk of identification. It also raises yet again the issue of truth. How can the reader know that what they read here is true?

As Laurel Richardson notes,

> claiming to write 'fiction' is different from claiming to write 'science' in terms of the audience one seeks, the impact one might have on different publics, and how one expects 'truth claims' to be evaluated. These differences should not be overlooked or minimized.
>
> (2000: 926)

Indeed they should not. We did fictionalise the stories we were told, presenting them under the headings of '*Confused, angry and actually betrayed: it was time to get out*', '*Timpson versus Regina*', '*How do you tell teenage children their father's been accused of sexual assault?*', '*It didn't take long for the rumour mill to start grinding*', and '*Nobody can prove anything for definite*'. However, within the stories we crafted, apart from creating characters, contexts and settings, we did not invent anything that directly related to people's experiences and perceptions of allegations of abuse as told to us. All that we wrote came straight from the narratives we were given, sometimes using the words the people themselves had used. It is the case though, that we didn't include everything because some events and occurrences were so singular that it would have been impossible to entirely disguise and anonymise them. We could, were we asked so to do and with the necessary permissions from the people who spoke to or wrote for us, produce notes, audio recordings or written accounts to demonstrate the basis of these composite stories. Obviously we wouldn't want to have to do this, given the confidentiality arrangements and agreements we entered into, but the evidence is there and we ask our readers to trust us.

There is one exception to this and that is with respect to '*Nobody can prove anything for definite*'. It was never our intention to speak with any students who made allegations that they later said were untrue. Our overriding concern was with the teachers' side of things but, following comments made by reviewers, we briefly entertained the idea of including accusers in the research. We rejected the notion though, on the grounds that it would be ethically too problematic and potentially harmful to all parties involved. However, as our work progressed we did hear what could be described as incidental stories relating to young women accusers and the backgrounds to the allegations which they had made. These stories came from accused teachers, from staff in schools and from our own contacts who, being aware of what we were researching, shared their own experiences. These included the father of a girl who had had a long standing and, what was shown to be, indubitably fantastical obsession with a teacher at her school; and also from a woman who, when at school, had been friends with a girl who had lied about abuse in order to cause trouble for a teacher she didn't like, seeking to get others to join in with the falsehood.

After thinking long and hard about whether or not to write a student accuser's story we decided to go ahead, keeping close to the various accounts we had been given. Having written the narrative, we showed it to a number of people, with our main concern being whether or not they found it believable. Essentially, we were applying the test of verisimilitude (see Bruner, 1986) here, while accepting that there are multiple verisimilitudes (Todorov, 1977: 83), that stories can have verisimilitude yet be deliberate lies (Sikes, 2000), and that events which did occur can seem unbelievable (Lincoln and Denzin, 1994: 578). Despite these caveats, it was important to us that readers could connect and could make imaginative contact with what we had written. Virginia Woolf suggests that

> the writer must get into touch with his [*sic*] reader by putting before him something which he recognises, which, therefore, stimulates his imagination, and makes him willing to co-operate in the far more difficult business of intimacy. And it is of the highest importance that this common meeting place should be reached easily, almost instinctively, in the dark, with one's eyes shut.
>
> (1992: x)

Andrew Sparkes makes a similar point when he talks about 'active reader-ship' (2003: 69) and it is this that we were aiming at. We wanted to tell a tale which readers could engage with, making their own sense of the story by drawing on 'personal meanings gathered from outside the text' (ibid). If they were unable to do this with our student accuser's story then we would have scrapped the piece. However, the feedback suggested that our construction had 'worked'. The following comments are representative of what readers said:

> This could be my 13-year-old niece talking – you have captured that tone so well, the things she is interested in and the way she is so much pleasan-ter out of school, her hopes and fears, her intelligence and the way it is put to such devastating and destructive use. You make the reasons for her alle-gation and the reasons she is believable really accessible and understandable. In short – this is a really believable account – it makes sense.
>
> (Yvonne)

> I know girls just like Teresa. And I can see them getting into that sort of situation.
>
> (Carrie)

> Scary stuff. I taught girls who were just like that. Mouthy, gobby, sweet-ies really but completely unable to back down once they'd taken a position. I know of a very similar case to the one in the story. It didn't go as far as yours but I bet if the guy concerned read this he'd be saying 'there but for the grace of God'.
>
> (Julia)

So we included it.

What can stories do?

Although fictional approaches to social research are often presented as new and contemporary, alternative and radical this is not actually the case. Consider this:

> If one is to show the school as it really is, it is not enough to be unpreju-diced. It is necessary to achieve some sort of literary realism . . . To be realistic, I believe, is simply to be concrete. To be concrete is to present materials in such a way that characters do not lose the qualities of persons, nor situations their intrinsic human reality . . . The purpose of [*this*] book, however it is used, is to give insight into concrete situations typical of the typical school. I have hewed to this line, and to no other. Whatever seemed

likely to give insight has been included, and all else, however worthwhile in other respects, has been excluded. A certain amount of fictional material has been included. This must be judged as fiction; it is good fiction, and it is relevant to our point, if it is based upon good insight.

(Waller, 1932 – *Preface* no page numbers)

Willard Waller wrote this back in 1932 in the *Preface* to what has become a classic text, arguably *the* classic text, on schools, teachers and teaching. He chose to use (some) fiction because he felt that it was through so doing that he could best represent the 'reality' (we might say complexity and messiness) of life in schools and because it would also allow him to portray teachers as ordinary, living, breathing everyday people. He points out that social expectations of how teachers should ideally behave, 'impose(s) upon the teacher many disqualifications' (1932: 45) and particularly so (and relevant to our project) when it comes to matters around sex.

Waller does not explicitly talk about how fictionalising can help to 'bring the written product of social research closer to the richness and complexity of lived experience' (Bochner and Ellis, 1998: 7), nor does he use words like 'evocative'. He takes what seems to be a far more pragmatic stance, appearing to take it for granted that 'good fiction' will give insight into 'concrete' reality. Edward Said makes a similar point when he states his belief that 'findings from research should be based on concrete human history or experience, not on donnish abstractions or on obscure laws or arbitrary systems' (Said, 1995: 238–239). Now, towards 80 years after Waller, we seem to be more concerned than he and his contemporaries were to signal awareness that texts are not innocent and neutral, and also to acknowledge the ways in which authors use various techniques in order to persuade (Baronne, 1995). We therefore tend to spell out that we use fictions because they

> evoke emotions; broaden audiences; illuminate the complexity of body self relationships; include 'researcher', 'participant' and 'reader' in dialogue; help us to think with stories; and . . . invite the reader-as-witness to morally breathe and share a life within the storytelling relation . . . *they* are a powerful means of conveying complexity and ambiguity without prompting a single, closed, convergent reading . . . The genre becomes an opportunity and a space where one may relinquish the role of the declarative author persuader and attempt to write as, and be represented by, an artfully persuasive storyteller.
>
> (Smith, 2002: 113–114)

This summary resonates with an understanding of stories as joint or collaborative constructions, involving writer and reader and, in our case, the people whose stories we are writing. Earlier on in this chapter we referred to Sparkes' (2003) notion of active readership and we also mentioned that we expected to find similarities in the stories that people told us. In *A Methodology of the*

Heart Ron Pelias advocates using forms of writing that promote 'empathetic scholarship' that 'connects person to person in the belief in a shared and complex world' (Pelias, 2004: 12). We see these participatory and connective elements and potentialities as essential if our work is to provoke sociological imaginations (Mills, 1970) and have any critical and transformative potential.

One of our key aims in undertaking this research is to make people aware of the consequences – the lived experiences – of accusations of sexual abuse. These experiences have, by and large, been ignored and silenced because, for reasons described and discussed in earlier chapters, the attention has been on the stories and experiences of the accusers. While we are not so naïve or grandiose (cf Troyna, 1994: also Phoenix, 2009) as to assume that our work will, or even could, make a difference, we would like to think that it might 'encourage compassion and promote dialogue' (Ellis and Bochner, 2000) around the way in which accusations of abuse, made in schools, are dealt with. We think that stories that embody and contextualise, stories that 'privilege evocation over cognitive contemplation' (Denzin, 2003: 119) can lead to empathetic connection and identification, even resulting in 'praxis, empowerment and social change' (Ibid: 133). Thus we would like to see our stories being read by headteachers, school governors, social workers and the police as well as by fellow academics. We believe that the stories have a place in initial and in-service teacher education where they can help to make people aware of an aspect of school life that people are often completely ignorant of until they find themselves in a situation where they or a colleague faces an accusation. Of central importance is the way in which our stories make clear that what happens in 'professional life cannot and should not be divorced from the lives of professionals . . . Once professional practice is located within a whole-life perspective, it has the capacity to *transform* our accounts and our understandings' (Goodson and Sikes, 2001: 71, original emphases).

The fact that people were willing to take part in our project suggests that others share our optimism.

Our people – who were they?

So who were the people we talked with? Where did they come from and how did we make contact with them? Our interest in teachers accused of sexual misconduct had initially been prompted by the story of a woman whose husband had been in this position. Having shared this tale and beginning to talk about the possibility of a research project, we discovered that between us, we were actually aware of around half a dozen instances of male teachers being accused of sexual abuse. In all of these cases the allegations had ultimately been shown to be unfounded, with the girls who had made the accusations eventually admitting to having lied as pay-back for such things as punishments, poor marks, or because the teacher had spoken to the student in a manner that she had found offensive. This group of 'known to us teachers', some of whom had gone to prison and none of whom were working in schools any more, were the first people we approached.

The way in which we made initial contact and broached the topic of taking part in our research varied depending on whether or not we had, ourselves, already met the accused man, or a family member, friend, colleague, or school governor, associated with an alleged case of abuse. If we had personal contact we simply got in touch and asked if they would be willing to talk with us. In the case of people who we'd heard about via an intermediary we wrote letters explaining who we were, what we were about, and asking if the person con-cerned would be prepared to talk with us. We offered institutional contact details – our websites and the names, numbers and addresses of our heads of department – so that people could check out that we really were who we said we were. For confidentiality and protection reasons, we are not prepared to say exactly how many teachers, family members, friends, colleagues or school governors we spoke to from this group but it was around a dozen. Then, as so often happens, when people got to hear about our work, the snowball started to roll and other potential participants were suggested. We approached these using the same procedures outlined above, and gained two or three more informants by these means.

Early on in our research we had made contact with F.A.C.T. which, as stated on its website,

> is essentially a campaigning organisation and support group. Our aim is to provide help and advice and to: campaign for justice and lobby for change; provide help and advice and support carers and teachers (and their families) who have been falsely accused of child abuse; raise public awareness concerning the reality and risks of false allegations of abuse
>
> (F.A.C.T. *About Us*)

F.A.C.T. has a substantial membership throughout the UK with regional groups throughout the country and links with similar organisations overseas. People who belong to F.A.C.T. are predominantly accused carers, teachers and those working in schools and care settings, and their families and supporters. Additionally other people, such as youth and community workers, sports coaches, health care and legal professionals, clergy and religious also belong, because they or someone they know has been accused of abuse, or because they want to lend their voices to protest against what they see as injustice. A num-ber of academics, criminal defence lawyers, justice groups, journalists, authors and politicians have associated themselves with, and contributed to, F.A.C.T.'s campaign and the organisation has had a role in briefing a Home Affairs Select Committee on Investigations into Past Abuse in Children's Homes (see Home Affairs Select Committee, 2002).

Inevitably F.A.C.T. and other such 'innocence groups' (e.g. False Allegations Support Organisation [FASO], People Against False Accusations of Abuse [PAFAA], and Support Organisation for Falsely Accused People [SOFAP]) risk misuse by people who are actually guilty. The same sort of truth issues that confronted us have even more import here given that some of these organisations mount large-scale campaigns, mobilising lawyers, the media, politicians and volunteers. Should someone who had been cleared as the result of such an exercise turn out to be guilty after all, or if they were to go on to re-offend, the negative repercussions for the organisation and the individuals who had supported them would be significant. The backwash could lead to them losing any credibility and having to close, thus depriving those who are genuinely innocent from receiving advice and support.

On its website F.A.C.T. makes it clear that they operate a policy of 'zero tolerance' regarding abuse of any kind. They require would-be members to declare that they are not guilty of abuse and will not allow membership to anyone found to be in possession of child pornography (see Zero Tolerance). However, as Michael Naughton, Chair of the Innocence Network UK (see Innocence Network UK) has pointed out, such declarations are not guarantees and the 'uncomfortable truth' is that 'not all victims of alleged false accusations will be innocent' (Naughton, 2007: 8). For their part F.A.C.T. does accept that they have to take innocence on trust and stress that they investigate suspicions that may come to their attention and will immediately withdraw support from anyone they discover to be guilty (see Zero Tolerance). This means that we too had to accept that, were we to contact and work with people via F.A.C.T., establishing the unequivocal truth was not possible for us, any more than it was for anybody else. Once again, we took that risk.

When we first got in touch with the organisation, the committee of F.A.C.T. invited us to attend their next bi-annual conference. When the date came round, one of us attended to say a few words about our work and to invite potential participants to come and talk about what was involved. Going to this conference turned out to be a revelatory, shocking and emotional experience and for this reason and in the spirit of ethnographic contextualising, an excerpt from notes made at the time describes what it was like.

> We had neither discussed nor really thought about what it was going to be like to meet a large number of people who were experiencing or who had experienced being accused of abuse and, with hindsight, I wasn't really prepared for the actuality. The conference was held, as it usually is, in the large function hall attached to a cathedral. Entering the room I was greeted by someone on the door who welcomed me and asked for my name. I explained who I was and was directed to the committee member with whom I had previously had contact. He again welcomed me, introduced me to various people and then left me to mingle.
>
> There were around 100 to 120 people there. The majority looked to be 50, 55-plus, although there was a scattering of younger folk. Only 2 or 3

people were not white. On first sight the individuals who made up the gathering reminded me of the members of my parents' bowling club because of their age and style of tidy dress, with most of the men wearing ties, sports jackets and flannels, whilst the women represented Marks and Spencer's various ranges with the emphasis being on the 'Classic' collection. As at bowling club meetings there was a handmade cards and old books stall and raffle tickets were being sold with the prizes – bottles of wine, chocolates, smellies and ornaments – laid out on a table. There were similar refreshments too in the form of tea, coffee and homemade cakes and I was strongly advised to have a piece of Veronica's (pseudonym) Victoria Sponge because it was to die for and would soon all be snaffled up. But it was when I started to talk to people and they to me, that all cosy similarities went out of the window.

I was told of husbands in prison, of children who stopped getting invitations to parties, of teenagers being asked to leave social and sporting clubs because of what their dads were said to have done, and of elderly parents dying before hearing that their sons' convictions had been quashed. I heard about home repossessions, about being mortgaged up to the hilt to pay for lawyers, and about physical and mental health breakdown. I spoke with men who had been on Prison Rule 45 Segregation (see Prison Rules / YOI Rules Relating to Segregation) for protection from other prisoners who had threatened or attempted to harm them. Throughout the day, during the coffee, lunch and tea breaks I heard more stories which made me sad, indignant, angry, uncertain as to whether or not I had the emotional stamina to carry on with this work and, at the same time, even more determined to bring these tales to a wider audience. And I left the conference with contact details of people who were prepared to be part of our project. A number of them eventually did share their stories.

Having said all of this about the conference, and we discussed it fully, it must be acknowledged that: abusers may be members of bowling clubs; abusers can be extremely good at creating identities which re-present them as safe, caring, respectable people; and that abusers lie. Further, if one of our own children said they had been abused by a teacher and the alleged abuser denied any wrongdoing, we would be inclined to believe our child and would do all in our power to get the teacher convicted. From such a position the people at the F.A.C.T. conference would have been viewed through a much less comfortable and benign gaze. On the other hand, if someone we knew had been accused of sexual abuse and if we believed that the allegation was false, we would feel outraged, would probably begin campaigning and lobbying on their behalf, and our involvement with F.A.C.T would be on a very different and engaged basis.

Following our discussion of impressions and experiences from the conference we came back to the view that injustices are perpetrated and serious damage is done to people's lives. Children are abused and some abusers get away with it, perhaps as a result of vigorously protesting their innocence. Some children make false accusations, which they also get away with. Children and teachers both need someone to speak for them and without in any way denying or diminishing the awfulness of abuse which, given our professional experiences and personal biographies we could never do, we try here to re-present the teachers' side of things whilst acknowledging the difficulties around truth. We find the notion, which we have heard expressed by child protection experts, that it is better an innocent adult go to prison than a child be disbelieved, both flawed and entirely contrary to our conception of justice and equity.

Reservations

We have repeatedly returned to our worries about being deceived and including an actual abuser in the group of people we spoke with, and have stressed our clear intention that, had we come across any information that suggested an offence had been committed, it would have been passed on to the police. This did not happen, although reservations about a couple of individuals led to us keeping our contact with them to the minimum, and deciding not to make use of anything they told us. There was nothing concrete or specifically incriminating about what these people said, and nor did they behave in any way inappropriately towards us. However, there was just something about them which didn't feel right and we decided to leave them out, trusting both to gut reaction and to our researchers' intuition based on long experience (see Moustakis, 1990, and Kvale, 2008). When we talked about this we speculated on whether or not the impression we got was just a consequence of how these people were and how they related to others. If this was so, and they were simply just the sort of person who comes over or could be perceived as being a bit creepy, it's possible that their strangeness was what lay at the heart of the accusations that had been made against them. We also decided not to go ahead and work with the relatives of some men who were currently in prison because, although they were willing to talk, it was clear that what they really wanted was for us to join, and lend our voices to, their specific campaigns. Regardless of the ethical issues such involvement would have raised, while these men were claiming innocence, their cases had not been disproved nor found to be lacking substance and so they fell outside our criteria for inclusion.

How we collected the stories and what we did with them

We collected stories in a number of ways. The majority came from face-to-face, audio-recorded interview conversations with those whom we'd approached to take part in the project. These recordings were then transcribed. Then there were the stories various people told us, sometimes off the cuff as it were, when they heard about our interest in the topic. Some of these came from folk we met at F.A.C.T. conferences, but others were offered in quite unrelated settings. When we were given stories in this manner we asked if it was okay for us to write them down and to use them in our research, explaining and emphasising that they would be unattributed and fictionalised. We got some written accounts too. These came from people who we weren't able to manage to meet in person but who wanted to make a contribution to the research. All of these stories, together with everything else that we knew about what happens following the making of an accusation, were the foundation for the fictionalised stories that we then began to construct.

On the basis of the accounts we'd collected it would have been very easy to write sensational, lurid, shock-horror narratives that would have, nonetheless, corresponded with some of the events and experiences that we were told about. However, we chose not to go down this route, preferring instead to write stories that, our evidence suggested, were more representative and characteristic of the sorts of things that tend to happen in the majority of allegation experiences. We are not, however, claiming that everything in any of our particular stories always happens, or that other things don't.

Writing the stories followed a similar pattern and, without giving too much away before readers reach that chapter, we will use *'How do you tell teenage children their father's been accused of sexual assault?'* as the example of how we went about the process. So: the first step was to sit down with all of the accounts given by family members and to read them over and over, looking for patterns and similarities. The next stage was to construct a cast of characters and a storyline that could be used to carry and enact the various experiences and perceptions that would be described in the story. Thus, we chose to have a family with four youngsters of different ages rather than a childless couple because the latter wouldn't have allowed us to make use of the data that we had about the effect of accusation upon teachers' own children. Strained relationships between husband and wife were common to all of the stories that we were told by wives but only one woman spoke openly about sexual matters. Nevertheless we chose to incorporate her account into the story because others had also alluded to difficulties in this area.

'How do you tell teenage children their father's been accused of sexual assault?' is told in the wife's voice, and both of the teachers' stories are similarly told as if by individuals. This is because we wanted to portray personal perceptions and experiences and it seemed best to do this through the first person. *'It didn't take long for the rumour mill to start grinding'*, however, uses a variation of the third person omniscient in order to allow us to show the various ways in which an accusation impacts on the life of the institution and the individuals who make it up. When it came to *'Nobody can prove anything for definite'*, as discussed previously, we were on different ground because we

had no data which came directly from a person who had gone through the experience we were storying. The decision to write using a diary format was based on our personal experience as teenagers and on our knowledge of how many young girls (and others for that matter) keep journals which record, interpret and re-present their lives and their thoughts.

We close this section by noting that our fictionalised stories of sexual abuse allegation are not unique. Others have written such tales and for various reasons. There is, for example, James Barlow's (1961) *Burden of Proof* (which was filmed under the title of *Term of Trial* starring Laurence Olivier, Simone Signoret, Sarah Miles, Terence Stamp and Thora Hird). The book and film tell the story of a schoolmaster accused of rape after he rejected the advances of an infatuated 15-year-old female pupil. Very little is known, or can be found out about the author, so it is not possible to speculate as to whether or not the story is in any way auto/biographical. Then there is Michael James'[1] (1999) *'That'll Teach You!'* which is also about an allegation and its subsequent aftermath. This author's work, however, is 'Dedicated to all family and friends who stood by me' and was 'initiated by actual experience' (1999, frontispiece). In our view, this book could be described as a revenge text on the basis of the sort of language that is used within it to describe characters. Thus the school bursar is described as a 'toss pot' (59), social workers are said to be 'anoraks' (69), and throughout the book, the teenage girls at the school where the accusation is made, are referred to as slags and tarts. Readers of our experientially based stories might like to seek out Barlow and James' books, and compare and contrast.

***

This chapter has given an account of how we went about doing and re-presenting our research. It wasn't an easy project to complete primarily owing to the problems it raised and entailed around truth, but also because of the consequences for us as researchers, academics and common or garden members of society. We have already described the difficulties we experienced when seeking initial ethical clearance to actually begin our project and we have, as well, discussed the moral panic that prevails around paedophilia. An aspect of this panic is the apparent suspicion aroused by any interest in a topic that links children, teachers and sex, regarding the 'real' motivations of the researchers concerned. As Sheila Cavanagh remarks,

> there is a curious way in which the topic of sex scandals implicates me as a researcher . . . I have had my share of raised eyebrows when I tell colleagues what I am writing about. People wonder why I am writing a book on teacher sex scandals and what this could possibly say about my own pedagogical practice or my ethics as a scholar. After all, who does research

on sex, particularly in the educational milieu, without moralizing or condemning what many people take to be obvious sexual transgressions and improprieties?

(2007: 192)

We have had experience of this sort of tarnishing by association and of being personally accused of paedophilia (Sikes, 2008) but this isn't something that gets easier. Like Tara Star Johnson we'll 'probably never become immune to personal attacks, [we] have grown to expect them and to think of them as an inevitable consequence of [our] choice to engage in this kind of research' (2008a: 7). On balance, we chose to accept the risk, and do the work because we believe it's important to bring this situation and the issues which arise from it into the public domain.

Chapter 5

'Confused, angry and actually betrayed: it was time to get out'

The last three years have been pretty good. If I don't work, my annual income is about £13,000, made up of my teachers' pension (with a hefty reduction because I took early retirement) and a little income from savings. The mortgage is paid off now, and both my daughters are well into university, so basic living (and even being able to attend most of Ebsfleet Rangers matches – sad but true!) is not really a problem. But I decided it would be silly to settle for just basic living at the age of 56, and so I've worked pretty regularly when not on a trip – like my stay in Australia last year – or visiting friends and family in the UK. I completed a basic EFL qualification, and so far have had two stints using it, in Shanghai and Damascus. The money isn't great, but is enough to make the experience of living and working in new environments relaxed and enjoyable. When at home, I've worked as a casual delivery driver, a painter/decorator, a greeter of coach and car arrivals at a huge pleasure park, and also as a carer on a fixed-term contract for a local voluntary organisation. As a result of all this activity, since retirement I've felt quite comfortably off, have never been bored or at a loose end, and have lived a stress-free life with real health benefits in comparison with the later years of my teaching career.

The prelude to this busy semi-retirement was an unbroken career of more than 30 years teaching drama and performing arts at four secondary schools in two different authorities. I was never particularly ambitious, and tended to move on when the potential for being bored manifested itself, rather than looking to move for promotion, and in my early fifties I was responsible for the performing arts curriculum and the work of a small group of colleagues within a much bigger faculty of a large mixed comprehensive. My role would not really be called even middle-management, and that was fine with me, as the idea of management and my idea of myself as a teacher never got on with each other very well. From an early stage, in the mid 1970s, I settled on trying to be a good classroom teacher. I enjoyed teaching and working with most pupils, and I really did (and still do) care about my subject. As a good and conscientious professional I went on many varied in-service courses, and accepted the out of normal hours work demands that came with the subject. Without aspiring to star status, I did a good job and enjoyed the positive feedback from pupils, parents and staff, and right to the end there were many aspects of the job that I valued.

My relationship to the job was affected by the particular circumstances of my family and domestic life. Having been single until my thirties, and thus professionally mobile, I then married in the early 1980s, a teacher at a nearby school, and by the mid 1980s we were divorced and each taking responsibility for our two daughters on a week-on/week-off basis. This longstanding (and in the event robust) arrangement gave me the half-time responsibilities of a single parent and to an extent structured the way that I did my job, as well as committing me to a lengthy drive to the school, as a house move became impractical given the pattern of childcare. Another effect was on the degree of informal and conversational support available to me as an adult male either living alone or with two girls. Karen and Emma were probably more caring and supportive towards me than many other daughters, and the circumstances made us a tight little unit, but the arrangement still left time for me to either work hard or worry hard at home, and I did a lot of both.

Looking back now, over 20 years I had gradually become more detached from the job, or at least from the changing mainstream idea of how it should be done and the various priorities that we were supposed to take seriously. What had once been quite simple and often enjoyable had been made complicated and frequently dispiriting, and this process had crept up alongside increased bureaucracy and a cloud of management-babble that many classroom teachers could not take seriously. For many years I had learned to pay lip service to the current imperatives and to complete the apparently necessary paperwork, while really focusing on the real job in the classroom. In my last school I guess my reputation was as an effective and no-nonsense teacher, but also as a quietly cynical and kind of semi-detached colleague who did what was needed but was unlikely to get excited by new ideas or demands. It was not a particularly easy school to work in, with a lot of challenging pupils, many with major problems outside school, and I was slowly becoming worn down. My feelings of stress were confirmed by my doctor's concern about my blood pressure and other clinical warning signs, and in my early fifties I knew that I was unlikely to resist the temptation of early retirement and that I would probably decide to retire before 60. So, in a sense, leaving the teaching profession early was no surprise in itself. The surprise – one that I am still recovering from – was what went on in the last couple of years and how it resulted in me leaving feeling confused, angry, and actually betrayed – and even more grateful to have got out with my health still intact.

While I don't think it was a big influence on the way I did the job, I was always conscious of the need to avoid situations and actions that could support claims of misconduct towards pupils. In my second year as a teacher, in 1975, my Head told me that a letter had been received from a pupil's mother saying that her daughter did not like 'Mr Chord's suggestive remarks and gestures'. I was offended and horrified, told him it was nonsense, and made it clear I would consult the Union. He advised me that there was no real evidence on which he could base any further action and suggested I shouldn't overreact as it could inflame the situation. I did speak to the union rep, but a couple of weeks later the girl's mother wrote again, to say that she now thought she had been wound up by her daughter and that she did not believe there was a substantiated complaint to be made. So the issue went away. The girl had been a regular truant, from my lessons and others, and a few weeks before the letter arrived I had seen her in town when she should have been in school. In making excuses to her mum she probably threw some verbal mud at me, but it didn't stick and I carried on with my career – but that was in 1975. There were no more complaints about my behaviour for nearly 30 years, not that I was expecting any.

In the meantime there were things going on that I couldn't help noticing. Occasional well publicised legal cases involving (usually) male teachers and (usually) female pupils, one of which was at a neighbouring school in the late 1970s, served as a reminder that the risks from any misbehaviour, real or not, were very high. In the mid 1980s a teacher in my own school went through two court cases before being found not guilty of sex with a minor and thus being responsible for the pregnancy of a troubled 15-year-old pupil. The school management team and most colleagues supported him throughout, although some were less convinced of his innocence (and he had married [and later divorced] an ex-pupil when she was only about 17). Anyway, this sort of thing, and a feeling that pupils and parents were becoming more likely to complain, plus increasing media coverage of all types of abuse and child protection, had a gradual effect on my own (and I suspect many others') teaching and relationships at work.

I was never a touchy-feely sort of man. Of course I hug my own children and so on and I'm not neurotic about it, but compared to many people I probably make much less physical contact with others in normal social situations. I don't casually put a hand on someone's arm or round their shoulder. In school, and particularly with pupils, I always avoided any suggestion of touching, and when it did occur on a number of occasions I actually told a senior colleague about it in case there was any comeback. For instance when a 15-year-old girl broke down completely in a drama class when we were reading Edward Bond's *Saved* – I hadn't known that she had recently been with her baby niece when she died, and felt terrible. I sat with my arm round her shoulder for a few minutes, and the situation passed over, but I immediately informed her head of year what had happened in case there could be any misunderstanding. I've done the same thing after having to break up some nasty fights, which can't be done without laying hands on pupils (in my experience, often girls) and holding on for a good few minutes if necessary. Obviously it's part of the job, but one that always made me feel vulnerable.

As I got older I probably became more careful and, like many male teachers, avoided one-to-one meetings with pupils. Closed doors were something else to be avoided, as conducting business in public was generally considered safer. Sometimes this approach (backed up by school policy and professional guidance) made me wonder what the world was coming to, but it was hard to resist. Two or three years before I retired a really keen GCSE pupil, who had missed some opportunities because of illness, asked me if she could come into school during the Easter holiday to use the recording studio to help complete her project. I had said I was going to be in on a particular day, to clear up my paperwork and check equipment for the summer term. However, I found myself telling this delightful and mature 16-year-old that I was happy to be responsible for her being in the studio, but that she should bring a friend with her. She looked puzzled and I explained that it was in both our interests to avoid any possible misunderstanding that could arise from our being alone for hours in an otherwise empty building. She agreed to bring a friend, but obviously thought I should chill out. In retrospect, I was confused too, as my attempt at self-protection had actually cast a shadow over a good and proper teacher/pupil relationship. If my explanation to her made sense, which of us was I saying I didn't trust?

Before describing my experience of the events which ruined the last couple of years of my teaching career, it is worth mentioning that the school went through a major trauma just after the millennium. During the summer vacation, all staff received a letter to the effect that a longstanding colleague (male, in his late forties) would not be returning at the start of term, having been arrested and charged with child abuse. Beyond that there was an official information blackout, but during the autumn term press coverage and the court case made clear that the teacher had groomed and sexually abused early teenage boys, mostly pupils of the school, over a number of years. He was sent to prison. We were all pretty amazed – he had been respected and liked – and nobody claimed prior awareness. With hindsight I remembered being surprised by his vehemence, in a conversation over a pint, about boys being feckless and apparently misusing cigarettes and beer. Court evidence suggested that such narcotics were being provided by him! I also remembered, some years earlier, being struck by seeing the almost intimate way that he administered eye drops to a male pupil. Why not refer him to the nurse? Anyway, beyond the wonders of hindsight the relevant thing is that these events had a real effect on the school, which lasted for years. The senior team (and I guess the Governors) were pretty rattled, and some senior staff moved on soon after; teachers were both shocked and increasingly careful about their own behaviour; parents were inevitably concerned; and pupils were both excited by a juicy scandal at their school and found that they had been gifted with a new narrative and rhetoric to use against teachers (and sometimes each other). The aggressive use of words like 'pervert' or 'perv', or references to someone being 'pervy' became much more commonplace. The school had become sensitised to such behaviour, all male teachers were now potential perverts, and the risks to a teacher of any such allegation being substantiated had been demonstrated in a very public way.

In late 2002 I was told by a library assistant (I had known her for years and her husband was a colleague and occasional drinking buddy) that she had overheard a group of Year 10 girls saying that they didn't like the way that I looked at them. They thought I was pervy and they were not going to allow me to look up their skirts. I thanked her for the warning, recalled that I had ordered at least two of the girls from my classroom for misbehaviour in recent weeks, and reminded myself to be even more proper than usual. I did nothing more about it because it didn't seem possible to do anything useful, and the lure of the Christmas break was very near. However, on the third Friday of the spring term, I had a message from the Head telling me to see one of his deputies on the following Monday morning. I was unwilling to spend a week-end wondering what the problem was, and made sure I spoke to the Head before the end of the day. He said he was not going to go into any detail but there had been some complaints from a parent (or parents? – it was all a bit vague) who were known to an un-named governor. He implied that they had sexual connotations but said I had to see the Deputy to discuss the matter. I was obviously anxious, and before going home to 'enjoy' the weekend, I spoke to my union rep to ask him to attend the meeting with me. He declined, saying he could not be involved as he was a member of the school's senior team! Unimpressed, I went off for the weekend. When the meeting with the Deputy finally happened (he cancelled without explanation on the Monday so we met on the Tuesday) I was accompanied by an experienced and trusted colleague who I had known for years. Inside the school my union provided no significant support throughout the ongoing process, and all my contact had to be with the regional office, which meant that the Union input was technically correct but pretty impersonal.

My initial response to the meeting with the Deputy Head was that it was both worse and better than I had feared. On the downside, it was conducted in a hostile and accusatory way. He was brusque, dismissive, and both I and my accompanying friend thought he was trying to bully me into admitting something. Overall it was a pretty demeaning experience. On the other hand, I was initially relieved that he did not make reference to any evidence or allegations concerning really serious sexual abuse, and I assumed that if anyone had claimed that I'd groped them (or worse!) then he would have said so. Instead, I was on the receiving end of an aggressive account of how there had been some complaints, and that a governor knew about the problem, and that this was not the first time that he had been aware of concerns about me. I was given no detail of when events were claimed to have happened, how many complaints there were, or in what form. It was even difficult to get out of him exactly what the complaint was about, but in the end he referred to me looking up girls' skirts and using the subterfuge of dropping things on the floor so I could bend down to get a better view. Obviously I denied any such thing, and made it clear that I would be seeking union advice. He said that he would now be investigating the circumstances and detail of the complaints. In the meantime I was not suspended but he instructed me not to discuss the situation with anyone in the school, as such issues should be kept confidential and I should not be seen to be getting in the way of his investigation or putting pressure on potential witnesses.

I left the meeting pretty confused, with all sorts of thoughts, questions and worries going round and round in my head, and got on with my normal duties as best I could. It was only over the next few days (which were lonely and isolated – it wasn't my week to have Karen and Emma so I had a lot of time to myself) that the nature of my situation became clear. I had been put into limbo while an unspecified investigation into undefined complaints by un-named people was conducted, and I did not even know exactly what I had been alleged to have done. Inevitably some pupils would know the complaint had been made, and would be looking out for responses and developments. Some staff might know of it too, but I couldn't check that out, or state my innocence, because I had been instructed not to discuss the issue with anyone in the school. In this situation I was expected to get on with the job, knowing that my good name and career were under serious threat. The ten weeks that it took to 'resolve' the situation were long and horrible, with measurable medical effects as my GP became increasingly worried about my blood pressure. The medication seemed to make it more difficult to sleep, and given the situation it was hard enough anyway. I wondered whether my death or incapacitation through a stroke or heart attack would make any impression on those responsible for the complaint or the way it was being dealt with, and in my lowest moments hoped they would feel guilty. Remembering reading it as a student, I dug out an old copy of Franz Kafka's *The Trial* and felt closer to it than was comfortable. Away from school I told a few friends what was happening, and their concern was at least a comfort. I told my daughters and they were outraged, but agreed to try to stay calm. This was important as they both had important exams coming up, and I was anxious that my troubles could damage their immediate chances and future opportunities. I told my ex-wife too, which was necessary but difficult in the circumstances, but she was as nice about it as I could have hoped.

I quickly made contact with the union official, and over the next few weeks sought regular advice. I think I got decent advice, and they did their job okay. In retrospect, I suppose that if I wanted more than objective technical guidance, this was my problem and not theirs. With loads of experience of such complaints and investigations, union officials just told me to stay calm and keep a detailed note of every conversation with anyone about the allegations, and to keep any written communication on the subject. Their basic position was that until there was a formal and specific allegation in writing, then there was little to be done and in the meantime I should be hopeful that nothing more formal would ever appear and that the whole thing would go away. I realised that from their point of view, I would only be a higher priority if the threat to my career became more concrete, and that they already had a heavy caseload. Accepting that, it was still ironic that one of my worst night's sleep (among many in the months of uncertainty) was after coming home to find on the doormat some post from my own union! In what was clearly meant to be a helpful leaflet I was advised what to do if the police turned up at my house unannounced to arrest me on suspicion of child abuse. With my anxious imagination already working overtime, I now had to deal with the idea that I was someone considered to be in need of that leaflet.

To my surprise and increasingly resigned anger, in all the weeks that the situation dragged on, I never received a specific account of what I was supposed to have done, when I did it, and to whom. But in a series of (usually perfunctory) exchanges with the Deputy Head the nature of the charges became clearer. It also became clear where the complaints had come from – a girl in the group mentioned to me by the library assistant, and one whom I had needed to discipline (through routine removal from the room) in the previous term. I had no choice but to continue teaching classes and workshops including this group, and felt quietly angry and uncomfortable. However it was something of a relief that the complaint(s?) as I gradually understood them simply seemed silly, although it was worrying that senior teachers didn't seem to think so. Offence had been taken that, in sessions aimed to develop voice control, I routinely require pupils (including girls wearing skirts) to uncross their legs when sitting. I also invite them to be aware of their diaphragm and its effect on breathing. Finally, I suggest that they should undo their top shirt button and loosen their tie. In conversations that even at the time seemed pretty surreal, I had to tell the Deputy that such measures were normal practice in voice or speech training or singing sessions, that I had been doing much the same for 30 years, and that I wouldn't know how to do it any differently. I was even able to report that a female Ofsted[1] inspector had observed me teaching a similar session in the previous year, including all the 'offensive' elements, and no negative comment had been made in a positive write-up on the lesson. His response to all this was to look unconvinced and continue to imply that such behaviour was dubious, and amounted to 'asking for trouble'. It was as if, whatever the truth of the matter, it could only be my fault that someone had complained. I even found myself demonstrating (in the absence of any pupils!) the practical difficulties in trying to look up the skirts of girls sitting at desks in a normally laid out classroom, particularly in the split second it takes to cross or uncross legs. Although I had said all I could to explain myself, I was still very worried, and had a lot of time to ponder the way that what I considered to be normal good practice could be interpreted and reported in a lurid way. How many buttons were to be undone? Did I look down their shirts too? Was talk about the diaphragm suggestive? Did I drop that pencil twice in 25 minutes? I felt increasingly vulnerable because any normal action could be misinterpreted in a malicious way, and on the basis of what seemed to be no more than tittle-tattle it seemed to be that I was assumed guilty and could not really prove my innocence.

I almost became used to living and working in this uncomfortable limbo. Regular enquiries to the union received the response that no news was good news and it seemed likely that the investigation was going nowhere. However, after a couple of months I prevailed on the union official to write formally to the Head, pointing to the lack of apparent progress or information and strongly suggesting the need for closure and a resolution to the longstanding hiatus. I believe there was then a telephone conversation, because when I next spoke to the union official he told me that in the more than two months since my first meetings with the Head and Deputy there had in fact been no further investigation, and it was now accepted that there was no basis on which any further action could or would be taken. Apparently the LEA's advisory service had confirmed that my description of good practice in teaching voice sessions was unexceptional and correct. However, contrary to what had been said at the start of the process, the Deputy had not interviewed the pupil responsible for the complaint; he had not made any report to the Head; and the Head had not asked him for feedback until the letter from the union was received. The union official told me that the Head would be writing to the girl's parents to resolve the issue, and also to the union to confirm that the matter was closed. From the point of view of the case-hardened official, all had gone much as expected. For myself, there was huge relief that the nightmare was over and that the threat to my status and reputation had disappeared.

However, I was left with a general feeling of frustration and anger, and aspects of the 'resolution' only added insult to injury. The letter sent to the girl's parents by the Head included the following: 'Now that I have had time to investigate the complaint which you made concerning your daughter we have been advised that singing with crossed legs is not advisable as the diaphragm is restricted. Mr Chord was therefore following standard practice. We have spoken to Mr Chord and do not intend to take any further action in this matter. Nevertheless I am sorry if your daughter was in any way upset by this incident.' The letter sent to the union by the Head included the following: 'I have spoken to Mr Chord and told him there will be no action taken following the recent complaints by parents. I believe he had been informed of this by the Deputy who conducted the interview. I have apologised accordingly.'

Apart from the continued slippage between singular and plural (complaint or complaints, parent or parents?) as if it didn't matter, the Head had offered an apology to the girl and her parents for an 'incident' in which I was wholly blameless. At the same time, if the reference to an apology in the letter to the union means an apology to me, then it was a lie as I never received any apology from either the Head or Deputy. This lie was additional to the misleading implication that a serious investigation had been conducted by the Deputy to whom the Head had delegated the responsibility. In the circumstances I was very angry and felt that senior management had acted in an insulting way which betrayed a total lack of concern or respect for my career, professional standing, or general well-being. The union official agreed that I had much to be angry about but stressed that from their point of view it was a 'good result' and that I could now get on with normal life and work with no stain on my record.

I was pleased and occasionally euphoric that it was all over as the union official said. However, because I felt I had been treated pretty badly, and that it was not acceptable that I should be expected to put up with ten weeks of deep anxiety on the basis of no serious evidence and yet receive no acknowledgement or apology, I consulted a solicitor at my own expense to see if any recourse was available to me. After reading my record of the last few months' events and talking with me to check he understood what had happened from my side, the solicitor advised me to let the matter drop. He said that current workplace legislation would not be very helpful; it would be necessary to prove that the Head had failed to follow proper procedures, and that would be very difficult. To bring a case would be expensive, and the expense would be mine. In the meantime I would be pitched against my line managers (and in reality the LEA itself) while still trying to do my job, and there could be more mud thrown in my direction. I was grateful for his advice, even if it depressed me to learn that I was apparently without the ability to do anything or to seek redress for the way I had been treated.

Over the next few months, while continuing to teach my classes and carry on as normal, I tried to understand what had happened. How was it possible that a 30-year career had been dragged through the dirt and I had been caused months of fear and anguish on the basis of little more than petulant gossip from one or two pupils with an axe to grind? The Deputy had made vague references to heads of year having known of complaints but once it was all over, and the instruction to stay silent had lapsed, I asked all the year heads if they had been involved in any way and all denied having received or passed on any complaints. So I was left to conclude that it had really all been about a single letter from a single parent, and that the apparent fact that the parent had access to a school governor had also played a part. The Head and Deputy felt they had to be seen do something, but actually did almost nothing beyond putting me under threat and pressure. In retrospect it could be said that in reality they had simply stonewalled and let the issue fade away by not putting any energy into it. This had been effective in defending their personal positions, and also the position of the school, but it had been achieved on the back of my own discomfort. I could appreciate that the senior team must be affected by the 'rights culture' that had grown over the last 15 years or so, with pupils much more willing to stand up to authority, parents more likely to complain, and the threat of legal action more evident. They were no doubt also terrified of the possibility of more negative publicity and media coverage of another tale with sexual connotations coming out of their school. However the rights and well-being of the teacher as a human being and employee (in this case me!) seemed to have been forgotten. The Head and Deputy had overreacted initially, had probably realised there was no real basis for action, and then just let the matter fade away. When it was all over, there was no change in the way that staffroom colleagues dealt with me at all and there was a degree of understanding and sympathy, but from the Head and Deputy and some other senior team members there was a new reserve. I think they were both being careful and feeling embarrassed.

To an extent, life returned to normal. Friends sympathised, and Karen and Emma relaxed and sailed through their exams and on to the next stage of their lives. My problems certainly had an effect on them, if only through teaching the useful lesson that the world is often unfair and we do not always get what we deserve, but there was no lasting harm done. But the same was not true at work. For days at a time it was possible to ignore what had happened and to get on with my teaching, and the parts of the job that I valued most still gave me satisfaction. Yet every so often incidents occurred that showed that on the pupil grapevine it was common knowledge that I had been the subject of a sexually related complaint, and this knowledge could be used against me when required. Sometimes it would manifest in a pointed unwillingness by some groups of girls to meet my eye or acknowledge my requests or instructions in class or on the corridor. Their male peers might deal with me with a half smile or repressed snigger, while being formally polite. It was typically low-level nuisance that I could do little about without the risk of looking strident and foolish. The same was true of the distant mocking shout of 'pervert' as I got out of my car in the morning to start another school day. I know I was not the only male teacher to be on the end of this welcome (and at least one female teacher was occasionally treated with calls of 'lesbo') but in my case it was certainly not random and it had an inevitably corrosive effect on my inner feelings and my professional capability.

After a couple of terms of this more challenging (or actually threatening) working life, I reluctantly admitted to myself that in professional terms I was irretrievably 'damaged goods'. In my mid fifties, and conscious of the ongoing risks associated with high blood pressure and stress, I did not fancy the idea of trying to move on to another school and start again with a clean sheet. Actually I doubted that, in the age of easy communications and pupil-oriented websites where teachers could be discussed with impunity, this escape strategy was realistic any more, and a dodgy reputation would possibly travel with me. Psychologically and emotionally I was at a low ebb and even began again to wonder if in some way I was the author of my own misfortune and that my behaviour really had been responsible for the difficulties and accusations. Did I simply and unavoidably look prone to abusive acts or at least thoughts? Was the problem that I was known not to be married but to live with teenage daughters? Perhaps my normal facial expression, when not serious or angry, is too easily interpreted as leering or suggestive? Do I smile too much? All these thoughts and many more were with me too much of the time to allow much inner peace, and I came to the conclusion that doing the job was no longer worth the candle. All that remained was to plot a course that would see me into retirement at a time of my choosing.

Over the years I had seen colleagues, with greater or lesser cause, take substantial periods of sick leave. Sometimes this was unavoidable given obvious ill health, but in other cases it could be described as defensive and precautionary (and in a much smaller number of cases might be categorised in the staffroom as exploitative). A number of friends argued that in the circumstances, given that my working life had been irreparably damaged by the action of senior staff who could be said to have failed in their duty of care, I should take the opportunity of going on medical leave for a term or two before finally resigning. It seemed unlikely that I would be assessed as requiring early retirement on the grounds of ill health, but there was little doubt that my GP would sign me off on the basis of stress and high blood pressure. Although I could see the argument that after 30 years' conscientious effort there could be some justification for such a strategy, I decided that I could not do it without risking an even greater loss of self-esteem. I set myself a date for leaving, at the end of the school year, two and a half terms away, and kept the letter of resignation stored in my computer at home, waiting to be used. It was reassuring to check it sometimes after a bad day, to prove that I really was going to get out.

Near the end of the final spring term of my career, before I had announced my intention to take early retirement or submitted my resignation letter to the Head, a colleague who worked as a Learning Mentor came to see me. She had found a Year 10 girl hanging around on a quiet bit of corridor during class time, asked what she was doing, and had been told that Mr Chord had sent her from the studio and instructed her to go to the referral room. This was true. She was new to the group but in the two weeks she had attended she had been repeatedly difficult and was damaging the experience of other pupils, so I had ejected her. However, she was now in an angry and emotional state and told the Learning Mentor in no uncertain terms that she was not going to go to referral no matter what she or Mr Chord said! It was obvious that the girl was in some distress, and probably not just about my class, so the colleague walked her down to a seated area in the foyer where they could talk in a calmer way. Things seemed to be going okay but after ten minutes, when it was suggested that she should now go to referral as instructed, the girl lost it completely and ended up crying and shouting in a quite busy part of the building. Anyone passing heard that she was not going to do what Mr Chord said. She hated Mr Chord. He was a perv who told girls to undo their blouses so he could look at their boobs. Why was he allowed to be a teacher when the Head already knew he did these things, and looked up girls' skirts? It was obvious that this was really a smokescreen for many other issues and problems that had nothing to do with me and, as the Learning Mentor pointed out to the girl, she had barely been in my class and so couldn't know these things were true, but they were said loudly, vehemently and in public.

I thanked the colleague for alerting me, and asked her to prepare a written report of the events and pass it directly to the Head. She did so, and the result was total silence. The issue was not raised with me, and from conversation with relevant colleagues, I am virtually certain that the statements made were never raised with the girl. So the Head presumably did not believe the claims to be true (otherwise he could not have ignored them, could he?) but he also did not think it appropriate to discipline a pupil who had publicly defamed a member of his staff and made it more difficult to do his job in the future. It was now apparently okay for a pupil to peddle damaging gossip about a teacher, and very loudly, without attracting any sanctions. No senior member of staff even sat down with her to make it clear, that no matter how upset she was, such unjustified outbursts would not be tolerated and that she would be sent home or suspended if there was any repetition. Had I needed any confirmation of my situation at the school and the wider unhealthy nature of senior management in schools today, this incident told me all I needed to know. It was time to get out, and it was a great relief when I submitted my letter of resignation a few weeks later. My full-time teaching career was over, and it had ended in a way that left a very bitter taste in the mouth. Obviously I have moved on now, and three years on I am in a much more positive frame of mind, but there are still many occasions when I run over the events in my mind and try to understand where things went wrong, for me and for the system as a whole. However, I know that even if I am financially poorer for having taken early retirement, in every other way that matters, I am immeasurably better off, even if this does not stop me being angry about the circumstances that led to me embarking on a different sort of life.

Chapter 6

Timpson versus Regina

I really want to tell the story, my story, but hardly feel able to do it. One difficulty is that I still can't really understand how it can have happened, and how the professionals I worked with and the system we worked in can have allowed it to happen. Another problem is that it is very hard for me to know what other people were meaning and thinking, what they thought they knew, at each stage of the process. I realise that things must have looked very different from the point of view of the head teacher, or a governor, or senior LEA staff, or diocesan representatives, or my union officials, or the police, or members of the jury, or the children who were interviewed and gave evidence – but it's very difficult for me to know how different, or different how. Actually it's impossible, as the system seems to be based on keeping most participants from communicating with each other and, as the person the whole process was focused on, I felt pretty much in the dark for most of the time. One thing I can be sure of now is that different individuals and groups were responsible for what happened in very different ways. Some took deliberate decisions, others took the easy way out and let the process take them along and tell them what was expected of them, and others were probably totally confused. I'm sure the children were. They ended up basically saying what they had been coached to say, and I worry about the lessons they may draw from the whole business. Anyway, I can only tell the story as best I can, from my own point of view and with my own interpretations, and let others make their own sense of what was going on.

The big picture of what happened is easy to outline. In my fifteenth year of teaching similar year groups, at the same junior school, and dealing with the pupils in essentially the same way that I had always done, I was informed of complaints from some parents about the way I had touched their children in class. While I certainly touched my pupils when appropriate, I could think of no event that seemed out of the ordinary and could not offer a specific response to the complaints (which were anyway fairly vague). Although most of the 'incidents' must have occurred when other adults were in the room, and *all* when the classroom was full of children, I was suspended. More than six months later I was charged with sexual assault, and was prevailed upon to resign. More than a year after that, at the end of a five-week trial, I was found not guilty on some charges, but guilty on four others, with 'no verdict' on a string of others. Following a consideration of 'reports' the judge sentenced me to six months in prison. I served three months among 'Category A' sex offenders before my release, an interesting but sometimes terrifying experience that I would not recommend to the average white collar professional worker. Three weeks after leaving prison, at the Appeal Court, three senior judges ruled that my conviction had been unsafe and that I was thus not guilty. My brief inclusion on the register of child abusers came to an end. However, the 'no verdict' charges technically still stand, and this may hinder any attempt to remove my name from the famous 'List 99' of adults who must not be allowed to work with children and young people.

My current position, many months after the Appeal Court ruling that overturned my conviction, is that I am unemployed (and feel unemployable), with my teaching career shattered, living on benefits, regarded as a fair target for abuse from some of my neighbours, in a state of shock, wondering if I will ever get any satisfaction, apology or compensation from a system that I feel has let me down terribly, and with no idea where my life can or will go from here. It has been an awful three years, and I doubt if I would have got through the experience without the support of friends and family who, like me, must have found it hard to know what to think for much of the time. This has been the biggest threat and challenge of my life, and one that it will be very hard to recover from and get my life back on track, so it will be difficult to tell the story in a calm way – but I will try.

The school is a quite large, denominational primary/junior, drawing from families in a mixed but generally comfortable suburban area on the outskirts of the city. It had gone through a number of phases during my time there. Following a relatively golden period with a stable and friendly staff group, with the departure of the former Head a few years earlier the atmosphere had changed. By 2005 I guess 30 teachers had left in the previous four years, unsettled by the more 'blame-oriented' approach of the new Head. As a result, the place felt more fragmented and less supportive, with a relatively distant Head, and results and inspection reports began to reflect the change.

I never considered myself a star teacher, and had no great ambition to climb the career ladder, but after 15 years I was a solid and successful classroom teacher. My experience with Year 5 and 6 classes gave me lots of confidence, and I knew how to bring the best out of all sorts of pupils, and results were good. I enjoyed the job, which was a good thing after four years' training and not being interested in any other type of work. Generally I think children liked me; I could make the class laugh, and 'discipline' was never a problem. I never shouted, having learnt that keeping the volume down was more effective, and letting the children get used to really paying attention to what I was doing and what I wanted from them at different stages of a lesson.

For some years I had been Maths coordinator, and in early November 2004 I met with the Head and the Deputy to discuss my survey of how the subject was being dealt with across the school, with an eye on the next Ofsted visitation. In the course of this routine 30-minute meeting, there was perhaps a three- or four-minute interlude when the Head said that there had been concerns from some parents at the way I had apparently touched their children in class. The clear impression given was that the matter was not being treated as a serious complaint. I accepted the information and reassured my managers that I was always appropriate and that of course I understood that it was sensible to get to know children before judging how and when they could be touched. The Deputy commented that it was best to be circumspect, and I agreed. The discussion was not presented as a formal warning in any sense, and no written communication from my line managers followed. Whether or not a note of the discussion was made at the time became a bone of contention later on.

At that stage I never imagined the issue would come up again, and got on with my teaching for the rest of the term without any particular incident or fuss. Nothing happened with any pupil, and nothing was said by any adult to give me cause for concern. I saw no need to change the way I had always been in class. Many of my current Year 5 class were familiar as I had taught them on occasion in the previous year, and the group settled down pretty well. I had never touched children for the sake of it, but had always put a hand on a shoulder or given a pat on the back when appropriate. If I sat down on a child-sized chair next to a pupil to read with them or check their work, then it was unavoidable that knees or hands might touch, but this never seemed to be a problem. My approach was to simply be normal and careful, and in years of teaching the issue had never arisen – and for many lessons I was not the only adult in the room, with classroom assistants, parent volunteers or student teachers frequently present. However, my confidence that it was unnecessary to make any change in the way I worked with the pupils blew up in my face and a nightmare began. On the last Thursday before the Easter holiday in late March 2005 I was abruptly told by the Head that a number of written complaints from parents had been received, that it was a serious matter and that it would soon be out of his hands. I was shocked, upset and amazed. I had a sleepless night, and spent a miserable day teaching (alone with the class) on the last day of term, the Friday that probably marked the real end of my teaching career.

In the last week of the Easter break, the Head telephoned me at home to say I was suspended and should not return to the school the following week, pending necessary meetings and investigations. When the police and social services were mentioned I realised that the whole thing had suddenly become very serious, but even then I had no idea of how long it would go on for or that my life was going to be changed for ever. From then until the following October, when I was actually charged with indecent assault, I was in a terrible and confusing limbo. There were meetings with the Head, LEA and diocesan representatives, school governors, child protection social workers, and police detectives. I was repeatedly interviewed by the police, latterly under caution. The detail of what happened and when during those months is just too dense for me to be able to report in full, and I was anyway in no condition to keep a complete record. I stayed in bed a lot and just seemed to exist from day to day, waking up with a sense of increasing dread. Once I understood the level of threat, I got organised with a solicitor and sought advice and support from my union. This was reassuring in a way, but it was always obvious that these were busy people with lots more to worry about than me and the threat to my good name and career.

As weeks went by, and I tried to defend myself in one meeting or interview after another, my biggest problem (shared with the union officials and my solicitor) was to find out what was being said about me and what I was being accused of. It all seemed very vague and amorphous. It seemed that a number of parents were claiming that I had touched their children in improper ways, but it was difficult to find out exactly what that meant. There seemed to be no suggestion of a major sexual assault, or of anything happening outside the classroom, which was almost reassuring, but I could not rebut claims that remained unspecified. With hindsight I think that the police and social services were busy talking with parents, children and I guess teaching and other colleagues, to find out if there was a case that they could take further. For me, getting information was almost impossible. I was forbidden to speak to any of my colleagues (and friends) at the school, and they were warned against any contact with me. In a vacuum, I spent painful hours trying to remember any events or actions that could have promoted or justified the nightmare I was experiencing, but could only think of normal instances where I touched one pupil or another in circumstances that for years had appeared to be unremarkable.

Now, with time for reflection, having heard from some uninvolved parents and having seen papers disclosed for the various legal proceedings, what was going on seems clearer. The original complaints in November 2004 had been from two families who were vague about what was supposed to have happened. For the rest of the term my propriety and professionalism became an increasing subject of gossip and innuendo among some parents at the school gates, and some began to contact each other at home. In an era when the involvement of any male in working with young children makes them a suitable case for suspicion, I suppose this should not have been a surprise, but it seems to have got out of all proportion and generated a momentum of its own. I think that for a number of parents I became defined as an odd and dangerous character, who something should be done about. I think whether or not children did go home with stories of things I had done that were worrying to them, some parents kept asking them whether I had touched them. In their minds I had been re-created as a real abuser, a risk to their children, not the sort of person to be alone with pupils in a classroom; perhaps they just didn't like the look of me and doubted the reasons for any grown man wanting to teach young children.

Some of their children, who spent five or six hours a day with me, no doubt picked up these concerns and, effectively sensitised to seeing me as a threat, and eager to please, started looking out for things to report. Among a very small group of pupils, my touching behaviour became a subject for conversation and even an area of competition ('he touched your hand! well he touched my . . . !'). Out of all this, in March 2005, three families wrote again, and some were shocked at the level of response their complaint provoked. At least one parent thought she could just inform the Head, leave it to him to deal with the issue as he saw fit, and that she and her child would not be bothered again. There was much unwillingness to expose the children to police interviews (or possible later court proceedings) and in this period it was hard for the police to identify specific charges. But the time that all this took meant that there was ample opportunity for the parents to talk to each other, with detectives, and with their children, and it does not seem too strong to say that the actual charges, and the nature and wording of the children's statements, emerged almost by negotiation from this process, while I could do nothing but wait to see what would happen. I will come back to the 'evidence' that finally appeared when talking about the trial.

At the same time, the Head and other colleagues were being interviewed to see if they had ever witnessed any incident of improper contact on my part. Since, other than the Head, no one was called to give evidence I am confident that all responded negatively (and I later saw signed statements from the classroom assistant and another colleague I had often shared classrooms with to the effect that my behaviour was always appropriate and that I treated all children the same). Senior staff could hardly say otherwise, as they had been happy for me to be with young children in the classroom and elsewhere, on my own, right up to the last day before my suspension. For all that, I have no sense that the Head took any stand in my defence at this stage, and throughout the process he merely went along with what was expected of him, taking the line of least resistance, following child protection guidelines (just when I felt in need of some teacher protection guidelines!) and risking as little personal or professional damage as possible. In the process of documentary disclosure before my trial, I later found that during this period an additional parent came to the school and told the Head that her daughter said I had touched 'her bottom'. The Head took note and said the issue would be followed up, but the following day the girl's mother contacted him again to say that she had spoken to her daughter very carefully and was absolutely satisfied that she had made the story up in order to be 'one of the group' and have something exciting and personal to report. The mother was sure there had been no substance to the claim. The Head dropped the issue, but my defence team had not been made aware of it, although it now seems highly informative about how the whole issue had arisen and was being sustained.

As the police became more convinced that they could build a case against me, towards early summer the tone of the process changed, and interviews became more formal, finally under caution with my solicitor present. I was arrested and bailed, and then could only wait and see what the system would decide to do to me. I found out in October 2005, when I was charged with 16 counts of sexual assault, and then at yet another Magistrates Court hearing was sent for trial at the County Court. Had I known then that there would be a 13-month wait for that, I would have been even more upset. I wasn't looking forward to trial and (possible) punishment, but I was already finding the whole business an enormous mental and emotional challenge. I spent many days and nights on my own, distressed and endlessly trying to make sense of what was happening. How could I be accused of any kind of assault on children in my classroom (a full and busy classroom) without me being able to recall in detail any of the events that were the basis of the charges against me? Although I kept up a reasonably secure public face, inside I knew I was close to collapse. On many occasions I wondered if my life was worth going on with. All this could happen when I had no sense of acting in an indecent way (let alone committing any assault), yet my life could be destroyed, and on occasion I wondered whether it was worth staying part of the world? If I had not been lucky with the local press coverage of my Magistrates Court appearances, and in my friends and family, I know I might not be here now.

When I was first suspended I told nobody about it – I suppose I still hoped it would all just disappear. But after five or six lonely weeks I spilled the beans to an old friend from my own school days during one of our regular trips to the pub. He heard it all and didn't react with horror. He joined me in the disbelief that it could really be happening, and showed he cared about me as a friend and that he would continue to do so. It was a big relief, and over the next few weeks I let my circle of friends know what was happening, just as it seemed natural to do it and without too much fuss. I heard from a couple of friends from the school too, and although they could do nothing to help it was good to know they cared and that they didn't believe what they were gathering about my situation. Among all my friends, and having lived in the same area for almost my entire life I know a lot of people, only one showed any concern or hostility. Actually it was the wife of an old friend, who I didn't really know to the same extent. She was obviously embarrassed (and probably worried and confused as in the past I had occasionally been an emergency babysitter for their three toddlers) and preferred if I didn't go to their house. It was difficult too when we were all invited to some other friends' wedding, as she clearly was not happy being in the same room as me or at the same table. But this was the only such problem, and anyway I occasionally managed to have a drink with her husband during his lunch break.

Telling my family was another big step. My parents have retired and moved across to Scarborough, so I knew that they would not see local newspaper stories when and if things went that far, but after a couple of months I visited them and outlined what had happened. As expected I received solid support and reassurance, just as I did earlier when I practised the disclosure on my younger brother and his wife. As they lived near me it was important to tell them before any court appearance and news coverage. Our elder sister lives abroad, and when my brother told her about it all, as I had asked, it was very good to get a supportive message from her. But all the welcome emotional support couldn't change what was happening, and when brief items in local papers followed my appearances in the Magistrates Court (for bail I think – I lose track) I was mortified and really frightened. But the newspaper items, with my name and address, didn't get noticed except by people who were expecting them, and to my relief there were no public scenes or embarrassment at this stage. That came later, ironically after I had been found not guilty!

At the end of October 2005, when I had been charged and it was clear that I would face a trial in due course, I was summoned to a meeting with the Head, some governors, and LEA and diocesan representatives. When the union official asked what the purpose of the proposed meeting was, it was made explicit that the assumption was that the outcome of the meeting would be my dismissal. Both my union and my solicitor wrote detailed letters of protest against this idea, arguing that it was against natural justice and also contrary to good practice guidelines which say that external legal proceedings should be completed before internal disciplinary mechanisms could be applied. They argued that the meeting could not be fair, as I could not defend myself without prejudicing the future court case, and a decision to dismiss me could itself be taken as evidence against me that would be used by the prosecution. These letters were rebuffed and it was made clear that the meeting would go ahead whether or not I attended or was represented. I was confused and in despair that they were so determined to get rid of me and trash my career even before I had been tried and found guilty. The idea seemed to be that the existence of complaints and allegations was sufficient grounds for ruining a teacher who had taught in the school without incident for 15 years, and they seemed able to do as they liked, whatever guidelines and commonsense said. I was a problem and they wanted to get rid of me quickly. My response was to resign. Friends have said that this was a mistake and that I should have sat tight and left them to take the decision to sack me, but I was feeling so depressed, confused and hurt that I was becoming unable to face more meetings and threats. My response was to want to find a hole and hide. Anyway the result was that from that September I was unemployed and living on benefits while waiting and preparing for my trial.

There isn't much to be said about the next 12 or 13 months. For long periods there was no news and nothing to be done. It was hard to see what sort of preparation made any sense because it seemed even harder to work out how to defend myself against the charges, and until late in the day my solicitors didn't know what evidence was going to be presented by the prosecution. So

I spent a lot of time just killing time and worrying. When I did some casual temp work in an office, the complications of going off and then back on benefits were so frustrating that it was easy to lapse into lethargy – which can't have been good for me. Anyway, when the trial finally began in November 2006 it went on for five weeks. I was terrified of it ending and the possible result, but willing it to end because the strain of sitting through it all was intolerable and I began to feel hopeless and exhausted. After a few days of it I moved in with my brother and his family and was never more grateful for not being an only child. I said it took five weeks, but progress was often at a snail's pace as the legal professionals did their thing, and we only managed four-day weeks as the judge always seemed to have other pressing engagements on a Friday. Throughout, I was an anxious spectator as my defence team had decided not to put me forward as a witness, deciding that I could only repeatedly say I didn't do it, and that the risk of my being pulled to pieces by the prosecutor outweighed any advantage. The strategy was to query the status and integrity of the evidence against me, and to appeal to the common sense of the jury, and this was successful in some cases but unfortunately not others.

When the necessary information was disclosed by the prosecution before the trial, it was clear that their evidence and 'witnesses' would be limited to some pupils – all girls, and to parents, the Head, and the detective in charge of the investigation. Actually of course, only the pupils had first-hand accounts of what I was supposed to have done, as nobody else could claim to have seen or experienced anything. The adults could only report second-hand hearsay information, and it was clear that some of the children had only said anything at all after their parents had asked them (having had their anxiety raised by other parents contacting them). So the police interviews with the children were obviously going to be very important to the outcome of the case and, with my solicitor, I read through them again and again (and became more and more angry and depressed). In the end there were five children whose evidence would be presented to the jury. Each was providing the basis for two or more charges of assault. Presumably if there had been other potential witnesses, either their parents had said they were not to be involved or their statements did not meet the needs of the prosecution.

Anyway, from reading the transcripts it was obvious that the police had needed to work very hard to get statements from most of the pupils that could in any way be taken to mean that something wrong and bad had happened to them. For instance, if a child said that I had touched their knee, the interviewer would ask if I had touched them anywhere else. If the child didn't give another instance of touch, the interviewer would ask the same question again – two or three times over the next few minutes – until in some cases the child agreed with the suggestion that I had touched them. Any teacher knows that children of eight or nine will try to give the answer that an adult wants to hear, and repeating questions in that way was telling them that there really was something they should be saying, that they should be reporting. In most cases the questions were asked repeatedly, until the 'right' answer was given. A number of children, even in the course of formal interviews, said at some stage that they had not been bothered by anything I had done. They said sensible things, like that some people touch more than others and that I was just being me, and that I was kind, friendly and polite! But ideas like this were discounted, not fitting into the story being constructed. Similarly, if the girl couldn't remember what she had been wearing on the day of one of the incidents (and if I was supposed to have touched a knee, the difference between a skirt or trousers seems quite significant) then the interviewer always led them towards opting for a skirt rather than trousers. Also, the interviewers worked at getting the children to use particular words to describe what I was supposed to have done. If a child said I had patted them on the back, the interviewer in effect tried to get them to describe my action as stroking their back (or, worse, their neck). In some cases the children rejected these attempts, but in others gave some level of assent. Finally, as I was being accused of touching these pupils variously on the head, the hand, the knee, the back, the shoulder and neck, and only once in the region of 'the bottom', with most of the touching being through clothing, it was a problem for the police to show that this was sexual assault. As none of the children had ever shown fear or run from the room etc., the best that could be done was to get them to say that they had felt 'uncomfortable'. And that was what most of them said at some stage of the interview, on cue, and I was sure as soon as I read the transcripts that they had been primed to come out with such a helpful yet vague word. As I said earlier, all the children's evidence was actually the product of weeks or months of talking and anxiety, involving their parents and then the police. Some of the parents had even set up amateurish role-play sessions to help themselves to understand what had happened and their children to remember! Given all this, I couldn't see how such statements could just be accepted as original and untouched by adult input.

When the trial began, the formality of the process seemed to take over and the truth of what had really happened (i.e. nothing beyond the normal and ordinary) became more and more distant. Only nine of the charges were proceeded with, in part I think for economy, but also because parents were unwilling to expose their children to further pressure. The judge and jury had the transcripts of the interviews with the children, but the courtroom watched full videos of the conversations they were based on. Watching the children (who I knew much better than did the adults interviewing them) confirmed my impression from the transcripts. They wanted to help but were at times a bit confused about what was expected of them. One showed some irritation when she had to insist that she did not mean 'stroke' when she said 'touch'. Another, who had said that I had once touched her 'bottom' when (in my own recollection) ushering her back to her seat and out of the way of other children carrying chairs, was asked to point to the place I had touched her.

In response she touched what can only be called her back. Generally, the girls recounted incidents that in themselves were hard to understand as sexual assault, but they all said they had felt worried or uncomfortable about what had taken place. There was no cross-examination of the children, and I was glad about that as I still felt that in a way they were as much victims of the situation as I was. My barrister argued that there were problems with the interviews as unblemished evidence, but for the jury I think the damage had been done. No smoke without fire . . .

My barrister gave the detective in charge of the enquiry a hard time about how evidence had been collected, the style of interviewing, and the judgements made. The suggestion was that the investigators had decided to define me as being interested in young girls, and had not even approached any boys for information even though there were as many boys as girls in my class. They had also acted on the basis that I had been given a formal warning at the meeting about Ofsted in November 2004, which was clearly untrue. In one interview with me the detectives had waved some lined and handwritten sheets of paper that they said were the Deputy's notes of the meeting, but these notes were never passed to the defence team, and the Head had actually said that no notes had been taken. When it was his turn, the Head gave evidence for the best part of two days. A lot of it was about how the process had started and what the parents had said and so on. When it came to how he had dealt with me, he was in a difficult position. He had no choice but to agree that prior to this process he had never had real concern about my behaviour with children, and that no other staff member had reported anything to the contrary. He needed to justify why he had been responsible for leaving me to work in classrooms with children even after the initial complaints had been received (let alone after the letters in March 2005 that led to my suspension). His response was to fall back on guidelines and procedures and to argue that he had done what was required of him at all times. He gave the court a false impression (I think from ignorance rather than malice) about how often I was the sole adult in the classroom during the period on which the complaints were based. Between the classroom assistant, a student teacher doing observation and then practice lessons, and also a volunteer (a grandmother who had been coming in to support individual children's reading on many afternoons for years) I had actually been accompanied by at least one other adult for between 80 and 85 per cent of the classroom periods in question. The Head seemed to know nothing about the volunteer, but my barrister could do little more than suggest he was wrong.

So, beyond the ritual statements and summing up from the prosecution and defence barristers, the jury learnt little more than that some children had stated that I had briefly touched them on various parts of their bodies (none normally classed as erogenous) and that they didn't like it and so in the end had told their parents. Some had raised the matter only after they knew about the investigation. The events had all taken place in normal classroom situations, in the presence of many other pupils and more often than not while other adults were in the room. In some cases, for instance when I was sitting beside a pupil on another child-size chair to hear reading, I would have been carrying at least a pen, a book and a clipboard to hold my recording sheets for noting progress and problems. My hands were already full. I thought it simply stretched common sense to interpret such a situation as an opportunity for a sexual assault, or not to recognise that if my hand (the back of my hand!) or my knee had touched a child's hand or knee it was simply unsurprising and accidental. But the jury found me guilty on four counts (but not guilty on four others, with a 'no verdict' on the rest) and I was absolutely devastated. The worst that I had imagined over the previous 20 months had come true, and it was a good job that I was staying with my brother that night as I was in utter despair.

It may be wishful thinking, but I think the judge was worried by the verdict. Anyway, she asked for reports before passing sentence, and so passed another five weeks with me hanging around waiting for something else nasty to happen to me. I twice met with a probation officer who was appointed by the court to make an assessment of me prior to sentencing. Although we talked at length, he did not speak to others who had known and worked with me for years, and he didn't seem to have read all the paperwork produced in the course of the investigation and the court proceedings. I felt quite relaxed about him and what he was likely to say, as in talking through with him how I thought about my job and how I had worked with my pupils for 15 years he never seemed to be surprised or concerned. So it was a very nasty surprise when he told the court in his report that he thought that I had demonstrated 'classic grooming behaviours' in the way I dealt with pupils. At the end of the long legal process this trotting out of a trite and inappropriate bit of prejudicial textbook jargon seemed par for the course. A little learning can be a dangerous thing; this part of the report only made any sense if it was first assumed that I had long-term improper sexual intentions towards my pupils, and even the dubious evidence presented in court had not shown that to be true. Anyway, the judge sentenced me to six months in prison, which I knew should mean 'only' three if I was well behaved. She had an option of giving me a suspended sentence, with compulsory attendance at a heavy-duty course at which sex offenders had to sit around and talk with each other, and therapists, in order to confront their wrongdoing, accept the error of their ways, and learn to control their offending behaviour. Although I didn't relish the idea of prison, I really couldn't have gone through such a course as the first requirement would have been to confess to being a paedophile and talk about my crimes. I think the judge knew that, and chose prison as the least bad option for me. I still left court with a black cloud hanging over me and with a brick in my stomach. Even though I knew they believed in me, at that moment I felt even sorrier for my family than I did for myself.

So, after 20 months of slow-moving disaster, I immediately found myself in a big city prison, miles from home, as a proven sex offender. That made me (a teacher who had never had any dealings with the police until this story began) a high risk prisoner alongside career criminals and people who had done truly terrible things. On arrival, the staff dealt with me in a straightforward way, and gave me a choice between entering a block made up of mixed everyday prisoners who would be very interested in why I was inside, or a wing populated by sex offenders (including domestic abuse, child sex, prostitution etc.) but where the general rule was that no questions were asked and everyone tended to just get on with being there. I was worried by the need to tacitly accept my status as a sex offender but had been advised to choose the second option, and was assigned to a cell with a man of about my own age who was quite near the end of a longer sentence. I suppose the staff were keeping an eye out for me as a new and at risk inmate, but it felt as if I was just left to get on with it. The first few weeks were awful. Prisoners spent most of the time in their cells. I had nothing to do, and was too upset and frightened to sleep much. My nightly tossing and turning annoyed my cellmate, who was obviously an experienced criminal and prisoner and considered pretty hard. I worried he might attack me which made it difficult to relax enough to sleep. But after a few weeks I calmed down, settled into the miserable routine, started to read loads of books from the library, talked quite a lot with Mick my cellmate, and on his advice took the opportunity of a job in the kitchen that kept me busy and out of the cell for a few hours every day. The pay also added in a small way to my spending allowance for chocolate, the telephone and stuff.

Once I had a normal relationship with Mick, and told him why I was there, I felt more secure and the rest of the sentence passed without more difficulty. I was never given a bad time by another prisoner and ended up feeling quite safe, but it was an eye opener to spend three months mixing with some who were content to admit they had committed murders (including wives and children), extreme violence, and other very nasty sexual crimes. Mick was inside for a range of offences which seemed to include robbery, conspiracy and grievous bodily harm. He had lived his entire life with the risk of prison, but his official job was in 'security' and he worked the doors at clubs and pubs. He had also taken the opportunity this job offered to run prostitutes, and had committed acts of sexual violence, which was why he was on my wing. We had little in common but had at least lived through the same history of music and sport, so it was possible to talk. I had no visits at all during the three months inside, and didn't really want people I cared about to see me there, but made as many telephone calls as possible (not easy, with queues of men behind you) to friends, my parents and my solicitors, who were working on an appeal petition. I wrote a lot of letters, which also helped kill time, and I think seeing me writing motivated Mick to write to a woman with whom he was expecting a baby. He had talked of his fear of losing touch and his guilt about not being there for them, so I hope things were okay when he was released a couple of months after me. Anyway, at the end of my sentence I left HMP without fuss, and after a night or two at my brother's place and a trip to see my parents I returned quietly to my flat. Being in prison was something I will never forget, but once it was over it seemed just a pointless interlude in the whole process and didn't really connect with everything else that had happened, or to me as a person.

As soon as I was found guilty my solicitors filed notice of an intended appeal against the verdict, and while I was in prison the case was prepared and papers were submitted to the Appeal Court. I had kept up with things by telephone but it was still a welcome surprise that the hearing was to take place only three weeks after my release from prison. After the slowness of the original trial, the appeal hearing took only an afternoon. It was limited to the three senior judges (there was no jury), the two legal teams, and myself, with few others present beyond the court officials. The judges had already seen all the papers from the trial as well as our submission. Each barrister made a statement, and the judges asked some questions. The prosecutor could do little more than rehearse the case made during the trial, but my barrister challenged the grounds for the guilty verdicts in a comprehensive way. He argued that police procedures in collecting evidence and identifying witnesses and passing information to the defence team had been flawed, that the children had been improperly led during interviews in order to produce statements helpful to the prosecution, and that information about the presence of other adults in my classroom had been misrepresented. He was able to summarise what I was meant to have done (i.e. touched their heads, hands etc. in a busy teaching situation often with other adults present) and to query the common sense of interpreting such actions as having an element of a sexual assault. He summed up by saying (and it was hard for me not to cheer when I saw the judges smile and nod in response) that had I been a female teacher it would have been inconceivable for such a case to have been brought. He argued that I had in effect been victimised for being a male teacher working with young children.

Whether they believed this last point or not, the judges ruled that the original guilty verdicts were unsafe, and ruled that I was not guilty on the four counts for which I had been sent to prison. Obviously I felt vindicated, extremely emotional and light-headed. It was very important to me that my family and friends could feel that reassurance and know that their faith in me had been justified, so I was grateful for the decision. But, of course, the Appeal Court ruling could not undo the damage that had been done to my life, finances and career, or take away the experience of disgrace or the frightened nights spent in prison. The ruling also did not automatically apply to the 'no verdict' charges that were never actually considered at my trial. They were much the same as the others on which I had now been found not guilty, but they still stood, enjoying some sort of legal half-life for the time being. Anyway, still grateful for my first good result after two years of defeat, I went home to try to get some rest and recuperation, and then to investigate what I could do and needed to do about trying to recover some of what had been taken from me.

I lived quietly for a few weeks, without much to do, or actually without much that I had to do, except regular depressing visits to the benefits office and occasional contacts with my solicitor to explore whether any channels to seek redress were available. I suppose I was surprised that returning to my flat and using the nearby shops and so on seemed to go without any problem or embarrassment, because this was something that had worried me a lot when in prison. My original guilty verdict and prison sentence had been fully covered in the local paper, but the coverage of the Appeal Court ruling that set the guilty verdict aside was much more sketchy and hard to find. 'Good news' doesn't sell papers, I guess. So it was a relief that I seemed to slip back into my locality without any obvious difficulty, but this feeling suddenly evaporated about two months after the successful appeal. I was in the local benefits office, dealing with the (to anybody who has previously always regularly worked and received a salary) mine-strewn labyrinth of questions and forms required to maintain an adequate income to live on. With no warning I suddenly found myself the target of verbal abuse from a middle-aged woman who I dimly recognised as living near the same street as where my flat is situated. In front of 25 or 30 people she pointed at me in a contemptuous way, saying that I was a child-abusing paedophile who should still be in prison and should never be allowed among decent people. The shock and hurt was enough to make it feel like a physical assault and, although the response of the other people present was quite restrained, I was afraid that a physical attack was actually possible. The office staff were quite good and told the woman her behaviour was unacceptable; I said that what she had said wasn't true, and got out of the office and away from the public gaze as fast as I could. The last I saw of my accuser that day was her looking righteous and triumphant, telling anyone near her what she took to be the facts of my case and my perversion.

I hoped this outburst would be a one-off event, but was soon disappointed. When it dawned on me that it was almost exactly six months since I began my sentence, the timing of the attack made some sense. Some people who had read of my conviction and sentence (and had then seen nothing of the harder-to-find coverage of my later successful appeal) had probably made a mental note that they could start abusing their 'paedo' neighbour in six months. I had actually been back in my flat for nine or ten weeks but either these public-spirited bullies had not seen me, or they had not been looking out for me yet. Obviously I felt very uncomfortable and seriously worried. I had been found not guilty but was still the target of abuse and perhaps worse, but there was no remedy in sight. A press advertisement to announce that I had been found not guilty of indecent assault on a number of eight- and nine-year-old girls seemed likely to do more harm than good! Anyway, over the next few weeks my flat was daubed with spray paint ('pervert' etc.) twice, and my front door hit by eggs and tomatoes. The (already imperfect) paintwork of my car was scratched, and abusive messages were painted all over the windows (with interesting spellings including 'pido'). I contacted the police each time and they were as polite as I could have expected, but they could be of little help as I had no way of knowing who was responsible. They thought it was probably 'kids', reassured me that there seemed to be no organised vigilante process underway (which could have made things very much worse), and suggested installing CCTV. I followed this advice, but nothing came of it as, to my massive relief, these sporadic incidents stopped after a few weeks. Perhaps the guilty parties had been put right by others who knew I had been cleared, or perhaps they suffered from an attention span as limited as their spelling. Either way, it will still be a long time before I feel fully secure and relaxed in my flat or on the streets where I live.

That brings my story virtually up to date. I am currently looking into what needs to be done in order to remove the no verdict charges from my record. Natural justice would suggest that, having finally been found not guilty on those charges I was originally found guilty on, these others should not simply be left 'on the table', with some sort of legitimate claim on my good name and integrity, but there is apparently no easy or automatic way of striking them off my record. Apparently they can't be reconsidered as the parents do not want their children to be involved any further. When I was released from prison I had to sign on to the register of child sexual abusers, but was removed from it three weeks later by the action of the Appeal Court, which was a huge relief. But the existence of these no verdict charges means that my name remains on the famous 'List 99' which bars access to jobs in teaching or with children. I can do nothing about the fact that the investigation, charges, and what has happened to me since, will always be disclosed by an enhanced Criminal Records Bureau check if I apply for jobs involving children and young people, but to be on 'List 99' with the no guilty verdict against me seems very unfair and even cruel. I am also looking into possible channels of complaint or even compensation. I think my head teacher (and thus the governors and LEA) was less than professional, failed in exercising a duty of care towards me, and took the line of least resistance throughout – which left me vulnerable and dispensable. Then the police procedures, in particular their selective creation and use of evidence and their prejudicial approach towards me, were obviously unfair and unprofessional. In both areas I am asking my solicitors to investigate what lines of complaint and possible source of redress are open to me. But it's a very lonely and bleak position to be in, although I am also talking with my union on the professional aspects of my situation.

The bottom line is still that I am not yet 40, an unemployed former teacher with a damaged record, no obvious source of income, and serious stigma attached to me in spite of being vindicated in court. The whole process has cost me towards £100K (my loss of salary, pension implications etc.), and I was never rich before it started. Although I have come through the last two years without really serious mental or emotional damage (I hope!), I remain hurt and scarred by what happened, prone to depression and with much lower confidence and energy levels than I previously enjoyed. It is not clear how I can rebuild a career or even any income-earning capacity, as all my qualifications and experience are in the employment area where I will now have most difficulty in getting a job. I really enjoyed teaching in the junior age groups, but must face the reality that I am never likely to get the chance to do it in the future, no matter how long I wait. I might be able to use my teaching skills and maths and literacy expertise in working on basic skills teaching with adults, but even there I may hit concerns about my 'record' and the fact that some of the adults may actually be only 16 or 17, or 'vulnerable' in some other way. So I am finding it very hard to make decisions and set a course for the future, and it is difficult not to feel sorry for myself and even bitter. Without my friends (and former colleagues who have broken cover following the successful appeal), and my family, it would be all too easy to just give up and spend the rest of my life as a victim – but I won't do that.

When I look back and try to understand, beyond my own hurt I still feel angry and sad. What happened was not just about me; it said a lot about a crazy system and the stupid way that people think nowadays. It is so normal and legitimate to raise concerns about improper behaviour with children, and the procedures are so skewed to react in favour of their 'protection', that there are no safeguards for adults and professionals caught up in the process. I think I was a victim of a small number of parents (actually, mothers) who, beyond being suspicious of a man doing a 'woman's job', really didn't like the look of me. By school-gate gossip they created a climate in which every action I took was worried about and reported back to them by their children in my class. The amazing thing now is that the children didn't lie. They said I had touched their knee or their hand or their shoulder, and no doubt I had. What really damaged me was that they also said that they didn't like it or that they were uncomfortable with it. This means that, from somewhere, they had been made 'aware' of things in a way that I (and any other adult present in my classroom) was not. I suppose this is what people mean when they refer to young children today being 'sexualised'. But if that is what they were, they did not get that from being with me in my classroom, so perhaps their parents should consider their own responsibility. Then their allegations of being touched were translated by the legal process into their having been sexually assaulted, and the logic or balance of that escapes me completely.

Anyway, these parents via their children defined me as a threat and a problem, and my Head rightly responded to their complaints, yet declined to make any stand in my defence, even though my record was long and exemplary. I think child protection procedures made it difficult for him to have done so even if he had wanted to. After that, the combative nature of the investigation and judicial process took over, and I barely stood a chance. It was only later that I discovered that some other parents (including a child protection social worker!) had been appalled by what was being said at the school gates during 2004 and 2005 and thought the whole thing to be a witch-hunt, but they had felt unable to intervene. Overall I think that, for the jury to have found me guilty at all, they must have been swayed by the general media emphasis on child abuse and the feeling that they should be 'better safe than sorry' in their verdict. I understand it, and obviously want children to be protected, but this approach leaves professionals like me in a hopeless position. I laugh now when I see news stories or official statements about how more men are needed in primary/junior schools or in nurseries. When government and local authorities encourage this but still leave current processes as they are, they are inviting young men to gamble with their lives and their career prospects. I loved my years teaching young children, but knowing what I do now I would never advise any male to risk following the same path.

Chapter 7

'How do you tell teenage children that their father's been accused of sexual abuse?'

At the time it had seemed like a good idea to take advantage of the fortnight's holiday we get in October now that our authority's gone on to the four-term year, so I'd booked a cottage just outside Brighton. I'd thought this would be a perfect place because if we got tired of doing stuff around and about it wasn't far up to London and the shops and the museums and what have you. We hadn't had much time as a family during the summer because the kids were on various camps and sports activities – all at different times of course – and Rob had been busy getting ready to start his new job as head of science at Bouchard High, so I was looking forward to the break and to us all being together. It was a lovely cottage too, really luxurious and much more expensive than anywhere we'd been before but I'd decided to push the boat out because the new job meant quite a bit more money and since Bouchard is much, much closer to home than Leesmith was, we were saving on driving costs too.

On the Saturday morning, getting ready to leave and during the drive down, Rob was quite ratty and snappy but I didn't really think any more about it because he's always been one of those people who take ages when you're going out. Our next door neighbour had noticed it over the years when he'd seen us sitting in the car, waiting for Rob, because his wife is one of them too and we'd made a bit of a joke about it. In fact, Gordon had been out washing his car on Saturday, and he'd made a sarky comment to Rob as he was, finally, locking the door. I was a bit surprised when Rob got in the car and said 'Stupid bastard' in a really aggressive fashion, far more nastily than was called for, because even if Gordon was being irritating, it wasn't like Rob to call folk names.

The cottage was totally lovely, every bit as good as it'd looked on the website and the kids were delighted. I hadn't told them there was a hot tub in the garden so when they saw that they were straight out to put it on and get in. I was pleased about that because, to be honest, I was a bit apprehensive about how the older two were going to be. Claire had already had a strop about why did she have to come with us when her friends were allowed to stay at home on their own and she'd be missing Carrie's party and going shopping and hanging about and getting behind on her driving lessons and so on and so on. I'd just said this was probably going to be the last holiday we'd have as a family before she goes to university next year and that her presence was non-negotiable. Sam didn't make as much of a fuss – as long as he has his Playstation he's usually happy – but he had had a chunter about why a fortnight and did I realise he'd miss Scouts and rugby and table tennis? The fact was that what I'd said to Claire was probably true: this was likely to be the last time we'd all be together on a holiday and I did find that sad.

I'd seen a Tesco just a few miles down the road so when I'd unpacked our stuff and Lucy and Emma's and put Claire and Sam's bags in their rooms, I suggested to Rob that we go and get the shopping. He'd been mooching around since we arrived, looking at the gadgets in the kitchen and switching on the tellies and trying out the satellite. We've not got that at home so I knew it'd be another plus when the kids discovered it, not to mention the fact that there was a telly in every bedroom. We love shopping on holiday: we usually treat ourselves and buy things we wouldn't normally have and Rob is great at saying 'oh go on, get that, we're on holiday' so when he said 'no, you go, I want to go for a walk', I was surprised and a bit hurt. We're one of those couples who do things together. We've never gone in for separate nights out or different hobbies like some people do. Ever since we started going out, during our PGCE year, we've been us – Rob and Kate – and then, when we had the kids, we were the Greene family. It might seem odd to other people but we've always done shopping together when we could, and especially on holiday, so Rob saying he didn't want to go was weird. I think he could see I was upset and he explained that his back was aching from the drive and he didn't want to be sitting down straight away again in the same sort of position. I could see that that made sense so I went on my own, but all the while I was out it kept niggling at me because he'd never suffered from his back before. It would fit though, with why he'd been a bit quiet and short on the journey so I bought some extra ibuprofen and a tube of Radiant Heat and I went in for some extravagant shopping therapy to make me feel better!

When I got back the kids were out of the tub and ensconced in their rooms where they'd discovered the tellies and the satellite channels. The twins came out seeking crisps and snacks and told me they wanted to live here forever and Sam shouted 'good skills ma' which was all very nice. While I was putting the food away Rob came in from his walk full of the beautiful scenery and what a great place this was and how clever I was to find it and had I bought some steak because if I had, he'd cook dinner – so all was well with my world again.

On the whole and on the face of things, we did have a good fortnight. The cottage was fantastic, the weather stayed dry and bright, the kids didn't fight and argue and we had some super days out but . . . something wasn't right with Rob. I couldn't put my finger on it but he just didn't seem to be his usual self. There was nothing that was particularly obvious or dramatic or different, but every now and then he seemed preoccupied or distracted and there were a few times when he was really snappy and bad tempered. It was out of character and the kids noticed too since he's usually really easy going. If any of us said anything he said his back was hurting or that he had a headache but as soon as he'd said this he seemed to make an effort and started behaving 'normally' again. I have to say that I was worried, especially as when I'd asked him a few times if anything was wrong he got quite nasty and said would I get off his back and that nothing was wrong except that I kept going on at him. After that I didn't ask but I did start fretting that something was up and I became frightened that either he was really unwell – cancer loomed in my mind, as it does – or that he was having an affair. It didn't set my mind much at rest when he was really nice either because I became all paranoid and was thinking he was only being okay to throw me off the scent, as it were. But this is probably making it all sound worse than it really was. We did have a good time; it was just that, generally, we get on so smoothly and well, that any change stands out like a sore thumb.

We got home on the Saturday and the Sunday was spent getting ready to go back to school and work. We had a bit of a do with Sam when it turned out he had had homework but had spent the time when he'd said he was working, watching TV. Rob got very, very angry and really laid in to Sam, calling him a lazy sod and saying he'd fail his GCSEs and end up in a dead-end job. I thought Rob had overdone it with the invective but Sam was in the wrong and maybe he did need a bit of a wake-up call.

Monday morning was the usual rush. Claire got impatient with the twins for the amount of time they were in the bathroom and stormed out saying she wished we were back at the cottage where there were en suites. Rob was in the kitchen at this point, sort of hanging about and he muttered that he wished we were back there too because it was a lot less hassle. I thought this was an unusual thing for him to say because he's always quite happy to get back to work as a rule. I was also a bit surprised that he hadn't left before the rest of us, as he always does, but I was in too much of a rush, getting my bags together and shepherding the girls into the car to take that much notice. As we followed Rob out of the drive though, Lucy said, 'isn't it odd that Dad's so late this morning?'

We're a bit old-fashioned and I gave up work when we had Claire. I was happy to stay at home and we decided that it was best for the kids and not that bad money-wise because of what we'd have had to spend on childcare. To be honest too, I hadn't much enjoyed teaching and I didn't want to make a career in it so when the twins went to school I'd done a librarian course and had got a half-time job-share at the children's library in town. My partner and I, Sue, mix and match our hours and this week I was doing mornings. My plan had been to come home at lunchtime and have a blitz on the ironing before everyone got home from school but when I turned into the drive, Rob's car was there. I assumed that he'd nipped back because he'd forgotten something – he could do that now he was at Bouchard – so I was completely unprepared to find him sitting slumped at the kitchen table.

My first thoughts, obviously, were that he was ill. When he lifted his head, hearing me come in, his face was ashen. My stomach did a somersault: there'd been an accident or a death, one of the kids or my mum or dad? But no, it was none of these things. Rob had been sent home from school, suspended until further notice, pending investigations into an alleged sexual assault on a Year 9 girl.

I knew he hadn't done it. There was no way he could have done it. Nothing about Rob would ever incline him to do such a thing. It was impossible. There was a mistake and it would all be sorted out soon. No question. So: what did we have to do? What did the union say? He had told them, hadn't he? When was this supposed to have happened? Who was the girl? What was the matter with her that she was saying such things? I just fired off loads of questions and Rob just sat there, holding my hands and looking as bad as I'd ever seen him look – like when his mum died a couple of years ago. 'Oh Kate, Kate,' he said.

He told me that he had had an inkling that there was going to be a formal suspension the day before we went to Brighton. On that Friday the Head had called him in and said an allegation had been made but that he was hopeful that, over the holiday, social services would talk to the girl and she'd withdraw what she'd said, namely that Rob had got her in a corner in the classroom and stroked her breasts. The Head had explained that, if this didn't happen, then Rob would not be allowed back to work until the case had been thoroughly investigated by social services and the police and it'd been established that nothing had happened.

I couldn't believe it. How could they do this? Wasn't it enough that Rob had said he hadn't done it? He had made it clear that he hadn't, hadn't he? Could it be that he hadn't been clear enough?

'Oh Kate,' he said again, 'think about it. If one of our girls said a teacher had touched her, wouldn't we want a proper investigation and the teacher out of the way?'

'Of course we would, but our girls wouldn't make up such wicked lies.'

'Well. Maybe Leanne's parents think that about her too.'

'But Rob, she's lying, it's different.'

'But we've got to prove it first.'

'So are you telling me that you're guilty until you're proved innocent? That's crazy, that's not how the law works.'

'It is in cases of child abuse.'

'But you're not an abuser.'

'They don't know that.'

During the rest of the afternoon we went round in circles. Or rather I went round in circles. I couldn't get my head around the fact that Rob had apparently been condemned on the word of a silly 14-year-old. Heaven's sakes, he could hardly recall who she was and yet she'd gone and done this. Why? Rob could think of no reason. And how long was this investigation going to take? Rob had asked the Head that and he'd said he had no idea but he hoped it would be quick because he needed a head of science.

The only good thing I could see in all this was that it explained why Rob had been strange during the holiday, which meant that I could put all thoughts that he was having an affair out of my head. I told him that I'd been frightened about this and it was then that he totally broke down and wept, saying that he'd decided not to tell me what was going on in the hopes that it would have all blown over by the time we got home. He said he was really sorry that I'd been put through these worries and that he'd been aware that his behaviour had been out of order at times but that he'd just been so wound up and anxious. He said that, in a way it was a relief that I knew now and that he didn't have to keep things hidden from me any more but he didn't think that we should tell the kids. I agreed with this. After all, this was all just so ridiculous that it was bound to be sorted out soon and there was no point in worrying them about something and nothing. But what would we tell them? We didn't want them thinking he was seriously ill or having tests for cancer or whatever. Emma and Lucy had a friend whose father had recently died of a brain tumour and who had been at home, looking really quite well, until right up to the end. I knew this had disturbed the twins because when we had had to tell them he'd died they'd asked how could that be because they'd been round playing with Izzy the previous week and Brian had seemed fine then. If we said he was stressed that might also cause anxiety so we decided to say that he'd been asked to prepare some new teaching materials and that the Head had told him he could do that at home. We knew it would seem a bit strange but Rob could tell them that this was one of the things that sometimes happened at Bouchard and they'd be none the wiser. In any case, I fully expected that he'd be back at work before the end of the week so there wouldn't be time for it to become an issue.

By the time we'd decided on our story it was 3 o'clock. I suggested that it wouldn't be a bad idea for Rob to go out and come in at his normal time. He could then announce his 'time out' to us when we were all together and it would seem more natural. This is what we did and apart from Sam saying he wished his chemistry teacher could work from home too, no other comments were made. After all, why should they have been? We'd always been honest with the kids, even when Rob's mum was dying we'd told them she was, so they had no reason to think we were dissembling. I can't pretend that I was happy with all this subterfuge but how do you tell teenage children that their father has been accused of sexual assault? Parents and sex don't fit well together at the best of times, let alone when something dodgy is in the frame.

So the rest of the week went by. I went out to work in the mornings and Rob stayed at home, reading and gardening and generally pottering around. By Friday I was getting impatient and was wondering why things were taking so long so I suggested Rob ring up Simon who was head of Year 9 and ask him what was going on. Si has been a friend of Rob's for years and really, it was through him that Rob decided to make the move to Bouchard. 'I can't,' he said, 'I'm not allowed to talk to anyone from the school while the investigation's under way, and they aren't allowed to talk to me either.' I couldn't believe this and it made me cross too. To stop people talking to their friends and colleagues is just awful because it creates a sort of isolation and distancing of someone who is already feeling out in the cold.

'I'll phone him up then,' I said.

'No Kate, you mustn't. It'd only compromise Si and it wouldn't do me any good to be seen to be trying to find out what's going on and maybe trying to influence people and get them on my side.'

'What do you mean? Don't be so ridiculous. You haven't done anything and I'm sure everyone knows that.'

'I doubt that many people know anything for sure about what's supposed to have happened. They'll know I'm not there and they'll know I've been suspended but that'll be about it. I've been doing a bit of research on the internet and I've found out that there's a procedure that has to be followed when this sort of thing happens and Bouchard are following it to the letter.'

'But what about the union? Hasn't the rep been in touch since she told you on Tuesday she would be doing all she could?'

'No. There's been nothing. But I suspect that's because nothing much has happened. I hate to have to tell you this, Kate, but what I've seen on the net suggests that sometimes things can take a long time.'

'What do you mean? Weeks?'

'Weeks, months even sometimes.'

And weeks did go by.

Every so often there'd be a snippet of news – mainly to the effect that investigations were proceeding – and Rob also had to go to a meeting with social services and to an interview with the police. On both occasions he was accompanied by Ralph, a retired head teacher who now worked for the union and who was, according to Rob, both knowledgeable and supportive. Rob didn't tell me much about what went on at these meetings but he did say the police interview was horrid, degrading and intrusive. Ralph, who had heard it all before, advised him to put everything out of his head and remember that the police were simply doing their job and that sometimes the people they had to work with were paedophiles and perverts.

At the beginning of the second week of the suspension we did learn the exact nature of the allegations. This girl, Leanne, had said that Rob had asked her to stay behind after a lesson. This much was true. Rob had kept her back in order to have a word because he was fed up with her disruptive effect on the class. Although she was obviously very bright and able, she clearly didn't like or didn't care about doing well in science and was, instead, putting her energies into mucking about, distracting her companions and sometimes even doing things that were potentially dangerous when they were doing practical experiments. Rob told her that if she didn't settle down he was going to have to have her excluded from the class. He said that while he was talking to her she stood there, in a typical, sulky, defiant teenager stance, head tossed to the side, one hand on her hip, the other tapping on the table that was between them, exuding 'I don't give a toss' and 'have you finished yet' from every pore. In effect, she was being given a second chance and the opportunity to mend her ways, but her story was that Rob'd told her she was getting low marks in chemistry and that, if she liked, he'd help her out with some extra, private tuition. She said he'd said there would be no cost to her parents and that nobody needed to know, it was just that he liked helping pretty girls. As he'd said this he was supposed to have put his arm around her and stroked her right breast. She said she was frightened but that, at this moment, a couple of her friends, wondering why she hadn't joined them yet had come into the room and had seen what was going on. Again, this had happened, but the reality was that these friends, a boy and a girl, had come into the room just as Rob was telling the girl to go and think on what he'd said. They, however, had made witness statements saying they'd seen Rob's arm round Leanne. With the desk in the way though, this simply wouldn't have been possible. Nevertheless, the fact that there was three people's evidence made the case against Rob so much stronger. This appalled me. How could three kids gang up in this wicked way? And why didn't their parents do something? After all, given that they were all minors, the families would all have to know what was going on. And if three people were implicated they would probably have talked to others and so the chances were that the whole school and parents and people in the local community knew about this too. How long would it be before word got back to our kids, especially as they all belonged to clubs and societies that were open to everyone in the area? They were almost bound to come into contact with Bouchard pupils or friends of such. And now Claire was 18, she went out into town, to nightclubs and pubs where she mixed with youngsters from all over. I could well imagine that there might be gossip doing the rounds about the pervy teacher. How awful it would be if she heard it and found out that it was her dad they were talking about.

Towards the end of the third week I told Rob we ought to tell them. After all, the preparing teaching materials story probably wouldn't work for much longer. My own parents were, I thought, already becoming suspicious. We hadn't meant to let them know anything was amiss but one afternoon, my mum had got mixed up about my shifts and she'd phoned to speak to me and Rob answered and had had to say he was working at home in order to explain why he was there at 2.30 on a school day. Now they were beginning to ask questions about when he would be going back and I was having to make elusive replies. Rob, however, refused point blank to let me say anything to anyone. In fact we had an argument, our first real argument connected with this business, over it. I gave way because he was so adamant and upset, but I was worried, as I thought that not saying sooner could have worse consequences in the long run.

I hadn't felt able to confide in anybody about what was going on but after this row I was so wound up that when I went for our weekly work catch up coffee with Sue I blurted it all out. She was lovely. She let me talk and talk and handed me tissues when I ran out. She chastised me for not having said anything before and said that she'd thought I seemed a bit not quite right. When I'd got over the first rush of words and crying she asked me if I believed Rob's story. My immediate reaction was to be affronted and I jumped in with a defence but she said,

'Hang on, wait, I didn't say he had done it. I just asked if you believed his account. It seems a reasonable question. And has he talked about why these kids might be making these allegations? Has he got any idea what might be behind it? Has he offended or upset any of them and this is their way of getting their own back?'

'He says he's gone through everything he can think of but other than telling the girl to pull her socks up and behave, he can't think of any other reason. I do believe him, Sue. If I had the least suspicion I couldn't live with him, mainly because our children are similar ages to the one he's supposed to have interfered with. It'd just be too disgusting.'

I know that. And for what it's worth, I really think you ought to tell them. It'd be so much better coming from you and you don't know how much longer this nightmare is going to go on for.'

She was right of course. I'd never dreamt we'd be in this position for more than a couple of days and now Rob had been off school for nearly four weeks. We were definitely feeling the strain and trying to be upbeat for the kids added to it. At least if they knew about what was going on, that'd be one thing less. But I didn't know how to tell them and I knew too, that in his present mood, I'd have to overrule my husband and that wouldn't be pleasant.

Living through all this with Rob wasn't in the least bit easy. When I'd occasionally fantasised about bad things happening, as you do, I'd always assumed that, in adversity, we'd be a strong team, supportive of each other and, basically, solid. But it wasn't proving to be quite like this. As soon as the kids went off to school every day, Rob seemed to retreat into a sort of self-centred egocentric bubble, leaving me to try and carry on as normal. And there I was, dashing around like a demented Pollyanna, trying to be all cheery and upbeat. It was as if he didn't recognise that I was affected by this thing too. After three weeks he hadn't offered to make the dinner once and while, at first, I'd not expected him to, thinking that he needed space and cosseting, I must be honest and say I was starting to feel some resentment. It really was coming to be all me, me, me as far as Rob was concerned. For instance, one day, in the second week, when I was working afternoons, I'd persuaded him to come into town with me, do a bit of shopping and then have an early lunch. We were sitting in Starbucks when this woman and a young girl, presumably her daughter, came in and sat on a sofa to our right. I suddenly noticed that they were staring at us and that the girl was chattering away, 97 to the dozen. I said to Rob, 'don't make it obvious that you're looking, but do you know that girl? Does she go to Bouchard?' He didn't know: after all he'd only worked there for a couple of months and had got to know very few of the children. Nevertheless he, like me, decided that they knew him and were talking about what he was supposed to have done. 'Let's go,' he said. So we left, leaving our paninis half eaten and all the way to the library Rob was going on and on about how awful this was for him. No mention of me and no mention at all of how bad it was for us as a family.

Anyway, on the Sunday after I'd had my chat with Sue I woke up early, determined to speak to the kids. Our normal Sunday routine is to have a bit of a lie in then I'll get up at around ten and make bacon sandwiches for everyone. Having thought about it all through the Saturday, I'd decided that I'd tell them when we were sitting down for breakfast. Having laid there for a while I got up at 8 o'clock, made a pot of coffee and took it up along with the papers, like I usually do. I flicked through the main section and the magazine, but I wasn't really taking it in. My mind was too much on plucking up my courage to go through with my intentions. By 9.30 I felt that it was now or never.

'I'm going to tell the kids this morning,' I said to Rob.

'I don't want you to.'

'I know, but I can't leave it any longer. If you don't want to be there then you'd better go out but I think it would be better if we did it together.'

I think he could tell that I wasn't going to budge on this. And, unedifying though it was, I was sort of fuelled by an unreasonable anger that it was through Rob that we were in this position and that, therefore, he ought to take some responsibility.

I went downstairs, made the sarnies and called everyone to the table. Rob sat in his usual place, glaring at his plate, looking as angry as I think I have ever seen him. My appetite was completely gone and I sat there, fiddling around with the mustard pot and sauce bottles but my mind was completely made up and I knew that I had to speak now or else I might bottle out. It felt a bit like diving from the highest board as I opened my mouth and said: 'We have to tell you something. A girl at Bouchard has accused Dad of assaulting her and that's why he's not been going into school.'

There was a stunned silence then Claire said 'What? What do you mean "assaulting her"?'

Rob was still staring down at his plate and I could feel that he wasn't going to speak.

'She said that he touched her inappropriately and because of that the school have had to suspend him until investigations are completed. Apparently that's the law, even in cases like Dad's where it's obviously lies and a load of rubbish.'

'What do you mean "touched her inappropriately"?'

'Well, she says he touched her breast.'

'Oh my God. That is so sick.'

'But he didn't do it.'

'Then why did she say he did?'

'Claire, it's your dad we're talking about here. We know he didn't do it.'

'Yes well, what did he do then? Why'd she make it up?'

'I don't know. We don't know. Probably she didn't like being told to stop messing about in class and saw this as a way of getting back at Dad. We just don't know yet.'

'And when will we know?'

'We don't know that either, the social workers and police haven't finished their enquiries yet.'

'The police? Oh my God. That is disgusting. How could you, you stupid man?'

And she stood up abruptly, knocking her chair over and rushed out of the room.

During this exchange Rob didn't move or say anything. Sam visibly blanched and the twins looked frightened; Lucy started to cry. I was amazed that Claire had behaved like this. I went over to Lucy and put my arms round her, telling her not to worry and that everything would be sorted out. At this point Rob stood up, said, 'So, are you satisfied now?', and left the room. I couldn't help myself at this point and though I definitely didn't want to do so in front of the children, I too wept.

The rest of the day was really horrible and took such a different track to our normal, comfortable Sunday. We all seemed to be existing around each other, almost on parallel lines as it were, all separate and isolated. It was odd and the roast dinner we usually have all together at around six o'clock just didn't happen because it didn't seem appropriate. Claire and Sam ensconced themselves in their rooms, and when asked if they wanted anything to eat, said they'd get their own food, thank you. After their, and my, tears, Emma and Lucy retreated into their twinness – as they do when they're upset – working on a Design and Technology craft collage project. They asked for beans on toast at around one and then went into the kitchen and cooked themselves some oven chips at 5.30-ish. Rob went out in the car not long after he'd stormed out of the kitchen without saying where he was going, indeed without speaking to me at all. I began desultorily working on my sewing machine, making up some fabric into curtains for the dining room but I couldn't really concentrate and as the day went by and Rob didn't return, I got more and more anxious. I tried ringing his mobile but it was switched off and I later found it on the work surface in the kitchen. There wasn't anything unusual in this because he's always forgetting to take it out or put it on, but I was getting worried. You do hear these stories of people going off and killing themselves, even though they're innocent, and while Rob has never ever been in the least suicidal, these weren't normal times. And then I got to thinking, but what if he did do it? What if he is guilty? And I felt disgust and repulsion both at Rob for what he might have done and with myself for even thinking he could have done it. I was so relieved when he came back at about six o'clock, when it'd been dark for quite some while and I was almost phoning the police. I asked him where he'd been but he just snapped 'out', then made a sandwich for himself, took it into the sitting room, put on the telly, watched it for an hour or so and then went to bed, while I carried on, messing about with the curtains in the dining room.

When I heard Rob go upstairs I wandered into the kitchen and poured myself a glass of wine from a bottle that had been opened and left on the table. I noticed the neck of another bottle poking out of the bin and, remembering that we'd drunk about half of it last night, realised Rob had had the best part of a bottle since he came in. This just wasn't him at all. He liked a drink but always complained he got a thick head if he had more than a couple, in fact, we really only kept wine in the house because I liked it. I don't ever drink on my own but, tonight I was feeling so on edge and I thought the alcohol might help me relax a bit. It was as if the atmosphere just wasn't right: everything was sort of uneasy and simply wrong and I had an awful, tight sensation in my chest and throat. If a drink could make me feel better, then what the hell?

Without wanting to make us seem like some sort of ideal, model couple Rob and I had never had a serious row or falling out in all the time we'd been together. I don't think we'd ever even spent as long without talking to each other as we had today. I just wasn't used to there being anything in the way between us and I didn't like it. Then Claire came in.

'Can I have some of that?' she asked, and without waiting for an answer filled a glass. 'I've been looking on the internet and I've come across this,' she said, passing me some sheets of paper, 'it might be useful.'

She'd printed off some information about an organisation called F.A.C.T., standing for Falsely Accused Carers and Teachers, which offered advice and support to people in the same sort of position as Rob. It might sound odd but simply seeing this print-out and reading that we were by no means on our own was a real relief. Then I wondered why Rob hadn't mentioned it. I knew he had done some research and surely this was just the sort of thing he must have come across. Maybe he had been in touch with them. But why hadn't he told me if they might be able to help?

Claire cut into my thoughts: 'He didn't do it did he, Mum?'

'No love. He'd never do anything like that.'

'I'm ever so sorry I said what I said this morning but I was really shocked and upset.'

'I know.'

'And I was really hurt that you'd not told us about it before. I can understand that you didn't want to tell the twins but to keep it from me and Sam wasn't right.'

'I know that too but we kept thinking it'd all be sorted and over and that there'd be no need for you to be worried. And your dad . . . Well, I think he was embarrassed for you to know this. It's really not something you want your daughter to hear, now is it?'

'But if he didn't do it, I can't understand that. He should know we'd not believe it.'

'Oh come on Claire. Think about it. It's just so sordid and nasty that he doesn't even really want to talk about it with me. As I said, we just hoped it would all blow over. I didn't imagine for one minute that it would drag on for as long as it has.'

'So why is it taking all this time?'

'They've got to do all the investigations properly. Your dad pointed out that if it was you who said you'd been assaulted by a teacher then we'd want everything done right.'

'Yes. But she's lying.'

'But they don't know that. There's procedures that have to be followed. When they're all done I'm sure it won't be long before it's all over.'

'Some of the stuff on this website's about people who've gone to prison and it's taken ages for them to be proved innocent. They've been in prison for years, Mum. For things they haven't done. Look what it says here, "If you have been falsely accused of child/adult abuse you should always seek advice from an experienced and competent solicitor at an early stage, and throughout the investigative period." Has dad got a solicitor?'

'He's got the union involved and a guy called Ralph is working with him.'

'But is he a solicitor, Mum? It looks to me like it's important.'

What Claire said about people being in jail really scared me. I hadn't thought for one minute that prison was a possibility. If Rob hadn't done anything then the investigations were bound to reveal this and that would be that. Surely.

Claire went on, 'How long is it now?'

'Six weeks since the allegation was first made because we had the fortnight's holiday and now Dad's been suspended for a month.'

'Do you mean you knew when we were away? Oh God, Mum. I do wish I'd known because it explains why Dad was so strange. Me and Sam wondered if he might be having an affair.'

That hurt. To think that the kids had talked about Rob's behaviour and had worried too was really upsetting. And so was the fact that I'd not even noticed they were concerned. I'd been too wrapped up in my own anxieties to see what was going on with my children.

'I'm sorry. Oh Claire, I am so, so sorry,' and for the second time in a day I cried.

She was lovely, bless her. She put her arms round me and said the sort of 'don't cry, it'll be alright' things I'd always said to her and the others when they were hurting and although it was nice to be comforted like this, I really felt quite pathetic and inadequate because it should have been me being strong for them. When I'd cried myself out and pulled myself together she said,

'Look. You really do need to check that Dad has got the proper advice and it might not be a bad idea to see if these F.A.C.T. people can help.'

'You're right. I will talk to him about it. And Claire, I am sorry I didn't speak to you and Sam.'

The truth of the matter was that, with the exception of my 'confession' to Sue, I hadn't spoken to anyone, including Rob, about what was going on, about how it was affecting us and about what was going to happen, or rather, about what might happen. And Rob didn't have much to say anyway. Now I thought about it, it was a bit like that saying about living with an elephant in the room and trying to pretend it wasn't there. While we weren't quite at the Basil Fawlty, 'don't mention the war' stage, I could see that we weren't that far off. Whether it was the wine or the cathartic effect of crying with Claire, I decided that this state of silence couldn't carry on and I determined that I'd speak to Rob in the morning. I didn't have to wait that long though because, as I crept into our bedroom, trying to make as little noise as possible, Rob switched on the light.

'I've behaved badly today,' he said. 'I should never have gone out like that, especially as you were right about telling the children. I'm really sorry, Kate. I just hate all this and the way it's making me useless and snappy and scared. I'm scared, Kate, and I don't think I can cope with this waiting around for something to happen for very much longer.'

He sounded so down, forlorn, and contrite and so much in need of reassurance so I got into bed and put my arms round him, just like Claire had done with me. We made love then and I realised that, not only had we not done this since the start of the whole business but that we'd barely even touched each other. Without either of us saying anything about it, it was as if the allegation, being sexual, had sullied and got in the way of mine and Rob's physical relationship, as well as everything else.

Afterwards, when we were lying there, Rob told me that he'd spent the day aimlessly driving between and wandering around shopping complexes off the motorway. He said that, initially, he had felt really angry with me but that almost as soon as he left the house, he'd realised that his crossness was misplaced, that it was the case that the children did have to know and that it was better that we tell them. Then it wasn't long before he'd begun to worry about me and about how anxious and frightened I was likely to be feeling, not knowing where he was or what he was up to. Even so he'd not been able to phone and tell me he was okay because he felt so ashamed of himself, both of his behaviour in the morning and also with regard to the whole situation we were facing. He explained that he felt entirely responsible for the mess and, in addition, that he considered himself to be a total failure as a husband, father and teacher. I told him I didn't see it like this at all but, rather, that he was the victim of a silly, naughty – not a malicious, evil, wicked – girl. Then we did talk, and I mean talk properly, about his embarrassment and shame: about his feelings about going back to work at Bouchard and about the way in which people often think there's no smoke without fire. He spoke of his fears that the case would get into the papers and how awful that would be for all of us and about how we'd probably have to move. To be honest I felt sick when he said that, partly because it hadn't occurred to me that it could come to this and that our entire lives could be turned upside down by lies and false-hoods, but also because it made me aware of the agony Rob had been going through in his mind, thinking all this through. Then I felt inadequate because he hadn't felt able to share these thoughts and realising the pointless-ness of this sort of vicious circle, I said,

'Rob. We have got to stop this keeping things to ourselves. We're in it together and we need to be straight and honest with each other, and with the kids, if we're going to get through, otherwise it leaves room for doubt and suspicion. Okay?'

'Okay.'

'And whilst we are on this, Claire showed me some information about an organisation called F.A.C.T. that's for people who have been falsely accused. Perhaps we should contact them.'

'I don't know, Kate. I've seen that site and I asked Ralph about it. He wasn't very encouraging and said that, for a start, they dealt with more seri-ous cases and that also getting involved with them could look suspicious – as if I had done something. I don't know, he just didn't seem keen.'

'But they say you should have a solicitor and that makes sense. Is the union enough?'

'Well, they do have solicitors if necessary and I'm sure Ralph knows what he's doing.'

'Claire told me that there are people who have been in prison for years for something they haven't done. I couldn't bear it if that happened to you.'

'Stop it love. Go to sleep and let's put today behind us. I'll say sorry to the kids tomorrow and I just hope that they'll understand.'

On the Wednesday that followed that grim weekend I was on mornings and I'd not been long back when the phone rang. I was actually in the bathroom, sorting the washing when I heard Rob say 'Hello Ralph,' then 'Oh God,' and finally 'Thank You': this last in a flat voice. My stomach turned over. I went to the top of the stairs. Rob was sitting on the bottom step, his elbows on his knees, his head in his hands, and the receiver dangling down on its cord from the wall mounted set. 'What is it? What's happened, Rob?'

You know how they say drowning people see their lives flash before them in a split second? In the minutes between me hearing Rob say 'Ralph', and his reply to my question, my future revealed itself in what could be described as gory technicolour detail. I saw myself sitting in courtrooms, telling the children their dad had been found guilty, visiting prisons, speaking to reporters as part of the 'Rob Greene is Innocent' campaign I'd mounted, and God knows what else.

'It's over.'

'What do you mean?' Over could, after all, mean either way.

'The case has been closed. Apparently there were too many discrepancies in the stories Leanne and her friends told for the allegations to hold water so there's insufficient evidence to proceed any further.'

'But why has it taken so long? They could have worked this out immediately.'

'I don't know. I suppose it's just all the procedures they have to follow and overstretched services and everything. I'm just thankful it's finished. I was just about at breaking point. I don't think I could have taken very much more.'

And nor did I.

In the immediate aftermath of Ralph's call we sat there, on the stairs, arms round each other, both weeping in the relief from the tension and stress of not knowing what was going to happen next and the fear of the worst possible outcome being realised. Neither of us could wait to share the news with the kids so we decided to pick them up from school, stopping off on the way to buy champagne and Rob's favourite steak ready for a celebratory meal. And we had a wonderful evening. Even Claire's cultivated cool sophistication and Sam's usual taciturnity were compromised by their delight and they joined in wholeheartedly with Lucy and Emma's over-the-top gaiety and jollification. We all went to bed in a better state of mind than had been the case for a long while.

Perhaps it wasn't really surprising that, in the euphoria of the moment, the implications of the fact that there hadn't been a declaration that the allegations were lies didn't occur to me. All I had heard and cared about was that Rob wasn't going to be going to court, let alone to jail. The nightmare was over, we could get back to normal and I could start doing something about Christmas, which I'd more or less completely ignored. The events of the past weeks were, in my mind, already all in the past, a story to tell and dine out on, maybe.

Although Rob would have gladly gone in the following day (even with the faint hangover induced by all the champagne) he'd been told to return to school at the start of the next week. What I could barely believe however was that he was still expected to have those appalling children in his class and also, as far as we could see, they weren't in any way going to be punished. I had thought that, as Head of the Science Department, Rob had some say over who he taught, but apparently not. Ralph did strongly recommend that the kids concerned, and Leanne in particular, be moved to another school within the Authority but the Head, Dr Smith, wouldn't countenance this. It seemed that he was too concerned about any potential negative local reputation that such a measure might give rise to. Indeed, he actually seemed to be annoyed with Rob and the impression he gave was that he held him responsible for the whole episode. I'd expected the Head to be supportive and sympathetic, but not a bit of it. On the Monday morning when Rob went back Dr Smith even called him in and told him to be careful, emphasised that he would be personally keeping an eye on him, and that if any more 'funny business' happened he'd be 'down like a ton of bricks'.

Going back, therefore, didn't turn out to be quite the relief we'd expected. Things were not the same as they had been before, or at least that was how Rob felt. Whilst other members of staff didn't – or weren't supposed to – know exactly what had happened or the nature of the allegations that'd been made, there'd obviously been a lot of speculation and people seemed a bit cagey. I'd been hurt that, as the weeks had passed by and Rob hadn't returned to school, no one from Bouchard had got in touch. Rob had said that he understood this because they weren't allowed to talk to him about anything to do with what was going on but I still held they could have given him a ring or sent an email or a card just to say 'thinking of you'. I would have done that had any of my friends, or even acquaintances, been in this situation. I felt Rob had been particularly let down by Simon even though Rob's view was that it would've been just too difficult for both of them to be together and not discuss the matter. Even now though, when Rob had suggested they go for a drink, Simon had made what sounded like lame excuses.

Of course, it was entirely possible that we were simply being paranoid and reading in things which weren't actually there. It was also the case that Rob was still very much a newcomer at the school and being away so soon after starting there meant that he hadn't had the chance to begin to establish relationships. Nevertheless, and despite all our attempts to provide rational explanations, Rob did feel, as he put it, a bit like Typhoid Mary. It was as if he was in some way a potential source of contamination and people were wary of coming, or being seen to come, too close. We did think though that when he went back in January everything would have settled down and be, if not forgotten, at least over and done with.

It wasn't quite like this though. On the first day back Rob had a Year 8 class which had something of a reputation for being badly behaved and difficult to handle. The lesson involved a practical and after he'd given a demonstration of the experiment, Rob began, as usual, to go round the class to see how they were getting on. As he approached a group of three girls, a lad across the other side of the room shouted out in a sing song manner, 'watch out, watch out, there's a perv about'. This led to uproarious laughter and then lots of shouting and offensive and obscene banter that Rob wasn't able to stop. He couldn't leave the room because of the chemicals that were being used so he called into the prep room for the technician to come and when she did he asked her to go and get Mrs Longson, the deputy head.

By the time Mrs Longson arrived the class was in uproar. They had behaved as if Rob was simply not in the room and he had had to listen to their pornographic accounts of what he was supposed to have done to Leanne and a whole harem of other young girls. According to the classroom *News of the Worlds* he had been sacked from his previous job for having sex with students in the stock cupboard as well as for downloading paedophile images on the school computer. This was known to be true because Catherine's cousin was at Leesmith and knew all about it. And it wasn't just girls who were at risk either because someone's brother in Year 9 had caught Rob hiding behind a cubicle door in the boys' lavatory, masturbating while watching the lads peeing.

As if all this wasn't bad enough, the fact that Mrs Longson's appearance occasioned immediate silence made Rob feel even more ineffective, inadequate and humiliated. He didn't stay to hear what she had to say but walked out of the lab and made straight for Dr Smith's office.

The Head's secretary, June, seeing him coming and obviously aware that something was seriously amiss, got up from her desk and stood in front of the door, effectively barring Rob's way. 'He's got someone with him at present. Will you take a seat, Mr Greene?'

There wasn't long to wait. After about five minutes the door opened and the lab technician came out, saw Rob and scuttled out of the room without acknowledging him. The secretary went in, closed the door, and after another few minutes invited him to enter.

According to Rob, Smith had a face like thunder. He asked for 'an account' of what had happened. Rob told him and when he'd finished he asked the Head what he was going to do, meaning, about the pupils. However, Dr Smith's reply made it clear that his concerns were quite other when he said, 'What am I going to do? I'm going to tell you to go home and if there's anything you've left in the science block tell June and she'll get it for you. I'm going to take advice from the authority and I suggest that you contact your union immediately to do the same. I told you I didn't want any more trouble and I'm not having it.'

'But I was subjected to an unacceptable and obscene barrage in there. I was harassed. Those children need to be punished and it needs to be made plain to them that this sort of thing can't happen.'

'Indeed, Mr Greene. It can't. And that is why I am telling you to go home,' then, and in a softer tone, 'Why don't you go to your doctor and see if he can give you something to help cope? As soon as we know what the LEA advise, we'll be in touch.' And he stood up and opened the door. His parting shot was, 'Don't forget to tell June what you want her to fetch for you.'

June had obviously been appraised of what was to happen. She was also, Rob thought, deeply uncomfortable and embarrassed and didn't look him in the eye. He told her where his coat, bag and laptop were and sat down to wait, feeling, he said, in a strange state of shock, anger and disbelief. He'd never, in all his career, been unable to control a class and it was this, rather than anything else, that was preoccupying his thoughts when Mo Longson came in, clearly on her way to report to Smith. 'Are you alright?' she asked, then without waiting for a reply, 'Bloody foul mouthed little monsters. If I had my way I'd. . . .' but before Rob could learn what she'd do, the Head's door opened and without looking at Rob he made a sweeping gesture with his arm, ushering Mo into his office. As she went through she turned and grimaced in what Rob took to be sympathy.

To give June her due, as soon as Rob had left, she phoned me and warned me he was on his way home. She said she thought I ought to be prepared and that I should know that Rob was extremely upset. I told her I appreciated her call but then asked her, unfairly, what sort of a place Bouchard was that these things could happen. Poor woman mumbled she was sorry.

When Rob came in we just held each other for a while and then he went to phone Ralph who was not, it turned out, that surprised. He'd seen similar things happen time after time. Apparently, teachers who have been accused of sexual offences often experience taunting, abuse, and fantastical embroidering of what they are supposed to have done, and are even more likely than their colleagues to have further allegations made against them. He told Rob to wait and see what the LEA and the school had to say and that the union would support Rob in what he chose to do, but that his personal advice was to think about early retirement, taking a pension and doing some other kind of work. When Rob pointed out that he was only 53 and had four kids to support through university, Ralph said, exactly, and that he presumed that Rob wanted to be around to be able to do this.

Having been in this line of work for a good few years Ralph had a library of stories of teachers who had tried to carry on but whose reputations kept coming back to haunt them; of people who had applied for teaching job after teaching job all over the country who, for some given reason or other, but always really, because of their history, were never appointed; of nervous breakdowns, premature deaths from stress-related causes; and of suicides committed, it would seem, out of sheer desperation and a sense of letting down one's family. He said it wasn't impossible that Rob could continue at Bouchard but that now, following the classroom incident, it would be difficult, even if, which seemed unlikely, the children concerned were suspended or expelled. Nor was it beyond the bounds of probability that he could get another teaching job somewhere local or further afield, although the chances were that that wouldn't be easy either.

Now, five years down the line, I can see that Ralph's assessment was pretty much accurate. Rob spent a couple of months in a sort of no-man's land while the LEA and the school were supposedly discussing what to do, then there were a couple of terms' sick leave on grounds of stress, which the union recommended that he take. During this time he must have sent off and applied for a hundred or so jobs, starting with head of department posts but as these applications yielded nothing, at lower, and finally at basic levels. There were a couple of interviews but these weren't successful. We'd reconciled ourselves to him going anywhere and, if necessary, living in rented accommodation during the week but although I and the children, the twins especially, anguished over this, we might as well have not wasted our time worrying because nothing came of any of it.

Before the sick leave period was up Rob decided that he would go down the early retirement route. We'd looked into it and decided that we could manage, not least because the children would then become eligible for EMA and university grants if Rob didn't manage to get other work. And of course, I could go back full time now, in fact, I had been thinking about doing so ever since Lucy and Emma went to secondary. We wouldn't be starving, even if we had to be more careful.

It worked out okay really money-wise, because just around the time Rob decided to go for early retirement, Sue's husband got a job in Scotland which meant that she would be leaving. As soon as I heard about this I went to see the chief librarian and said that I was interested in full-time work now. She told me I'd have to apply but knowing this, they advertised a full or part-time post. It was all a bit stressful because someone better than me could have come along, so the interview was nerve racking, but I did get it!

As for Rob: the sick leave wasn't a scam. He did really need it. It's odd but it was the fact that he'd been unable to get the class quiet that really distressed him. While he knew he hadn't done the things he was alleged to have done and nothing could take that knowledge away, he'd always seen himself as a competent teacher and now that identity or image didn't, in his view, apply. Nor was he prepared to accept any explanations as to how and why he had been unable to control that class on that occasion. It took him some time and some counselling to come out of the depression but once he did he made a real effort to put things behind him and move on. He got a job delivering cars which most of the time he does quite enjoy. He's also taken on an allotment and has got really into growing organic veg to the extent that he's thinking of applying for another plot and maybe selling some produce to a local deli.

The kids were very upset at first and they did have some anger which they took out on Rob and me, Claire in particular. They all experienced hearing other youngsters saying things about their dad and though he's never admitted it, I suspect that the black eye Sam got a couple of days after Rob was sent home from school was the result of a fight. They're all okay now – Claire is in her first job, Sam's in his final year at uni and the twins are in Year 13 – but they did have a lot to cope with which makes Rob feel bad sometimes because he feels responsible. One lasting effect on them, and on me, is that they are very sceptical about what you might call institutional justice. They saw what happened to their dad and they, like me, now know that the seemingly impossible can happen to anybody. I would never have believed that someone's career could be ruined in such a casual sort of a way. I'm also disgusted with the way in which Bouchard School, or rather Dr Smith, treated Rob. I know all about the need for schools to have a good image and reputation but what about loyalty to staff? If Rob had assaulted that girl then that would have been another matter, but even so, I would have expected different treatment – not that he should have been given the benefit of the doubt – I'm not so naïve as to believe that teachers never do bad things to their students – but that he would have been treated respectfully and as innocent until he was proved guilty. Having said this though, I've had to learn the hard way how the law when it comes to child abuse doesn't really do that. Yes, children do have to be protected and there are some evil people out there but it seems to me that innocent folk can become victims simply because of how the law works and I don't think that is just.

We are certainly very different people now as a result of all this and not necessarily for the better. Rob and I did nearly split up more than once and I honestly don't think we'd have had those near misses if that girl hadn't made her poisonous allegations. I never really thought that Rob had touched her but there were times when I did blame him for keeping her behind that day.

It's great that good people do want to become teachers but I have been so relieved that none of our kids have wanted to go in for it. Teachers aren't safe. None of them.

Chapter 8

It didn't take long for the rumour mill to start grinding

Vee had decided that nothing, but nothing, was going to stop her from being in the chair at Toni and Guy's at quarter past five that afternoon. She wasn't sure exactly how many hairdresser's appointments she'd had to cancel – it was at least three and possibly could even be five but, whatever the exact number, it was now impossible to ignore the widening expanse of grey where her colour had grown out. Catching sight of herself in the mirror on the way to sixth form assembly, she'd hated what she'd seen and had strengthened her resolve to leave school dead on the dot of four. Jean, Vee's redoubtable PA, had been enlisted to make sure that she got away and so, when Sally Braithwaite, Head of Year 11, was shown into her office at a quarter to four, Vee knew it had to be about something pretty serious.

'Jean told me you need to leave by four,' said Sally, 'and I'm really, really sorry but I'm afraid I honestly don't think this can wait. Natalie Brown, Olivia Knight and Becky Woodward have just come to me and made allegations about Jim Barlow. Natalie Brown says she's been seeing and having sex with him for the past nine months and Olivia and Becky say he's been coming on to them, getting them in the geography room stock cupboard and touching and trying to kiss them. They're in my office, all really upset and in a right state. I got Bronwen to sit in with them while I came to see you.'

Clearly the hairdressers' was off.

***

As Vee turned into the drive at twenty past nine, Malcolm opened the front door and held out a large glass of red wine.

'Thought you'd need this love,' he said, exchanging the Beaujolais for Vee's briefcase.

'Don't I just. I'm absolutely knackered.'

'Well, supper's ready as soon as you are. I decided you'd probably be able to do with something substantial when you finally got home so I've made one of my everything in the pot chicken stews with *ta dah* dumplings. And I've made you an appointment with Lucy for nine on Saturday morning: she'd had a cancellation come in just before I rang and I thought you'd be able to make that. She said just to call her tomorrow if it wasn't any good.'

'You are a star,' said Vee, starting up the stairs. 'Let me go and get my suit off and I'll be right there.'

***

The stew was delicious and the dumplings were so good that Vee ate far more than she knew was wise. She was well aware of her tendency to comfort eat and even though the consequence was tight waistbands and self-loathing, there were times when her attitude was a) needs must when the devil drives, b) she would definitely go to the gym first thing on Sunday morning, and c) the occasional overindulgence wasn't, indeed just couldn't be, as bad health-wise as hitting the booze. Having just entertained that justificatory thought, and as Malcolm emptied the last dregs of the bottle into her glass, she realised, with a bit of a sobering jolt, that she hadn't been aware that she'd drunk anything like as much as the unequivocal evidence revealed.

***

They'd had very little conversation over the meal, concentration having been focused on eating and on debating the pros and cons of dried, over fresh, thyme but now that they were finished and had moved into the sitting room, Malcolm asked,

'So what's happened then? I thought nothing bar an earthquake was going to keep you from the hairdressers' today.'

'I'm afraid it looks like we've probably had the equivalent. Some kids, three girls in Year 11, have accused a male teacher of very, very serious sexual misconduct, stretching back nine months in one case, and whatever the truth of the matter, we're likely to be in for a difficult and uncomfortable time. I was so late back because I've had to speak to the LEA and the area child pro-tection committee people and the girls' parents and Sharon Golding, the new Chair of Governors, none of which was a lot of fun. And then I had to brief Bill and we had to think about what we're going to do tomorrow and how we're going to handle it. God, I really do not need this. And I'm not supposed to talk to anyone about it, not even you. The LEA and the child protection folk were really strong on that. I've probably told you more than I should have done already.'

'What do you mean?'

'The rules are that it has to be kept entirely confidential at this stage and no one in or outside the school, apart from those who have to know or who're involved in the investigation, are to be told anything. Heaven's sakes, even the person who is alleged to have done this doesn't know at the moment and muggins here is the one who has to break the news that they've been sus-pended in the morning.'

'Suspended?'

'Yes. The alleged offences are so serious that he can't be in school until it's all sorted out. So as well as the thing itself there's cover to arrange and then people are going to be asking questions about where their colleague is and we're going to have to fudge it for as long as it takes. One of the first things the child protection woman told me was that these cases can drag out and she said not to waste time about getting in good supply. I must say she was quite helpful but I'm going to have to get on to the union tomorrow and find out all I can and also see if they can put me in touch with somebody else who's had to deal with this sort of thing. It's a minefield and there's a lot of room to make mistakes. Whether or not anything did happen, the shit can hit the fan and the school can be damaged, regardless of the harm done to the individuals concerned.'

'Do you think it's true?'

'I don't know. Obviously I wouldn't have thought so because I wouldn't want to think we'd got anybody who'd do that sort of thing working at Farrowdown anyway – although nobody would knowingly employ a known abuser, would they? And in any case, ever since Soham[1] and Ian Huntley and CRB checks and List 99 and what have you, it's supposed to be much more difficult for them to slip through the gaps. But do you remember, when the kids were at school and before we came here, that scandal at the Church of England High School where the Head of RE had been carrying on with a 13-year-old, taking her to his mother's house and God knows what?'

'Yes I do. Ally was in his son's class, wasn't she, and he'd come to our birthday parties. Didn't he bring that bingo machine as a present?'

'That's right. Then another time he brought a Little Mermaid doll and he really was Mr Favourite as a result. Ally insisted that he sat by her at the tea and she went round saying he was her boyfriend for weeks after! He was a lovely child, really sweet and ever so polite. There was a daughter too, a bit younger than him. I knew the wife a bit, Kate her name was, 'cus I'd met her once or twice at school concerts and parents' evenings and the kids' parties and she was also in a group of friends with Lyn and when Lyn was minding Ally – they all used to go to toddler group together and swimming and stuff. I remember one night, after it had all happened, nipping into that 8 Til Late shop on Alsop Road and she was working there. She'd changed her hair and I said, "you look fantastic!" because she did. And all she said was, "re-invention is better than a cure". And that's stuck with me. If I ever saw the boy or her, I thought about that – "re-invention is better than a cure" – and about how dreadful it must have been for her because it was all in the papers and the fact he was Head of RE at a church school somehow seemed to make it worse. Poor, poor woman. He went to prison for a very long time partly, I think, because she was so young and it was really so abusive of his position. I can't imagine what his mother was up to either but apparently he'd lied to her too, about the girl's age and about his so-called unhappy marriage. Lyn told me

Kate had immediately divorced him and that she'd said she wasn't going to move away because she hadn't done anything wrong except trust and marry the wrong man and I thought how brave and how right that was. It's really stayed in my mind and it all came back to me as I was driving home, what it must have been like for her and her children. I went to a day conference put on by the union about sex and schools not long after I'd become a head and I remember thinking about her then and how I thought I hope I'm never in a position where I have to deal with anything of the kind, which was naïve really because it does happen, and I know it happens more often than anyone'd like to imagine.'

'If one of the girls who've made these accusations said it'd been going on for nine months, why's she decided to complain now? Seems a bit odd that. I seem to recall that in that case you've been talking about, with the RE teacher, the child's mother found out and brought things into the open.'

'I don't know why it's come out now. And I can't ask any questions myself. The child protection people take responsibility for the enquiry so I have to wait on them. But I have to say part of me really wishes it had all stayed under the carpet, especially as we're expecting an Ofsted any minute now too. Still, I just have to wait and see. Maybe everything will sort out sooner rather than later but I need to go to bed now. I've arranged to meet Bill at 7.15 tomorrow to plan strategy for the day and I said I'd bring breakfast so I'll just get those croissants out of the freezer and put them on the kitchen table so as I don't forget.'

***

Bill Hatgreaves dialled the number and looked out of the window. Down in the car park he could see Jim Barlow getting into his car and Vee opening the rear door and depositing a laptop and a couple of carrier bags on the back seat. He saw her reach through the window and place her hand on Jim's arm in what looked like a comforting sort of way. Then the phone was answered.

'Hello? Rimton 732495.'

'Oh hello. Mrs Barlow?'

'Yes, who is that please?'

'It's Bill Hatgreaves. Deputy Head at Farrowdown. Mrs Barlow, I'm phoning to tell you that Jim's coming home and he's a bit upset. I thought you ought to know. There's been an allegation made against him and we've had to send him home while investigations are made.'

'Is he alright? What sort of investigations? What allegations?'

'I think it's best that Jim tell you when he gets home. I just thought it would be a good idea for you to know he's on his way and that he's upset. I'm sorry, Mrs Barlow. I don't think he'll be long. He said he'd go straight home. Try not to worry but he's going to need some support and I thought I should warn you.'

'I don't understand. He's not hurt is he?'

'No no. Nothing like that. But he'll be with you soon. As I said, Mrs Barlow, I'm really sorry to have to phone you like this but I thought you should know. Get the kettle on and that. And be ready. Do take care won't you.'

'But what's going on?'

'Oh I'm sorry, Mrs Barlow, there's someone at my door. I must go. Goodbye.'

Well, I made a right cock up of that, thought Bill, as he put down the phone, wishing both that he hadn't put himself forward for the job and feeling embarrassed for his obvious lie. But it had been the utter bewilderment on Jim's face as Vee'd told him what had been alleged and that he couldn't stay in school that had made Bill decide he'd ring the wife. He remembered seeing her only a couple of weeks ago when she'd come to pick Jim up after a parents' evening. She'd looked very pregnant and he'd felt a touch of envy, wishing he had a settled relationship, let alone the startings of a family.

Bill glanced at the clock and saw that it was half past nine. He'd only been in school for two hours and it felt like he'd already done a full day. But lunch wasn't until half past twelve, he was teaching all afternoon and Tuesday night was canoe club which meant he was unlikely to get away before seven if the boats were to be properly cleaned and stowed. Hours to go yet then. Still, tonight was also the night when he usually treated himself to an Indian from the Koh I Noor, a pint in The Crown next door while his order was being prepared, as much of a bottle of red as he felt like, and crap telly. Sad and unhealthy maybe, but it was a change from his normal evening routine of get home, work, make a sandwich or something on toast, more work, then bed. A man needed something to look forward to when he lived alone and there seemed little prospect of ever finding the time to change that state of affairs. And at least he had something to look forward to this evening. He couldn't imagine that Jim Barlow had. God, fancy having to tell his wife he'd been accused of having an affair and touching up pupils. Natalie Brown had said it'd been going on for nine months. The length of a pregnancy. What was Mrs Barlow going to think so close to giving birth? Would she think there was anything in it? Only a husband and wife know what goes on in a marriage and Bill was only a colleague, not a friend, of Jim's. They didn't even teach in the same department so Bill had no real knowledge of what the man was like or of whether there were any grounds for thinking he might have done what he was accused of doing. Certainly nothing untoward about him had come to Bill's attention, either formally or through staffroom gossip. There were a couple of other blokes who he did have his suspicions about though, not that there'd ever been any complaints or anything, but he'd seen the way they looked at the girls and how some of them hung around the sixth form coffee bar. One Saturday he'd seen Damian Jackson in a nightclub with a Year 13 girl but she must have been over 18 because the bouncers were checking everybody's ID that evening and even though, strictly speaking, no teacher could have a relationship with any pupil in the school where they taught, regardless of age, Bill didn't really think intervening was any of his business here. After all Damian was what?, 24, 25 at the most and he only taught in lower school anyway. Bill couldn't really see anything wrong in that. Lots of schools had cases where teachers had married pupils. In fact, his mum's best friend had married her teacher the summer she left school – back in 1947, so it was hardly anything new. As far as Bill could see his 'aunty' Doreen had hardly been abused and taken advantage of and while 'uncle' Wilf, her husband, had always seemed a colourless and nondescript little man, Doreen often told the story of being smitten and falling head over heels in love with him when she walked into his maths classroom on her first day at grammar school. But of course, the law was different then. Even so, clearly there were cases and there were cases and although some were obviously wrong, illegal and prosecutable, as this case with Jim Barlow would be if it was proven, others, Bill thought, couldn't be seen in quite so clear a light.

***

The plan that morning had been that Bill intercept Jim as soon as he arrived at school at around quarter past eight and ask him to come up to the Head's office. Nothing too unusual in that and it'd been Bill rather than Jim who might have appeared to look uneasy to any casual observer. When Vee'd told Jim he'd been accused of an improper sexual relationship with one girl and of sexual misconduct and harassment involving two others, his response had been 'who is it?' Vee'd told him that, in accordance with policy, the investigation would be being undertaken by the local child protection people, not the school, and that they couldn't tell him anything. Jim'd said 'one of them's Natalie Barlow isn't it? I thought she'd got over her crush or whatever it was on me and now she's saying this. It's not true. I've not had anything to do with her, nothing at all but I could've done if I'd wanted. She put it on a plate. Threw herself at me and made it plain that,' at which point Vee had intervened and stopped him, saying it was better if he didn't say anything except to the investigators. She'd also explained that the requirements were that he didn't talk about any of this with anyone at all from Farrowdown and that nobody in school, except those immediately involved was to know or would be told anything either. She asked him if he wanted anything fetching from his classroom because he had to leave the premises and not return until the all clear was given. Then he started again, saying he hadn't done anything and that he was an idiot and why hadn't he told anybody the girl'd been infatuated with him. And Vee'd just said, 'Don't, Jim. You'll be able to tell all this to the investigators but it's complicating matters if we don't follow procedure. Now, is there anything you want us to get?' He sort of pulled himself together then and said he'd left his laptop in the geography stock cupboard, as well as a pile of marking because he'd had to rush off last night to take his wife to an antenatal appointment because she had a trapped nerve and couldn't drive. Vee asked Bill to get the stuff and as he left the room he saw Jim put his head in his hands. Poor sod, Bill thought as he went down the stairs of the admin block, those little personal details like the wife's trapped nerve, somehow seemed to make the whole thing seem so much worse, more poignant.

***

Vee watched Jim drive away then walked briskly back to her office. She didn't want to see anyone at the moment or to have to answer any questions as to why Jim Barlow was going home. Everyone would assume the baby had started and she didn't want to have to prevaricate.

Bill stood behind her desk, looking down at the telephone handset, which was clasped in his hand. Hearing Vee enter, he lifted his head and spoke,

'I rang Mrs Barlow to let her know to expect Jim home and to tell her he'd be upset.'

'You didn't say why?'

'I said there'd been allegations made and that we'd had to send him home while investigations were being carried out. It was him talking about her trapped nerve and that. I just didn't think she should be totally unprepared in her state.'

'No, no. You were right to do it.'

'She wanted to know what it was all about and she sounded like she was beginning to panic and I'm ashamed I pretended someone was at the door and put the phone down. I didn't feel I could hedge it though, Vee.'

'No. Don't worry. I just hope he does go straight home now though else she'll be really worried. I'll leave it an hour then check that he is there.'

'Did he say anything when you were going to the car?'

'Not really. He just repeated that he hadn't done anything and that he should have told somebody that Natalie Brown was infatuated with him – and he's right. He probably should've done. He asked me what was going to happen and I told him what I know – which is precious little really. What do you think, Bill? What do you think from how he reacted?'

'He seemed totally gobsmacked to me. He was obviously shocked but who wouldn't be to have that chucked at you first thing in the morning? I don't really know him, Vee, but his wasn't a name I would have expected to hear in connection with this sort of thing.'

'No, nor would I. But you can't ever know for sure about what people are really like, can you? I just hope to God he didn't do it, for his sake and for ours.'

***

The bell had just rung for morning break and the staffroom was quickly filling up. From her place in the coffee queue, Liz Jenkins shouted across to Val Borthwick who was walking out of the room, a steaming mug precariously balanced on a pile of books,

'Are you going to organise the collection then?'

'What collection?'

'For Jim's baby. I've just had to cover for him. I saw him come in this morning but then he must have gone straight back out again so I'm assuming Lisa must have rung to say she'd started.'

'Well I don't know anything about that. No one's told me. But then I'm only head of department.'

***

It didn't take long for the rumour mill to start grinding. By the end of the day it had been ascertained that Lisa Barlow hadn't gone in to labour and people were beginning to wonder why Jim had come in and gone out in the way that he had done.

The following morning, Bill Hatgreaves who had responsibility for arranging supply cover, called Val Borthwick in to discuss a possible long-term replacement for Jim. Val already had someone lined up for Jim's paternity leave and, giving Bill the woman's telephone number, suggested that he try her first. Then she asked,

'What's this all about Bill? Is Jim ill? I didn't like to phone last night, especially after Karen, who's friendly with Jim's wife phoned up to see if she was ok and got a very curt response from Lisa, and the impression that her call wasn't at all welcome.'

'Jim's not ill.'

The silence dragged on.

'So? Why isn't he at work?'

'Look Val, it's a confidential matter. I'm not at liberty to say anything more. OK? I'll ring Helen Parkinson immediately and see what she says. With a bit of luck she might be able to start tomorrow. OK? Right. See you later then.'

Feeling very dismissed Val left the office and, as the bell had just gone for break, made her way to the staffroom. Picking up a coffee she went over to the corner where she generally sat when she allowed herself the luxury of a rest and a chat. More usually she grabbed a mug in passing, made herself a drink in the departmental stock cupboard cum office, or went without. Often there simply wasn't the time. Today though, feeling brushed off by Bill, anxious about the implications both for the department and for exam results of potential long-term staffing problems, and worried about what might be wrong with or for a junior colleague of whom she was very fond, she felt she deserved a bit of time out. Immediately she sat down though, Brian Fothergill, Head of History, asked her what was going on with Jim.

'I don't know Brian. Bill says it's confidential and that he might be off for some time.'

'So it isn't anything to do with the baby then?'

'I honestly don't know but I don't think it is'.

'I think our Master Jim has been a naughty boy' said Keith Smithson.

'What are you on about Keith?' asked Val.

She didn't like the man much. He was always ready to gossip and slag people off and a bit of a letch where women were concerned. She'd also got the impression from the way in which she'd seen his head of department repeatedly asking him if he could get his reports completed before parents' evening, that he was a lazy so and so.

'I think he's in trouble because of some little girlies.'

'Oh for God's sake, Keith. Don't be ridiculous.'

'I'm not being. What's the usual reason for someone to be suspended? Either they've walloped a kid or they've interfered with one. Stands to reason.'

'Who's said he's been suspended? Bill never said that.'

'Oh come on, Val! They're talking about getting long-term supply and you've been told it's confidential. Two and two make four.'

'You need to be careful, Keith,' interjected Brian. 'You need a bit more evidence before you start jumping to conclusions. And think what you're implying about a colleague. It's dangerous stuff what you're suggesting.'

'What is? Are you talking about Jim Barlow and Natalie Brown?' Establishing by a quick scan of her colleagues' amazed faces that she'd upped the ante by coupling names, Anna Castle, who had been passing, sat down. Val, Keith and Brian stared at her.

'Do tell dahlink!' said Keith in a cod Marlene Dietrich voice. 'Spill zee beans.'

'Well,' said Anna in a breathy way that made it clear that she had a story to tell and was dying to tell it, 'I'm Natalie's form tutor. She wasn't in yesterday or today. She was seen the day before yesterday, in a right state, going in to see Sally. And, cincher, this morning Sean Webster asked me if she was away because of Mr Barlow dumping her.'

'Sean Webster's a nasty little toe-rag,' said Brian. 'I wouldn't believe anything that he said.'

'Nor would I usually but then Tara Forrester said it wasn't that that'd upset her but the fact that she'd found out he'd been trying it on with Olivia Knight and Becky Woodward.'

There was a stunned silence then a, 'well, well, well. What did I say?' from Keith Smithson. 'My wife went off sex too when she was pregnant.'

'Shut up, Keith,' snapped Brian.

But Keith had got the bit between his teeth: 'I wouldn't have thought he'd got it in him. Stupid sod. Look, but don't touch. That's my motto.'

'Spare us your masturbatory fantasies, Keith, please.' Val, shocked to the core by what Anna had said about her protégé, stood up to go. 'And remember,' she said as she bent to pick up her mug from the table, 'all this is supposition. There could be quite another reason why Jim had to go home.'

Sally Braithwaite who was walking by at that point turned round and looking at the group in the corner said 'Val's right. And remember, careless talk costs lives, even when it's unfounded. I'd keep your thoughts to yourself, Keith, especially those which originate from your nether regions.'

Keith's 'get her!' sounded pathetic.

***

Vee operated a simple access policy: if her door was open, she'd see all comers so finding it ajar, Sally Braithwaite walked straight in.

'Do you mind if I close this?'

'Not at all. Would you like a coffee? Or have you had one?'

'I've come straight from having one in the staff room where, I thought you ought to know, people are starting to speculate on why Jim Barlow's off. Keith Smithson is being a total slime bag, as you might imagine, but other people are beginning to chunter too. I think you should make that announcement now, Vee. See if you can put the brakes on a bit.'

As the person to whom the allegations had been made, Sally actually knew more about what was said to have happened than anyone else in the school. Right from the very start, when Sally had come to her and said she'd got the three girls who'd made the accusations in her room, Vee had been scrupulously careful to follow procedures. She would have liked to ask Sally for further details because she was worried in case the school – that is she herself, since she believed that this particular buck stopped with the head – might turn out to have been negligent. However she'd restrained herself, with the consequence that all she knew was that Natalie Barlow was claiming she'd been in a sexual relationship with Jim Barlow for nine months and that Becky Woodward and Olivia Knight were saying that he'd fondled and tried to kiss them. In a sense, the less she knew the less she had to dissemble, and there was something to be said for that.

The day after the disclosures, Vee, Bill Hatgreaves, Sharon Golding the Chair of Governors and Sally as the girls' head of year as well as the recipient of their confidences, had talked about handling the business and any immediate repercussions within the school. They'd been well aware that it wouldn't take long for the gossiping to start and because of this and on the advice of both the child protection woman Vee had spoken to that first evening and the NAHT[2] union guy, Vee had prepared a brief announcement

saying essentially that: a member of staff is currently on leave pending investigations; that the matter was entirely confidential; that policy and
procedure requirements were that it should remain so; and that it was
expected that colleagues would respect this confidentiality and would not
indulge in idle speculation or discussion either among themselves or outside
of the school. This announcement was what Sally was referring to.

Vee had mixed feelings about saying anything. On the one hand, flagging
up that there was a potential problem alerted everyone to it and could really
fan the flames for gossip and innuendo on the grounds that there was no
smoke without fire. Countering this though, was the need to try and limit
fall-out and negative publicity by impressing the importance of confidentiality. And of course, there was Jim Barlow himself and his family to consider.
Nothing had been proven, the man might well not have done anything.
Surely he deserved not to be discussed, accused and publicly named? Perhaps
Sally was right and now was the time to speak.

Naïvely, maybe, Vee had initially thought – had hoped rather – that
within a couple of days everything would have been sorted out, the allegations would have been retracted as having been based on a misunderstanding
and Jim would be back at work with no need for any public statement. She
knew now though that such a neat outcome was unlikely. In the, what was it?
barely 43 hours since Sally had come to her room on Monday afternoon, Vee
had been on a rapid learning curve. She'd read everything she could lay her
hands on that dealt with teachers being accused of sexual misconduct and
she'd spent most of last night on the internet, trawling for reported cases and
scaring herself half stupid with some of the horrors she'd come across. For
instance, there was one school in what she'd always considered to be a sleepy
seaside town where, over a number of years, 14 teachers had been investigated, three of whom were convicted and sent to jail. She'd read the report of
the review that the local Safeguarding Children Board had conducted into
that case[3] and while she could see that the headteachers who'd been at the
school during the period in question had made mistakes, and serious ones, she
still felt for them. It wasn't quite there but for the grace of God, because Vee
didn't think she would have made the same errors of judgement, but
nonetheless. Then there were the false allegations, some of which had been
proven and some where investigations were ongoing, often while the accused
were still in prison or after they were released and were continuing to seek to
clear their names. In fact, she discovered, the family of one of the teachers
from the seaside school was actively and vociferously campaigning for his
exoneration and release from prison because, they claimed, his accusers had
lied. These cases seemed particularly appalling to Vee. How could you
rebuild a life after being branded a child abuser? She doubted that anyone
could, and especially not without moving away and starting over in a different place if not another country. She wondered too if she would employ a

teacher who had been accused, even though they'd later been shown to have been innocent. It would definitely be risky because if word got out, parents probably would make a fuss. It all came back to that wretched no smoke without fire thing – and that's what was worrying her about Jim. He was young, he should have a whole career ahead of him and this had happened. If, as she fervently hoped, it turned out that he hadn't done anything, he was still going to be tainted, even if Farrowdown wasn't. And what about his wife? 'Re-invention is better than a cure' came into her mind again. Oh well, she thought, and called Jean into her room to send round the message that there was to be an extraordinary staff meeting at afternoon break.

***

Hardly anyone in 11C liked Personal and Social Education and the class got the impression that their form tutor, Miss Baldwin, wasn't keen either. Most weeks they got a comprehension piece which they were supposed to do and then discuss 'the issues' it raised but what normally happened was Miss Baldwin gave the sheets out and as long as they kept the noise down and wrote some answers, they could chat among themselves or get on with some work for an examination subject that really mattered. Miss did her marking.

Today's topic was Responsible Relationships and the piece they were supposed to read was about the effectiveness of different types of contraception. Sometimes, when it was something more important like this, Miss read it out to be sure everybody had had it so when the papers had been distributed she said,

'Right. I expect you'll have done this before but it's something that's well worth going over again especially as Mrs Braithwaite has a bet on with all the other year heads that nobody in this year's Year 11 is going to be a premature parent. As a Year 11 tutor I stand to gain because if we win we're going to have a proper night out on the proceeds!'

'It's a good job Mr Barlow's been sacked then innit!', shouted Sam Wordley from the back of the classroom. 'I know he don't shoot blanks 'cus I seen him with his wife a few weeks ago and she was so pregnant she was about busting.'

'Yeah well have you seen Natalie lately? She ain't been in school for weeks either so how do you know she's not pregnant too?' was Josh Kendall's retort. 'That's enough of that. Now, Christina, will you start reading please?' Miss Baldwin said in a frosty voice.

***

'I suppose you've heard that Jim Baldwin's got a son?' said Pete Deighton to Val coming up behind her as she was putting a box of marking in her boot.

'No. No I hadn't actually.'

'My sister in law, my wife's twin, had a baby yesterday morning and when we went in to see her, believe it or not, Lisa was in the next bed.'

'Was Jim there? Did you see him?'

'No. She was going home later on so Lorna my sister in law said, and he'd've been coming to fetch her I suppose. Thank goodness really because I wouldn't't've known what to say if he'd been there.'

'Well, congratulations and baby stuff would have been quite apposite I'd've thought Pete, wouldn't you?' Val said, drily.

Pete's embarrassment was clear as he mumbled, 'Well yes but you know what I mean. Still, better be off. See you tomorrow.'

Driving home Val didn't know what to do. When she'd asked Vee about contacting Jim, once it had become clear that he'd been suspended, she'd been told that she couldn't talk to him about anything at all to do with school or about why he wasn't at work. This had seemed such a tall order that, after a week of worrying and prevaricating about how to proceed and as Jim didn't contact her, no doubt because he'd been put under the same prohibitions, she had, much to her shame, kept pushing him to the back of her mind. Some mentor she was – not! And her sarcasm to Pete really was a case of the pot calling the kettle. She'd been just as bad, worse in fact because she'd considered herself close to Jim.

In normal circumstances the birth of a colleague's baby was a matter for great fuss and present buying. But was that appropriate now? Oh hang it, thought Val, of course it was. The baby wasn't anything to do with school or what its dad might or might not've done. There was a Mothercare at the Blossomfields shopping centre. She'd go and have a spend and finger her colleagues for contributions tomorrow. It was the least they could do and no one could say they were breaching procedure by celebrating a birth. She'd buy a bottle of champagne and some flowers and chocolates too and she'd phone Vee when she got home and tell her what she'd done. Maybe they could go together and deliver it all tomorrow after school.

***

Straight after she'd put the phone down in disgust, Val dialled Vee. 'Hello?' a male voice answered in a very abrupt and interrogatory tone,

'It's Val Borthwick, from Farrowdown. Sorry to trouble you on a Saturday but could I speak to Vee please?'

'Oh Val! Hello! It's Malcolm here. Vee's around somewhere. Probably in the garden I think. Just hang on a minute and I'll go and get her. Sorry if I sounded a bit off but you can't be too sure who's on the line.'

Indeed you can't, thought Val, as she waited to speak with her boss.

'Val? Is anything wrong?' Vee sounded out of breath and a bit anxious, 'I was just doing a spot of digging therapy. Works wonders: no calories, no liver damage and it's even good for you. I can recommend it.'

'I'm sorry to disturb you, Val, but I've had somebody ring me up saying they're from the *Daily Mail* and offering me money to talk about Jim Barlow "in my capacity as his head of department" as he put it. I said "no comment" of course but I thought you ought to know.'

'They've been on to me too. Repeatedly. From the nationals and the local papers. I've got Malcolm answering the phone and saying I'm not available for comment if he's here and if he's out, I'm just not picking up. They can leave a message – which I won't reply to. First few times I did answer and kept saying "no comment" but it gets hard and you don't want to give them grounds to say you're rude or you're hiding things by putting the phone down. If you can get somebody to screen your calls, Val, it might be worth it because I expect from now on they'll be doing what they can to try and concoct a story and what they can't find out they'll make up. I'd better say something to the staff on Monday 'cus I bet they'll be getting on to other people too by now. The union advisor has told me that it'll only get worse when the trial starts and we'll probably get the media circus camped out-side school, talking to kids and trying to present some sort of "school for sin" picture.'

'What must it be like for Jim and Lisa?'

'Dreadful. Absolutely hell. I heard she'd gone away with the baby and I hope that's only to avoid all this, not because she's left him or anything.'

'I feel really bad, Vee. I feel I've abandoned him.'

'You and me both. There's nights I can't sleep and I'm cursing the system and how it works.'

'I did go and see him, you know, after we'd taken the baby things but it was awful. Talk about the elephant in the room. All he wanted to talk about was his situation and how he hadn't done anything and how he should have told me that she was infatuated and obsessed with him and all I could say was yes he should have and that I wasn't supposed to talk about it. He asked me if I thought he'd done it and I said no, I'd never seen him behave in any unto-ward manner and then I felt that I shouldn't have said anything. I just couldn't go again. When this is all over I wouldn't blame him if he never said another word to me.'

'I know what you mean.'

'You don't think anybody would say anything to the press do you? They're so tricky and seductive it'd be easy to give some response which they could then twist.'

'I sincerely hope not. But maybe we do need to take some action. I'll phone Bill Hatgreaves and tell him you've been contacted and then I think we should ring round all the staff to warn them, if it's not already too late. Having prospectuses on line makes it so much easier for these journalists to find out people's names and track them down. Perhaps you could speak to the others in the geography department? It would help us get round quicker.'

'Yes, I'll definitely do that. In fact I'll do everyone in social studies. Let's do what we can to spoke those bastards' wheels.'

***

As it had become increasingly likely that there was going to be a trial, Vee had found it harder to keep her thoughts upbeat. Tomorrow, 13 months after the allegations were first made, the court case would begin and she was already tired, very tired, enervated really, yes, that was the best word to describe how she felt. Not a good state to be in, considering what was to come. As well as having to hear what was alleged to have happened described in graphic detail, in addition to having to witness the distress of the girls and of Jim Barlow who was still protesting his innocence and pleading not guilty, Vee knew that her management and oversight of the school was going to be called into question. She expected to be accused of negligence at the least and she was worried about the school's as well as her own, future. Would parents continue to want to send their kids to Farrowdown if they thought it would be putting them at risk? Would the governors declare they had no confidence in her?

Lucy, the colourist, broke into her thoughts, 'Are you wanting your usual, Vee?' 'I think so, please,' Vee replied. She reflected wryly that it was rather ironic that she should be here at the hairdressers on the eve of the trial whose cause had first been brought to her attention as she was trying to leave school to get her hair done! Normally she liked this sort of coincidence. Not this one though.

Lucy got down to work. She could see that Vee, who usually was a right chatterbox, was distracted and she expected she was worrying about that teacher sex business. Must be awful for her, but it was more dreadful for the lasses who'd been involved. You didn't send your kids to school to be abused. They were supposed to be safe there. Over the last few weeks Lucy had heard about the goings on at Farrowdown from a number of her customers. Apparently this teacher, Mr Barlow, would get girls in the stock cupboard and offer them money to suck him off. Disgusting. And he'd terrified the girl who'd finally told on him, the one he was having sex with, by threatening to interfere with her mother's car so that it would crash. What a bastard. And what about his poor wife? Mrs Oughton, one of Lucy's regulars, lived in the same road as the Barlows and she'd said how she'd not seen her, or the little one, for months. Gone away she thought and she thought too that it was just as well really because ever since Mr Barlow had been committed to trial there'd been reporters snooping around. One day Mrs Oughton had even called the police because there'd been this white van with two men sat in it parked next door. She'd thought they might be burglars but when the police had talked to them and they'd gone, the policemen had come and told Mrs O that they'd been reporters from the

Mail. Another time some blokes from the *Express* had come to her door and asked her if she knew the Barlows and if she'd ever seen any young girls there and she'd just said no: because she hadn't. Oh well, now the trial'd started the truth was bound to come out.

What they had been through since that first day! Vee reflected that nothing on her NPQH[4] course or at any conference or staff development event had prepared her for what it'd been like, leading a school where a serious allegation had been made. As to what the trial might bring, it was probably best to wait and see, batten down the hatches and sit it out. For some reason she suddenly remembered the antenatal class, before she'd had Ally, when the midwife had told them all to put their fingers in the corners of their mouths and pull and said 'that's what childbirth feels like'. Six weeks later, deep in labour, Vee'd understood why the second-time mothers in the group had looked very sceptical and why one had actually had to leave the room because she was laughing so much that she was in danger of wetting herself when the midwife'd admitted that she'd had to have a caesarean herself! That was another really good example of the rhetoric not matching the reality.

The way in which the staff had split up into camps had been surprising and very unpleasant. The divisions really had had a pernicious effect on the school community, spilling out and into lots of different areas of life. For instance, the school play nearly hadn't gone ahead because the drama staff, who believed Jim had been falsely accused, refused to work with the head of music who was convinced he was guilty. On a more general and day-to-day level the business seemed to have negatively touched and changed all relationships within the school and outside between the school and its wider community. Senior staff, middle managers, classroom teachers, students, governors, lunchtime supervisors, cleaners, local people, you name it, were all implicated by their association with Farrowdean. There was a lot of mistrust, suspicion, rumour, innuendo, accusation and tension in the air. And the confidentiality requirements really only made things worse. Now that the media was muscling in, the fact that barely anyone knew exactly who was said to be involved or what was supposed to have happened was hardly going to contribute to fair and balanced reporting.

At times it had felt almost impossible to do any work effectively. A good crop of examination results had helped a bit but what of the future? Vee realised that any return to 'normality' was going to take a long time and she wondered whether it would, indeed, be possible for her to continue to work at the school. It was so unfair. She truly believed that nothing she had done or omitted to do could have prevented what was supposed to have happened. What should she have done differently? It really wasn't a question of slamming the stable door after the horse had bolted and the union rep who'd been assigned to support her had confirmed this. He'd looked into all policies and procedures and had checked out working practices and had said nothing was untoward, that she ran a tight ship and that he didn't believe all the formality in the world could ever be proof against determined paedophiles, if that was indeed what Jim Barlow was.

'Is that okay then, Vee?' Lucy's voice broke into her reverie. Vee looked up, focused her eyes on the mirror and realised, to her shock, that her coiffure was complete. She hadn't realised so much time had passed. 'Yes, yes thank you it's lovely, Lucy. You've done a good job again.'

She fumbled in her bag and found a £10 note which she pushed into Lucy's hand as a tip. 'Thank you Vee, you take care and be strong now.'

Well, she'd try – and casting another, appraising glance at herself in the glass she could see that after Lucy's ministrations she'd certainly look good if she was caught on any cameras! Attagirl, as her old hockey mistress used to say, and with care, strength and a bloody good hairdo, she wasn't going to be cowed.

***

'Well!' announced Keith Smithson, apparently to anyone within hearing distance, 'so the trial has collapsed. Now we need to make sure that they don't try to send those little bitches back here, we'd none of us be safe.'

'We aren't safe anyway or anywhere for that matter, Keith. But I doubt you need worry. I expect they'll stay at St Mary's,' said Brian Fothergill.

'I think St Mary's should expel them actually, though they won't. I expect as is usually the case, no action whatsoever will be taken against them and I think it's appalling,' was Bronwen Tunnicliffe's response. 'And to think I believed them! I really did. I sat with them after they made their declaration to Sally and they were in a right state. Real Oscar performances I can see now, 'cus I was entirely taken in and I like to think I'm a tough nut. You're not a PE teacher for as long as I've been and not be able to see through acting. God, I must have dealt with an average of half a dozen cases of "please miss, can I be excused, I've got my period and I feel poorly" every lesson. I'd've never done any teaching if I hadn't learnt how to tell who was telling the truth. I really must be losing my grip.'

'I dread to even imagine what would have happened to Jim if Olivia Knight hadn't had her crisis of conscience and confessed they'd made it all up. He'd've gone down for a very long time I suspect.' Sanjit Singh shuddered at the thought. 'What on earth did those girls think they were up to? Jim must really have upset them for revenge on that scale.'

'As I understand it,' said Sally Braithwaite, 'Natalie Brown had been obsessed with Jim for quite some time. She considered herself to be in love with him and she convinced herself that he loved her but that he was stopping himself from professing his true feelings until she left the school and they could be together properly. She kept hanging round him and she wrote him letters, which he, silly fool, binned immediately. He didn't give her any encouragement except he didn't actually tell her to stop it and the fact that he didn't say that further fed her fantasy that he really did love her. She started hinting to her friends that there was something going on between her and him and eventually she told Olivia and Becky Woodward and Katy Culson that they were lovers and had been for months. Then she found out that Lisa Barlow was pregnant, I think she came in to school to collect something and the girls saw her. That really incensed Natalie, especially as Katy Culson said that she didn't believe that Jim was her lover, so she bullied Becky and Olivia into going along with this story which she said was to punish Jim for cheating on her. I suspect that as time went on it got harder and harder for them to tell the truth.'

'Bloomin 'eck!' said Keith, 'it makes my blood run cold.'

'The banality of evil,' mused Brian Fothergill.

'You what?'

'Hannah Arendt. She wrote a book about Adolf Eichmann and she said everybody has the capacity to be evil, even the most ordinary people.'

'I don't think they were evil,' Sally offered, 'I think they were just silly little girls who got themselves involved in something that ran away with them. Natalie though, now she probably does have some real problems.'

Val Borthwick who had been sitting listening got up abruptly at this point and said, 'Real problems, Sally? Tell that to Jim, tell it to Lisa. They're the ones with the real problems,' and she walked out of the staffroom.

Chapter 9

Nobody can prove anything for definite

Monday 16th April 2007

Krista's going out with Matty. Seems they were seeing each other in town over Easter. I'm pissed off that mam always makes us go stay at gran's in the holidays cus I never get to go round with my friends and though everyone thinks it's brilliant to go to Spain all the time they don't know how boring it is with all these old retired people and it wasn't that hot this time either. Mrs Agar is on maternity leave and we've got a new form teacher.

Tuesday 17th April 2007

It was a real laugh on the bus this morning. Daniel was mooning out the upstairs window and Jodie McAllister stuck her finger up his bum. Everyone was talking about it in form and Mr Frinton went ballistic. He's a stuck up git.

Thursday 19th April 2007

Frinton gave us a bollocking this morning because he said the cleaner had complained our room was the worst in Lower. He wouldn't stop going on and I turned round and said to Maddie he was having a right hissey fit and that he was an old woman and he shouted at me to shut up and sit in my seat properly. When the bell went and we were going to maths he stopped me going out the door and said 'Teresa, you will pay attention when I'm speaking. Got that?' Who does he think he is?

Friday 20th April 2007

I should have realised that cus Frinton is standing in for Mrs Agar, we'd have him for RE. That subject is such a waste of time and I don't think we should have to do it. I don't believe in god and religion only causes trouble anyway. The second world war was about the Jews, then there was Ireland and the IRA and that, and now there's the Muslins. Mrs Agar's alright cus she knows us and she wears nice clothes and tells us about getting drunk when she was at university and lets us do our RE homework in form time but Mr Frinton looks like a Christian. I bet he's a hippocrit.

Saturday 21st April 2007

Me and Lynsey went round town today. It was great. We went in Starbucks and met some lads from St John's. I really fancied one of them called Bryn who's in Year 11 and Lynsey liked his mate, Sam. We said we were in Y10 cus at our school Y11 boys who go out with Y9 girls get called cradle snatchers. Ronni Brown in our class started seeing a Y11 over Christmas but he dumped her a day after we came back cus of everybody in his year taking the piss. Bryn and me swopped numbers and when we were on the bus going home I got a text asking if I'd meet him in Barracuda next Friday night. Lynsey was a bit mardy cus Sam hadn't asked her. I'm going to have to think about how I can get out on Friday and what I can say to mam and I texted Bryn that I'd let him know.

Mam and Keith, Aunty Sue and Uncle Colin have gone to the club. I've got £10 for babysitting Kian. Dad phoned and said he's booked for Ayia Napa again at half term and Ruth has made sure that Charlie's dad won't be taking her away then so she'll be coming too. Should be good.

Sunday 22nd April 2007

Omigod! I am in lurve!!!!!! Bumped into Bryn and Sam at the ice rink this afternoon. We'd said we usually went and they said they'd thought they'd give it a go too. Must be interested. We've all arranged to meet after school on Wednesday. I think Bryn is gorgeous and a million times nicer than Matty.

Wednesday 25th April 2007

I HATE MR FRINTON. HES A BASTARD. Had RE today and we were doing about marriage. He was going on about how all religions said marriage was the place for sex and that it was better for kids to be brought up in families with both their own parents and that divorce was very sad. I said to Shaz that he was talking bollocks and he asked me what I'd said. I said nothing but he said he wanted to know what I'd really said so I told him. I said I'd said he was talking bollocks because divorce was better than kids growing up where there was fighting and that because of divorce I've got my baby half-brother Kian and my step-sister Charlie who is really nice and a mam and dad who're happy with their partners and that he was talking out of his arse. He's such a slimy, stuck up, sarcastic shit because he said it was a pity that I'd spoiled a valid argument with abusive language and that I'd now earned myself a detention this evening. I said I wasn't coming because he had to give 24 hours notice and it said so in the school rules so all smarmy and sarky he said he begged my apology and would see me tomorrow night. I was fuming and said I wasn't coming and then the bell went. Everyone got up to go and Frinton shouted that we would go out quietly in an orderly fashion. Cus I was at the back I was last out. He put his arm across the door and said that he would be telling Mrs Higgs the head of year and that she would inform my parents about the detention and I said well he'd better tell both my mam and my dad and that I'd tell them what he thought of divorced people. He let me go then.

We met the lads in Town Hall Square and went in the KFC there. Bryn and Sam had chips but me and Lyns just got Diet Pepsi. She told them all about my detention and though I wasn't very pleased about this at first they both thought it was ace and that I'd been right to tell him what for and I said Frinton was just a fuckwit. Sam said that there used to be a deputy head at St Johns called that but he'd left at Christmas and some people said he'd got the sack. I asked what he looked like and it sounds like the same person. Bryn said he was a right bossy sod, always putting people down and handing out detentions. I bet it is him.

I really, really, really like Bryn. He put his arm round me on the way to the bus station. He asked me about Friday and I said I wasn't sure cus I might need to babysit but I'd let him know tomorrow. I asked Lynsey if she was going out on Friday and she said she couldn't anyway because it's her grandma and grandad's ruby wedding. I don't think Sam has asked her and I don't see how I can get out. Glad I thought of Kian as an excuse. When I got in mam said she'd had a call from the school to say I was doing detention tomorrow for cheeking a teacher and that Ruth had rang to say they'd phoned dad too. I said I wasn't going to go and mam said if she found out I hadn't I'd be grounded.

Thursday 26th April 2007

One good thing happened and that's when I texted Bryn that I couldn't go out Friday he got back and we fixed to go to the pictures on Saturday. Everything else today has been crap though. In form Mr Frinton said in front of everybody that he was looking forward to my company at 3.35 in room 17. I said to Simon that Frinton'd be lucky because no way was I going and the bastard heard me and said think again lady. How bloody dare he. Last lesson was French and just as it finished Mrs Higgs came in the room and when I went out the door she said she was just walking with me over to room 17. Frinton must've said I'd said I wasn't going cus

Mrs Higgs was all oh Teresa you do need to stop being so mouthy and get yourself on track because you are clever and can get good GCSEs if you don't mess up with silly behaviour. I told her that Mr Frinton had been right out of order in what he'd said about divorce and that he was so sarcastic and disrespectful. She wrinkled up her face in a way that made me think she don't like him either but she didn't say anything to me cus teachers always stick together.

There were 4 other kids already in room 17 and Mrs Higgs said well you have got a lot of customers Mr Frinton and the way she said it you could tell she was sort of being critical but then she went away. Right he said. You can all take off your coats because you are staying. The others all did it but I weren't going to and I just sat there. He came over in front of my desk and kept banging on and threatening more detentions but he could see he would have to take it off me himself cus I wasn't saying anything and wasn't looking at him and I wasn't taking it off. He said he would be telling Mrs Higgs and arranging another detention but he did back off so one of the Y8 lads put his coat back on and Frinton said I advise you not to make an idiot of yourself like Teresa here. Get it off now or you will be seeing me again too. I said I was going to tell my mam and dad he'd called me an idiot and they'd be up and he might get the sack from here too. I could see that had shook him but he just looked at me all nasty like. Then he gave out paper and said we had to copy what was on the board 50 times. It was the pupils bit of the home school agreement that you have to sign every year that says things like Doing as I am told by all staff without question and Arriving at lessons with all the necessary equipment, being prepared to start work immediately and packing away quietly and quickly when instructed to do so and Not talking when the teacher is talking. I put my hand up and said, all proper and polite, please sir, what's the educational value in that? When I was at primary they said lines and copying were pointless activities. He said there is no value it's a punishment. Get on with it.

I wrote really slow cus I knew he couldn't keep us after half past 4 and by then I'd done it all about 3 times. He said right. You may go when I point to you and I don't want to see anyone here again. I was last to be let go and as I went out he said Teresa what has happened to you to make you as you are? You are a bright girl but you are doing yourself no favours behaving like a silly cow.

I can not believe he said that and I am really mad. I hate him.

Keith was waiting outside school. Mam must have sent him to check that I'd done the detention cus I'd said I'd get the bus. That pissed me off but Keith was cool and said he'd had loads of detentions when he was at school and that most teachers were tossers and little Hitlers. He told me this saying that goes something like those who can do things do them but those who can't do real work become teachers.

Friday 27th April 2007

I've decided I'm going to get Frinton for how he's spoken to me, treating me like muck and saying those things about my parents. It upset me him sounding off about divorce like that cus I didn't like it when mam and dad split up and I sometimes wish they were still together now even though there are lots of good things but he has no right to say anything at all. I'd read a story in *Take a Break* about a teacher who'd come on to this girl and he'd lost his job and been sent to prison and that gave me an idea so on the bus I told Lynsey that after the detention Frinton'd kept me behind when the other kids had gone and had come on all creepy and pervy saying I was a pretty girl and that he really fancied me and I said he'd put his arm round me and stroked my breasts and tried to kiss me but I'd pushed him away and run out. I acted all upset and hurt and that and Lynsey said he was a disgusting dirty old man. She said I ought to tell Mrs Higgs and that if I liked she'd go with me so as soon as we got to school we went to her office. To be honest I'd told Lyns cus I thought she'd start off a rumour but going to Mrs Higgs was even better though I was a bit scared she wouldn't believe it and I'd get into serious bother. Mrs Higgs said she had to finish off preparing assembly and could we go to form and come back at break or lunchtime but Lyns said that wouldn't be appropriate and she really didn't think I ought to have to go to form because of the nature of the allegations. That was an ace thing to say. Lynsey is right good at English and she likes all the police stuff on telly so she knows the proper words. Anyway, it made Mrs Higgs ask what she meant and she said Miss, Teresa has been sexually assaulted by Mr Frinton so I don't think she should go anywhere near him. I hadn't said anything yet. Mrs Higgs asked what do you mean, is this true Teresa? And I said yes and she said who had I told and I said only Lynsey and she said when had this happened and I said last night at the end of detention and she said why hadn't I told my mam and I said I hadn't liked to and then I started to cry cus I'd begun to feel really upset and sort of sorry for myself.

Mrs Higgs said not to worry and it'd all be ok and that she'd send a message to our forms saying we were here and that I wasn't feeling well and Lyns was staying with me. She said she had to go and do assembly but that after she'd be back and we'd talk. She told Lynsey to make us some tea or coffee if we wanted and showed her where the things were and then she went off. When she came back Miss Cooper the deputy head was with her and she asked me if I was alright and said Lynsey could go back to class now but that she and Mrs Higgs needed to talk to me and that Lynsey wasn't to say anything except that I was feeling poorly and certainly not to say anything about Mr Frinton.

Miss Cooper told me to tell her what had happened and I said that I'd been in Mr Frinton's detention last night and that after the other students had left he'd kept me back and said he fancied me and put his arm round me and stroked my breasts and tried to kiss me. She asked why I'd got the detention and I said it was because I'd got upset when Mr Frinton had said stuff in RE about divorce and my mam and dad were divorced and that what he'd said was rubbish and was dissing them and I said he was always going on at me as well. Miss Cooper said well, he couldn't have been going on at me that much cus he'd only been in school for two weeks and I said exactly. Then Mrs Higgs asked if Mr Frinton had said or done anything inappropriate before last night and I said no except he'd stopped me leaving the RE room on Wednesday and that he'd called me a silly cow. But I said he'd said I was a silly cow when I wouldn't kiss him back. And then I was feeling all upset again and I couldn't help beginning to cry and it was weird because it seemed like it was true and that he had done these things. Mrs Higgs and Miss Cooper were really lovely and said I mustn't get myself in a state. Then Miss Cooper said I needed to be absolutely sure that I had got things right and wasn't mistaken because this was a serious allegation which could have serious consequences and I got all offended like and said didn't they believe me? And they said, no no. Then Miss Cooper said they had to make some phone calls and was my mother or father at home and I said mam was and she said it was probably going to be best if I didn't go into class because I was upset but they'd get me some work and maybe I'd need to tell some other people what'd happened and then I had better go home. She said I wasn't to talk to anybody about any of this.

Mam arrived at about 11 with Kian and she came in and said why hadn't I told her or Keith when he picked me up and I said I'd been too upset and she said to Mrs Higgs that I'd seemed fine last night and this morning. Mrs Higgs said it could be difficult for people to talk about these things and that I'd probably been in shock. Mam asked what was going to happen and Mrs Higgs said they had to contact and inform the local authority and there might have to be some meetings and I'd probably have to tell somebody else what'd happened but this wouldn't be til next week and that until then I'd probably be best off working at home. She said she'd go round my teachers and get me some work and that she'd drop it in tonight after school. She said again I'd not to say anything to anybody over the weekend and then she said we could go.

On the way home mam asked me why I'd not said anything and I told her what Mr Frinton had said about divorce and how mad it'd made me. She said she knew I could be gobby but that I should have told her what had happened cus all school had said about the detention was that I'd cheeked a teacher and if she'd known why she'd have complained cus he had no right to be saying that sort of thing.

Dad came round after work to see if I was ok and he said if he got his hands on Mr Frinton he'd knock him into next week and that he had a mind to find out where the filthy pedo lived so he could go round and sort him out. Mrs Higgs arrived while dad was here and he asked her what the school was doing and she said everything was in hand and dad said it better bloody well be or else there would be trouble. Mrs Higgs said there was going to be a proper investigation and that dad should rest assured of this. She said everyone treated these things seriously and it was important to follow correct procedures. She said she could understand that he was angry and upset and that she would be if it was her daughter who'd made these allegations. Dad asked what would happen to Mr Frinton and she said it depended on the outcome of the investigations. Dad said he hoped to God that he'd get the sack cus he was sick and shouldn't be anywhere near young lasses.

Dad gave me £20 and said he'd pick me up at the usual time for lunch on Sunday.

Saturday 28th April 2007

I have had a brilliant day. Met Bryn at one and we went to see *Hot Fuzz*. Don't really know what happened in it though!!!!!!!!!!!!!!!!!!! !!!!!!!!!!!!!!! Afterwards we went to MacDonalds and had milk shakes. I told Bryn about what happened in the detention and he said he'd kill Frinton if he saw him. He said he thought he'd got the sack from St John's for touching girls up. We walked through town and he held my hand. I'm seeing him next Wednesday again.

Monday 30th April 2007

No school. Lynsey phoned and said that Mr Frinton hadn't been there and they'd had Miss Cooper for form. She said people were asking why I wasn't there cus Kerrie had seen me in town on Saturday and I hadn't looked ill then. Lyns said she hadn't told them exactly but she'd sort of hinted that it was something bad. I told her what Bryn had said about Frinton being sacked from St Johns for sexual abuse and then she asked me all about Saturday!!!!!!!!!!!!!!!!!!!!!!!!!!!!!!!!!!!!!!

Wednesday 2nd May 2007

Mrs Higgs phoned and said could we go in to school for a meeting Friday morning. Mam rang dad and we're all going to go. Mr Frinton won't be there thank goodness.

Mam wasn't very keen about me going into town after school time. She said I hadn't ought to see people cus it might compromise things. Not sure what she meant. So I told her about Bryn and that he went to

St Johns anyway. She was alright about it and even said that I ought to ask him round for tea.

Me and Bryn went to Starbucks. We had the biggest size mochas and I bought them. I'm rolling in it cus dad gave me that money. Bryn said he'd tried to find out some more about what happened with Mr Frinton at St Johns but no one seemed to know anything definite it was more like people just saying that was why he'd left all suddenly like. We're going swimming on Saturday and then I said would he like to come back to ours and he said yes. Omigod! I forgot he doesn't know I'm really in Y9. What shall I do?

Friday 4th May 2007

Felt sick when I got up this morning. Mam told me to be brave and to just tell the truth but that's what I'm scared of and that they'll find out I made it all up. Keith stayed home to look after Kian and dad picked us up. He said I was just to stay relaxed and mam said he needed to take his own advice but then she told him that there was a rumour that Mr Frinton had got the sack from St Johns for sexual abuse and he got all worked up and started saying what the fuck was the man doing working in another school then? He ought to be banned or in prison. Mam told him to calm down and that him getting aireated wasn't helping anybody.

When we got to school we went to the reception and were shown into this room where Mrs Higgs and Miss Cooper and this woman, Mrs Bilton, from the local authority or something were. We all sat down and Miss Cooper said thank you for coming and that the purpose of today was to hear my story as part of the formal investigation and that was why Mrs Bilton was here. She asked me to tell everybody what had happened and to take my time. I said I'd been in detention and when it was over Mr Frinton had kept me back when he'd let everybody else go and he'd said he fancied me and had put his arm round me and stroked my breasts and tried to kiss me but that I'd run away. Miss Cooper asked me why I was in detention and I said I'd been upset in RE because Mr Frinton had said divorce was bad and I admitted that I had used bad language but that was because what he'd said was rubbish and because he shouldn't say things he don't know anything about and cus I didn't like him dissing my family. I said he had been really sarcastic to me ever since he'd come to our school and he was always putting me down in form and he'd called me an idiot and a silly cow. Then dad said he didn't send his daughter to school to be spoken to like that and he was disgusted that Mr Frinton had even been employed after he'd been sacked from St Johns for sex abuse offences. When dad brought that one out I could see them all look at each other and Mrs Bilton said I beg your pardon where did you get that information from? and dad said it doesn't matter, the main thing is pedofiles shouldn't be working in schools and why are they? He said he thought there was a special list and checks to stop all this stuff and people like Frinton getting near to kids. Miss Cooper said I think your informant got it wrong Mr Connolly, Mr Frinton wasn't sacked and dad said well there isn't any smoke without fire and if it wasn't true how come these stories were going the rounds? Mrs Bilton said we're here to discuss Teresa's case Mr Connolly that's what's important at the moment. We really need to establish what actually happened I'm sure you can agree with that. I think they just wanted to shut dad up because he was getting right wound up and was beginning to get shouty. So then Mrs Higgs said now Teresa, these are really serious allegations that you've made are you absolutely certain that what you have told us is what truly happened? Dad said me and Sharon might be divorced but we have brought our daughter up to be honest. And Mrs Higgs said I'm sure you have but you must appreciate that we do have to ask these questions. Mam said of course we understand but Brian's upset. We're both upset and Teresa was nearly sick about having to go through with this meeting this morning. She can be a bit gobby but she's a good girl really. Mrs Higgs said I know that and she's bright and could do well in her GCSEs if she put her mind to it but the point at issue now is is the account she has given us about what happened at the detention an accurate one? Is it Teresa? And I said yes.

And that was it really. Dad went off on a bit of one asking what was going to happen now and were the police going to be involved. That scared me cus I didn't want things to get that serious and I didn't want to have to take a lie detector test like they do on Jeremy Kyle cus I didn't think I'd be able to pass it. Miss Cooper said she didn't know at this stage but we'd be kept informed. Mam asked about me going back to school and Miss Higgs said I should go on Tuesday cus it's a bank holiday on Monday. Dad said this bloke's standing in for her form tutor and he's her RE teacher. I don't want him coming anywhere near her. Mrs Cooper said not to worry and that she could promise there wasn't any chance of that at the moment. And then we went home. In the car dad was saying that it sounded as if Frinton had been suspended or something and I said Lynsey had told me he hadn't taken form all week so maybe he wasn't there.

I am a bit worried about what will happen if they do find out he hasn't actually touched me but I don't know how they can cus there wasn't any one else there so nobody can prove anything for definite so it's always going to be our words against each other. And anyway he did say those things and he was right out of order and it did upset me. He deserves to get in trouble.

Sunday 6th May 2007

Yesterday was really ace. Swimming was great and I wore my purple bikini I got for going to grans at easter but never wore cus it was too cold. Makes my boobs look really good. Bryn said he liked my belly piercing and we sat in the hot tub for ages. I know he really fancies me cus I could see!!!!!!!!!!!!!!!!! Afterwards we went home and mam and Keith weren't embarrassing thank goodness and Keith went and got pizzas. Bryn was lovely playing with Kian, he's got some little cousins but he's the youngest in his own family and he says he likes kids when they're funny and cute like Kian.

We went in my room and listened to music and lay on the bed and talked. I wish I hadn't told him I was in Y10 though cus it's really stressful. I was scared in case mam said how old I was and then I have to keep remembering like when he was looking at my class picture from primary and it said Class of 2003 and he said shouldn't it be class of 2002 cus I thought it was the year you started not the year you left. That's what it says on mine. I said they did it differently at Park Avenue. And he said, it's all American stuff anyway and he started talking about his prom and how he and his mates have hired this stretch Hummer and he's going with this lass Grace but she's only a friend like and everybody has to have a partner from in the year group, it's not like couples. I'm wondering if I ought to tell him I'm in year 9. I told Charlie about him and asked her what she thought and she said to tell him cus it sounds like he really likes me and he won't mind.

We went to The Mount for their Sunday Carvery today and I was a right pig cus I love their roast potatoes. Need to watch it if I'm going to carry on looking good in that bikini. Dad started talking about Frinton and what a slime bag he was and how he needed to get what was coming to him. Charlie said there'd been a 45 year old teacher at her school who'd been having sex with this girl in year 11 and her parents found out and told the police and he's gone to prison but the girl has went round saying he's her boyfriend and she loves him and that she'll wait for him and all that. She sold her story to *Chat* for £2,000. Ruth said there you are Terri, you could do that, make a few bob. I could as well.

Tuesday 8th May 2007

It was weird going back to school and on the bus and all through the day everyone was looking at me and coming round and asking if I was all right. Some of them are right nosy bastards cus they don't normally talk to me. On the bus this lad whose in year 8 and who was one of the people in the detention told me that all of them had had to go and see Miss Cooper and she'd asked them what'd happened. He asked me if it was true that Mr Frinton had raped me and Lynsey said that that was the rumour going round but she said she'd been saying he only groped me to try and stop it. We had Mrs Higgs for form and when I was going out she said ok Teresa? And I said yes and she said don't encourage the gossip will you. And I said I haven't said anything.

It were nice to be back with my mates because I'd got a bit bored being at home but I don't much like the way other people are talking about me and going all quiet when I pass and I heard some lads were saying things like Frinton must've been desperate to go anywhere near me. Some of the teachers were really nice asking if I was ok and that but Mr Courtney was right off and he's usually a good laugh. The worse thing though was when I walked into science Jonny Burrows shouted out you be careful Mr Henderson here comes Teresa the temptress. Can you resist her? And that was dreadful because everybody knows Mr Henderson is gay and he went ballistic. He sent Jonny to Mrs Higgs and made me sit on the front bench instead of in my normal seat. That wont fair at all because I haven't done anything.

Friday 11th May 2007

THANK FUCK ITS FRIDAY. Ruth rang mam to ask her if I can go into town with her and Charlie tomorrow to get some things for Ayia Napa. I'm meeting Bryn at 2 at skating so I said I could only go in the morning and mam said I had to change my arrangements and I said no and we had a real row and I ended up crying and telling mam I'd had enough of people being nasty to me all week at school how they'd been calling me slag and saying I'd been raped and stuff. She said she was sorry and she did understand how awful it'd all been and what a lot of stress it'd put me under. She told me that when she was 15 she'd gone to her cousin Rita's wedding and a bloke at the reception had followed her into the toilet and tried to do something to her but somebody had come in just in time. She said she had nightmares about it for years and people didn't understand how vulnerable young girls were and Mr Frinton was an evil bastard because he was a teacher and I should have been able to trust him. She rang Ruth back and arranged for us go in the morning instead and she gave me £15 too.

Saturday 12th May 2007

We got loads of stuff in Primark cus dad had told Ruth to get us whatever we wanted. Skating was good and Bryn came back after and said his mum had said would I like to go round there next Saturday for a change. I decided then that I had to tell him I was in Y9 cus if this is getting serious its better to do it now and as Charlie says he does seem to like me so I said it'd been Lynsey's idea and he said it didn't matter and he understood how you sometimes had to go along with your mates. He said he thought Lyns wasn't as mature as me anyway and that was why Sam hadn't seen her again. I feel so relieved.

Thursday 17th May 2007

Been so busy this week. Me and Bryn met in town on Tuesday and Wednesday and went round a bit. We really are a couple and we have got leather friendship bracelets!!!!! It was Bryn's idea.

Today I got called out of maths to see Mrs Higgs and Miss Cooper and that Mrs Bilton was there too. They asked me to tell them about what happened at the detention again and was I absolutely certain that Mr Frinton had said he fancied me and touched me and tried to kiss me and I said yes. I got upset cus they kept saying was I sure and I said didn't they believe me and that Mr Frinton was a pervert who shouldn't be near children and he certainly shouldn't call people silly cows and idiots and Mrs Higgs said not to get distressed but they had to be certain because the consequences of allegations of this kind were extremely serious. I said I knew that anyway without people keep getting on at me and how did they think I felt keep being asked and did they want me to take a lie detector. Miss Cooper said she didn't think there'd be any need for that so that's good cus I was getting worried about that again. When I got home I told mam they'd been on at me again and she phoned dad and he said it was about time this was all sorted and he wanted it out the way before we go to Cyprus so he'd phone school tomorrow.

Saturday 19th May 2007

I was really nervous about going to Bryn's but his mum and dad was lovely. His sister Rhiannon had come back from uni for the weekend cus it was her friends 21st and she was really nice too. Me and Bryn took his dog Shady for a walk and then we had tea and watched a dvd in his room. Bryn's dad took me home at 10 and Bryn kissed me when I got out the car right in front of his dad!!!!!!!!!!!!!!!!!

Wednesday 23rd May 2007

I've got to be interviewed by the police. They wanted to do it next week but mam said I was going on holiday so it's going to be when I come back on June 5th. I'm really shit scared.

Monday 4th June 2007

Ayia Napa was ace. Everything was great except not seeing Bryn but we made up for that yesterday when he came round. He loves my brown body!!!!!!!!!! We've got a new form teacher, Mrs Weston and we're having her for RE too. I had put the trouble out of my head but going to school has brought it all back. I'm dreading tomorrow.

Tuesday 5th June 2007

I went to school as normal and mam and dad came at 2. I'd thought I'd have to go to the police station but they came to school and we were in Miss Cooper's office. It was a young police woman and Miss Cooper and that Mrs Bilton. I had to tell them what happened and then the policewoman said was I absolutely certain that he had touched me and tried to kiss me or could I have been mistaken and I said no and she said what did I mean no? no that I wasn't certain or that no I couldn't be mistaken and I said no I couldn't be mistaken. She said she understood Mr Frinton had called me an idiot and a silly cow and had said things which I'd considered to be disrespectful to my mum and dad and she could see this would make anybody upset and angry and they might want to retaliate. Dad said what are you suggesting? And she said I'm not suggesting anything, I'm just exploring alternative explanations Mr Connolly. Well Teresa? And I said he did it. I was feeling all angry then and scared at the same time. I'm not going to change anything cus he is a bastard and nobody else was there to say anything else.

The New Courier

TEACHER DENIES SEXUAL ASSAULT

Today at Bankside Crown Court, Mr Kevin Frinton, a teacher from Great Stoughton High School, denied sexual assault but admitted calling a 15 year old female student 'an idiot' and 'a silly cow'. Fifty seven year old Frinton who kept the girl behind following a detention, is alleged to have told her that he was attracted to her, stroked her breasts and tried to kiss her. He claims that she was taking retribution for what he describes as his 'uncharacteristic, inappropriate and unacceptable language'. Frinton who has a previously unblemished record, took early retirement from his position as assistant head at St John's Comprehensive in April, 2006. Financial difficulties, attributed to 'unexpected divorce' had led Mr Frinton to return to work and he obtained a temporary maternity cover post at Great Stoughton which is where the alleged offence was committed. The case continues.

Chapter 10

EndWords

We began this book with a story about a young, female teacher who, having had an allegation of sexual abuse made against her, spent a nightmarish 24 hours before investigations established that she definitely hadn't done anything at all untoward. Rebecca's experience was bad enough but, as the composite stories of the people who contributed to our research have shown, it could have been a lot worse. Indeed, and as was explained in Chapter 4, things could have been much more appalling than we described, given our choice to re-present what might be called 'run of the mill' allegation experiences, rather than writing sensational narratives based on some of the accounts we heard. However, having taken that decision, as the deadline for handing our manuscript to the publisher loomed close we came across a story that we really felt needed to be included both because of its awfulness and its provenance. This account is contained in the Hansard Report for April 1, 2009 which transcribes a debate initiated by Paul Goodman, Conservative MP for Wycombe, and it begins:

> I am grateful to have secured this debate today. I want to tell part of the story of my constituent, Nick Cousins, because that will allow me to ask how a teacher who has never been found guilty by a court is now unlikely to be able to return to his vocation because, in effect, of the intervention of the Government and their agencies. The story raises serious questions about the balance – in our schools, in the education system as a whole, in government and in our popular culture – between the protection of pupils and justice for teachers, and about the consequences for those schools, that system and our education and popular culture, if that balance goes awry. It also raises profound questions of justice and equity.
>
> (Hansard, 2009, np)

We recommend that readers view the Hansard Report for themselves because the complicated and convoluted tale that Mr Goodman goes on to recount is not easy to tell succinctly and is best seen in its original form. Having said this, the gist of the story is that in 1998 Mr Cousins, a senior teacher at an independent school, was alleged to have behaved inappropriately towards a male pupil. An internal inquiry cleared him of wrongdoing and in 2001 he was successful in gaining a post as deputy head at a selective boys' state school. In 2004 two allegations dating back to the late 1990s were made by boys who had been contemporaries of the original accuser. In July 2004 Mr Cousins was arrested; in April 2005 he was charged with indecent assault; and in March 2006 his case came to trial. During this time he was suspended from school. The jury acquitted Mr Cousins on three counts but could not reach a decision on two further charges which were, consequently, left on file. Following this verdict the school set up its own internal inquiry and on the basis of the report produced by an independent investigator, reinstated the deputy head to his post. From this point on the case becomes increasingly complex involving: enhanced CRB checks; informal and unverified comments made in the so called 'soft box' of the CRB disclosure by a senior police officer; an investigation by the Department for Education and Schools (as the Department for Children, Schools and Families was then called); dismissal in August 2007; and acknowledgement in October 2008 by the governors of the school, that the dismissal had been unfair. In March 2009 Mr Cousins received word that the Secretary of State had decided not to bar or restrict his employment as a teacher. However, and in a manner reminiscent of the story we told in Chapter 5, the letter informing him of this, referred to his 'misconduct' despite no misconduct having been proven. Mr Goodman concluded his account by saying:

> Finally, I close by reflecting on what this story suggests not just for one teacher, but for all teachers, all schools, our education system as a whole, and our educational and popular culture. Not long ago, there was an imbalance between the protection of children and the autonomy of teachers. The former was compromised at the expense of the latter. That imbalance had to be addressed. By and large, I think that it has been. The protection of children should be non-negotiable . . . Ministers, the DCSF, local authorities, Parliament, the courts, schools, teachers and governors have no easy task in deciding where the balance lies. As I said earlier, there are circumstances in which there are grounds for proceeding against people even if they have been cleared in court, especially, perhaps, when child protection is concerned. None the less, there are, as I say, serious questions about whether this balance is now right.
>
> (Paul Goodman Conservative MP for Wycombe telling
> the story of his constituent, Nick Cousins, in a debate
> on April 1, 2009 – reported in Hansard, 2009)

Of course, in and of itself, this story says nothing definitive about, and cannot do anything to disprove or prove Mr Cousins' innocence or guilt. Nor does the fact that it was reported by an MP make any difference in this regard. The point we want to stress though is that this is a story, specific details aside, which is likely to be repeated and repeated unless there is a seismic shift in public attitudes and a change in the way that allegations are dealt with. In Chapter 1 we quoted various Secretaries of State for Education who have expressed concern about investigatory procedures and as we write (early May, 2009) a Children, Families and Schools Select Committee is undertaking a parliamentary inquiry into 'Allegations Against School Staff' and has invited written submissions on:

- the scale and nature of allegations of improper conduct made against school staff;
- whether staff subject to allegations should remain anonymous while the case is investigated;
- whether the guidance available to head teachers, school governors, police and others on how to handle claims of improper conduct by school staff should be revised, with particular reference to:
  - the procedures to be followed by disciplinary panels;
  - when suspension of the staff member concerned is appropriate;
  - when arrest of the staff member concerned is appropriate; and
  - the retention of records of allegations found to be false.
  (Children, Families and Schools Select Committee Inquiry, 2009)

The findings of and any consequences ensuing from this inquiry will unfortunately appear too late for us to report (in this edition at least). However we would not expect there to be any immediate improvement to the lived experiences of teachers, their families, friends, colleagues and schools. Although changes in procedure that could help prevent some of the distress and damage caused to those touched by an allegation are undoubtedly welcome, they alone cannot challenge what Sheila Cavanagh (following Foucault) describes as the 'colonizing . . . pervasive and deeply entrenched . . . master narrative of child sexual abuse . . . premised on the idea that children are innocent and asexual' (Cavanagh, 2007: 11–12). The normalising and normative influence of this narrative is such that any sort of questioning – and even academic investigation of and writing about it – is likely to be taken as evidence that such questioners and authors are not concerned to protect children, or are even *themselves* either potential or actual abusers; we have personal experience of this. The circularity of the argument appears to be impervious to challenge or disruption.

Cavanagh, and others (notably Steven Angelides, 2004; 2009), have made use of queer theory, adopting a queering approach to interrogate the master narrative, which they suggest has the potential to pervert all adult–child relations. This is essentially because the narrative is underpinned by the belief, which becomes an assumption, that adults always possess more power (be that physical, psychic or social) than youngsters and are therefore always able to assert overt and implicit coercive pressure simply because of their position and age.[1] Thus no adult–child relationship is exempt from this. Closer to home, in research which explored teachers' perceptions and experiences around touching children, Heather (and colleagues) illustrated the ways in which constant attention to, and concern about, the potential dangers of touch heightens teacher anxiety and actually perverts what was previously pure, indeed in itself bringing about corruption (see also Kincaid, 1998). This thesis was particularly informed and supported by a case study undertaken at Summerhill, A.S. Neill's unique and 'alternative' school. When Heather went to Summerhill and started asking questions

> about adults touching children, children touching each other, adults touching adults, it felt a bit 'pervy' as a subject for conversation, an attempt to unnaturalise what the subjects regarded as absolutely normal.
> (Piper and Stronach, 2008: 21)

Discomfort increased as it became increasingly clear these questions were introducing a sexual register and inviting people to see things under a different gaze to that which they had previously adopted. This is the sort of effect that the 'master narrative' of innocence and its concomitant premise that children never lie about sexual abuse, coupled with moral panic around paedophilia and child abuse has had. It distorts perceptions and understandings and it can lead to teachers being accused of sexual misconduct on the basis of actions and behaviours and comments that had quite another intention and motivation. It also, of course, lays a way open for malicious allegations to be made and believed. Acknowledging this is not, in any degree whatsoever, to suggest that children should not be protected but it does seem that in many places throughout the world, we have now reached a situation where adults in general, and those who work with young people in particular, are frightened. They are frightened of having their innocent actions misconstrued. Ironically, this means that children can end up losing out in a number of different and significant ways because adults don't want to put themselves at risk (see Brooks, 2006; Furedi and Bristow, 2008; Gill, 2007). It seems that adults' and children's and young people's lives are being impoverished and in some cases ruined, and injustices being perpetrated because of an apparent inability to approach child protection in a measured and judicious manner. Attempting to establish that wrongdoing has occurred does not and should not require that one party be assumed to be more likely to be telling the truth than the other. In the past the benefit was on the teacher's side, now it is in favour of the youngster. Both of these extremes are damaging and both can lead to contravention of the basic human rights to safety and to justice, which should be enjoyed by both pupils and teachers.

The difficulties we experienced in undertaking our research further highlight the parlous state we are in with regard to any consideration of school-aged children and young people, adults and sex. To date, very few academics have focused on these topics and those who have (notably ourselves, Sheila Cavanagh and Tara Star Johnson) have all felt it necessary to declare that we are committed to child protection and that we abhor abuse. Such declarations, in themselves, lay us open to charges that we protest too much and must, therefore, be seeking to construct a cover, an alibi for our own activities and proclivities, and an apology for abusers. When we have given conference papers and presentations about various aspects of this work we have always been told how 'brave' we are to be doing it. Rather than being courageous, and as we noted in Chapter 3, we see ourselves as having a responsibility to alert a wider audience to what is happening, in a similar way to that in which Mr Goodman brought Mr Cousins' experience to the attention of the MPs in the House of Commons. It is not just an academic or professional issue; it gets to the heart of key questions about the sort of society and culture we all want to live in and the sort of human beings we want to be.

In attempting to answer the question 'How could things be done differently?' we can only make tentative suggestions. It is necessary to remind readers of the difficulties we encountered in attempting to gain ethics approval and funding for a more comprehensive piece of research. Consequently our research to date has focused on the experiences of those caught up in the current system rather than on their and others' views of how things could and should be done differently. We hope subsequently to be in a position to fill this gap in knowledge, but meanwhile we can offer a number of considerations. Children and young people of different ages are not a homogenous category and the doctrinaire presumption that children never lie about abuse should be tempered by a contextual assessment of the relevant circumstances surrounding allegation against a professional, which would include the age and known characteristics of the child/young person. Further, we do not agree that following an allegation a teacher should immediately and automatically be suspended. We suggest a cooling down period of a day or so where teachers or others who know the child/young person well are able to talk with them in a non-threatening way. During this short period the teacher could still be prevented from having contact with students (going on a course, preparing paperwork for Ofsted, visits etc.) but crucially in a way that does not presuppose guilt. It seems very likely that a number of false allegations could be resolved at this early stage before everyone becomes entrenched in their polarised position, and where a child or young person who has lied and invested so much emotional and social capital in their narrative becomes unable to retract their allegation. We also believe the current system that prevents teachers from talking to their friends and colleagues to be inhumane. A situation can arise where a child who has lied is still able to talk to their friends and get their story 'right' but the teacher becomes isolated and disempowered from the start. It is perhaps surprising that any teachers are found not guilty, given this imbalance in the treatment of pupils and teachers. We would also wish teachers' anonymity to be preserved throughout, not just so as to preserve the anonymity of a child but because of the consequences of 'no smoke without fire' for subsequent career possibilities, and the vigilante type activity which such naming encourages. We appreciate full anonymity is impossible as children talk, as do parents, but a total ban on reporting could help to keep it local in the first instance (Facebook etc. aside).

Our cases suggest that once an investigation is in play, the interests of natural justice are not well served by current procedures. Thus the insights of other professionals, parents and children closest to the situation are not investigated in an open-handed way, but rather the priority is to build a case to support a prosecution. In almost every case there is likely to be a sizeable contrast between the investigatory resources of the prosecution and the defence, and of course the accused individual is forbidden to have any direct input. Given verdicts in child care cases tend to be on the balance of probabilities, these realities again make the task of proving innocence that much harder. We suggest the current judicial processes do not serve the best interests of either children or teachers in these situations. It may be that a process more akin to that which occurs in a family court is more appropriate, where the process is less oppositional and those involved are trained and better able to deal with the complex issues. Only if the need for a full criminal prosecution is then confirmed should the full prosecutory process be applied.

To suggest that a more rounded and even-handed investigative process would be beneficial in cases of sexual allegations against teachers (and other professionals in child care settings) should not be taken to indicate a 'soft' attitude towards teachers or child protection. Beyond the obvious principled issue of natural justice, and the more pragmatic one which can be summed up as 'why in current circumstances would a sane adult place themselves at risk by being a teacher?', is the fact that a more inclusive process would cut both ways. We may be concerned by stories of the type presented in earlier chapters, but we are just as concerned that actual cases of abuse are identified and dealt with. Current procedures can all too easily miss a pupil's story which needs to be read between the lines, and can also prove so intimidating that some real cases go nowhere as a more timid child clams up. Thus, a different type of process could have benefits for both teacher (as individuals and for the profession) and pupils, and also for justice itself. However, if an allegation is proved to be false, we think it is wrong that currently most young people experience no negative effects and are certainly not punished. The length of time the case often takes may be a contributory factor, but pupils should be made aware that there are consequences to their actions, and to allow false allegations to be exempt from normal sanctions sends a clear message that such behaviour is not considered serious and that it is easy to get away with it – it also implies doubt in regard to any 'not guilty' verdict. This is not the way to treat professionals who can be considered to have chosen a 'risky' vocation.

As an aside, it is relevant to mention the current vogue for 'therapeutic education' (see for example Ecclestone and Hayes, 2009). As with many government initiatives a contradiction is set in play. We currently simultaneously have teachers (and others) encouraged to not touch children any more, and not to put themselves at risk (keep the door open, a table between you and a pupil – see Piper and Smith, 2003) while teachers are also being encouraged to manage 'circle time', lead 'peer massage' and any number of other 'therapeutic' interventions aimed at increasing the 'social and emotional well-being' of the child. Yet, as all therapists know, 'counselling stirs up thoughts and emotions that we may be unaware of consciously. In most talking therapies, the therapist becomes the target of the strongest of these currents: they are loved and hated' (Leader, 2009: 32). It is perhaps hardly surprising then that teachers risk being targeted by vulnerable young people.

In telling the story in the way that we have, we are well aware of the extent to which we are asking readers to trust us. To trust that we have no nefarious purpose, and that the accounts that are the basis for Chapters 5 to 9 are 'real'. This trust mirrors that which we needed to have, when accepting that the people who we spoke to were telling the truth; and with regard to this, we repeat that we excluded every and anything that we had doubts about. However, we can not individually control the moral panic around child abuse and paedophilia, and expect trust therefore to be in limited supply. On the news this week (6th May 2009) Channel Four at 7.00pm gave voice for some considerable time to an anonymous social worker in Haringey discussing social work post the death of Baby P. Within a description of how difficult social work is and underfunded (which we would not dispute) the voice told viewers that the fact we are not hearing of large-scale abuse and huge paedophile rings anymore, is because there are not enough social workers and not enough time for active investigation. As Brendan O'Neill (2008, np) (leaning on Richard Webster) has said in relation to the Jersey children's home scandal (a case where it was assumed children had been killed and abused en masse – but little evidence surfaced in spite of massive resources being used to uncover them) 'child abusers are the new devil we all can rail against . . . those who ask critical questions about the facts can be denounced as "unbelievers" and "deniers"'.

This book has focused on accusations of sexual misconduct. According to the IRSC data referenced in Chapter 1 (DfES, 2004a), only around one-third of allegations made against teachers fall into this category. In fact, teachers are much more likely to be accused of physical abuse and when they are they face the same investigative procedures and the same potentially protracted period of uncertainty and suspicion. Hitting, restraining or in other ways physically hurting children who may themselves have been behaving in inappropriate or unacceptable ways does not seem to incur the same degree of public opprobrium as alleged sexual abuse: the legacy of 'spare the rod and spoil the child' is pervasive and tenacious. However, for a teacher accused of physical wrong-doing which they claim they have not perpetrated, the consequences for and effects upon their careers and their well-being are no different than for those faced with sexual allegations. Thus we close with an email sent to us by a head teacher, who heard of our work and wanted to share her experiences of the aftermath of being accused of inflicting physical harm.

> I feel that I have been deemed guilty . . . Indeed, I do not know the contents of the original allegation, or who made it, to whom. If anyone had bothered to phone my chair of Governors the whole issue could have been described to them, as I believe that it was resolved with the complainant within 48 hours of the incident.

> I feel bad for my staff who are having to cope in a school without a leader, and for the kids, many of whom already have significant attachment issues.

> I have been unable to contact people I work with because although I have been told I can talk to staff, we are restricted from talking about the incident, the allegation and the processes. So, the reality is that it is impossible to meet them. Ask yourself, in this situation, what is the first question on everyone's lips . . . 'What's going on?' and to say I can't talk about it would suggest to most people that I have something to hide.

> I have tried to avoid social situations where I would meet ex-colleagues who are bound to ask about the school, so I have become increasingly isolated.

> I did ask HR if I could attend a conference so that at least I could access mental stimulation and undertake some CPD. I was told that I could not do anything that would be seen to be within a teacher's remit. Thus, I have become professionally anonymous, unable to use my title to gain access to training and having to pay for any course I want to attend personally.

> My designated officer, who I was told would be my link to school and the developments of my case has not been told anything by the HR department so we have these depressing phone calls where he rings up because he has been told to keep in contact with me, but he has no information. In fact, he was not even told in December that the police (after interviewing me under caution) had decided that there was no case to answer.

> My designated officer attended a strategy group meeting held about me in November; the head of School Improvements in charge of this investigation originally denied that any such meeting had taken place. The LA Safeguarding Monitoring officer refused to send me the minutes of

the meeting and despite writing to ask her what was happening to my case, I am still suspended (22 weeks now) and becoming more and more anxious.

I can't access my school emails or I will be in breach of the conditions of my suspension, I have no idea what has been in the last six months of DCSF announcements; likewise Ofsted and all the other professional networks that I rely upon to be effective in my role.

All in all, I feel terrible, and I have even had to fight for professional counselling through the employee support line . . . *the authority* will only pay for three sessions!!!!

Sorry to dump this on you . . . but this is just scratching the surface, there's lots more examples. I know I need help, but I'm having to jump through hoops again to get more counselling, and I obviously need it!

The current Children, Families and Schools Select Committee's parliamentary inquiry that we refer to earlier in this chapter would benefit from a consideration of a test case ruling made in relation to nurses earlier in 2009. Four nurses had been suspended from duty and placed on a list banning them from working during an enquiry following a complaint about their alleged mistreatment of vulnerable adults under the Protection of Vulnerable Adults (POVA) legislation. However the Law Lords ruled 'that nurses have the right to be heard before they can be suspended from work under the . . . POVA scheme – which has been deemed to be in contravention of human rights' (Staines, 2009). It is expected that this test case will pave the way for at least another 50–100 such cases currently going through the European Court of Human Rights in Strasbourg. Words such as 'unfair and unjust' and 'disproportionate in their adverse effects on the rights of care workers' were applied to the care standards provisions applied to nurses. The process had resulted in one of the nurses going bankrupt and nearly losing her house if friends and family had not helped out, and another experienced both the loss of his home and the breakdown of his family. Being placed on the list and being suspended was often the result of 'flimsy' evidence and 'malicious rumours' and many of the same scenarios we have described in relation to teachers are mirrored by the experiences of nurses. It is expected that the test case will have repercussions not only for nurses but for other health care and care workers. We conclude, if nurses have had their human rights contravened by such treatment, then so too must have teachers. The only apparent difference is that one client group is vulnerable adults and the other is children. We hope that the current inquiry and future legal process reaches a similar conclusion.

Notes

Chapter 1

1. 'Rebecca' is a pseudonym. Rebecca is a long-term and close friend of one of us. At the time of writing she was 33 and had been teaching for around seven years.
2. The DfES (Department for Education and Skills) is now the DCSF – the Department for Children, Schools and Families.
3. In the February 2007 England and Wales Court of Appeal (Civil Division) case of 'Mezey vs South West London and St George's Mental Health NHS Trust', the judge, Lord Justice Sedley, stated that 'Suspension changes the status quo from work to no work, and it invariably casts a shadow over the employee's competence. Of course this does not mean that it cannot be done, but it is not a neutral act.' (England and Wales Court of Appeal [Civil Division], 2007)
4. The Scottish Commissioner for Children, Kathleen Marshall, spoke about the dangers of naming suspects in the 2004 McLintock lecture, *'Names Can Never Hurt Me': Does Naming Suspects Help Children?* (available at http://www.sccyp.org.uk/webpages/speeches.php).
5. The Criminal Records Bureau (CRB) does already record names of those against whom an investigation involving the police has been undertaken, whether or not it results in a conviction. Authorised enquirers applying for enhanced CRB disclosure can also see 'soft' information which chief police officers can add at their discretion (see Hansard, 2009). There is also 'Information held under Section 142 of the Education Act, 2002'. This 'information' – maintained by the Department for Children, Families and Schools used to be known as 'List 99' and it includes details of teachers who have either been banned from or who are considered unsuitable to work with children.

Chapter 2

1. See also Zygmunt Bauman (2006) who talks of *liquid fears* which are amorphous and which lack easily identifiable referents. He describes fear of the paedophile and of paedophilia as one such fear.
2. Some, such as Richard Webster (1998) have drawn attention to similarities in the sixteenth and seventeenth centuries when scholars accepted the existence of a society of witches who provided a focus for what could now be described as pornography for the educated elite, who were both fascinated and horrified – but who crucially suspended their critical judgement in accepting that witches flew through the air astride broomsticks, gathering together to engage in orgiastic worship of their master, Satan.
3. The term 'satanic ritual abuse' is often used interchangeably with 'sadistic ritual abuse', and other more inclusive terms that refer to any and all ritualistic abuse.
4. This same book also triggered a furore around notions of recovered memories and/or false memory syndrome – which we do not have space to cover here.

5. A version of the next few paragraphs appeared as a Battle in Print: 'Does Every Child really Matter – has the abuse panic gone too far?' by Heather Piper and Catherine Scott (2006) and is available at http://www.battleofideas.co.uk/C2B/document_tree/ViewADocument.asp? ID=274andCatID=42 (last accessed 29.4.09).

Chapter 4

1. Michael James is the pseudonym of one Mike Simpson (see Mike Simpson).

Chapter 5

1. Ofsted refers to Office for Standards in Education inspection of the school.

Chapter 8

1. 'Soham' refers to the 2002 murders of two girls, Jessica Chapman and Holly Wells, at Soham by a school caretaker, Ian Huntley. It turned out that Huntley had a police record for sexually abusing young girls yet this was not revealed when he applied for, and was appointed to, his post.
2. NAHT is the acronym for the National Association of Head Teachers.
3. Vee here is referring to the case of Headlands Community College, Bridlington (see Herring, 2008).
4. NPQH is the acronym for National Professional Qualification for Headship. All intending assistant, deputy and headteachers have to attain this qualification.

Chapter 10

1. See too, Paula Reavey and Sam Warner's (2003) edited collection in which a number of feminist authors look critically at the master narrative of child sexual abuse.

References

Allen, A., Anderson, K., Bristol, L., Downs, Y., O'Neill, D., Watts, N. and Wu, Q. (2009) 'Resisting the Unethical in Formalised Ethics: Perspectives and Experiences', in Satterthwaite, J., Piper, H. and Sikes, P. (eds) *Power in the Academy*, Stoke-on-Trent: Trentham Books: 135–52.

Angelides, S. (2004) 'Feminism, Child Sexual Abuse, and the Erasure of Child Sexuality', *GLQ*, 10(2): 141–77.

Angelides, S. (2009) 'Intersubjectivity, Power, and Teacher – Student Sex Crime', *Subjectivity*, 26: 87–108.

Atwood, M. (1996) *Alias Grace*, London: Bloomsbury.

Barlow, J. (1961) *Burden of Proof*, London: Hamish Hamilton.

Baronne, T. (1995) 'Persuasive Writings, Vigilant Readings and Reconstructed Characters: The Paradox of Trust in Educational Storytelling', in Hatch, J. and Wisniewski, R. (eds) *Life History and Narrative*, London: Falmer: 63–74.

Barthes, R. (1966) 'Introduction to the Structural Analysis of Narratives', in Sontag, S. (1982) (ed.) *A Barthes Reader*, New York: Hill and Wang.

Barthes, R. (1977) 'The Death of The Author', in *Image-Music-Text*, Glasgow: Fontana/Collins (Originally published in French, 1968).

Bauman, Z. (1991) *Modernity and Ambivalence*, Cambridge: Polity.

Bauman, Z. (2006) *Liquid Fear*, Cambridge: Polity.

BBC 1 (2006) 'When Satan comes to Town', *Panorama*, 6 January 2006.

Beck, U. (1992) *Risk Society*, London: Sage Publications.

BERA (2004) 'Revised Ethical Guidelines for Educational Research', available at www.bera.ac.uk/guidelines.html (accessed 3 October 2009).

Bochner, A. and Ellis, C. (1998) 'Series Editors' Preface', in Banks, A. and Banks, S. (eds) *Fiction and Social Research: By Ice or Fire*, Walnut Creek: AltaMira: 7–8.

BPS (2006) *Code of Ethics and Conduct*, available at http://www.bps.org.uk/the-society/code-of-conduct/code-of-conduct_home.cfm (accessed 1 February 2009).

Bradley, A. (1994) 'A Morality Play For Our Times', *Living Marxism*, 63, January 1994.

Brooks, L. (2006) *The Story of Childhood: Growing up in Modern Britain*, London: Bloomsbury.

Bruner, J. (1985) *Actual Minds, Possible Worlds*, Cambridge MA: Harvard University Press.

Bruner, J. (1993) 'The Autobiographical Process', in Folkenflik, R. (ed.) *The Culture of Autobiography: Constructions of Self Representation*, Stanford CA: Stanford University Press: 215–35.

BSA (2002) *Statement of Ethical Practice for the British Sociological Association*, available at http://www.britsoc.co.uk/equality/Statement+Ethical+Practice.htm (accessed 1 February 2009).

Burgess, R. (ed.) (1989) *The Ethics of Educational Research*, Lewes: Falmer Press.

Butler, P. (2009) 'Main Headline', *The Guardian*, 7 February 2009: 1–2.

Butler-Sloss, E. (1988) *Report of the Inquiry into Child Abuse in Cleveland 1987*, London: HMSO.

Campbell, B. (1987) 'The Hounding of Dr Higgs', *New Statesman*, 31 July 1987, London.

Campbell, B. (1988) *Unofficial Secrets*, Reading: Virago Press.

Canella, G. and Lincoln, Y. (2007) 'Predatory vs Dialogic Ethics: Constructing an Illusion or Ethical Practice as the Core of Research Methods', *Qualitative Inquiry*, 13(3): 31–353.

Canella, G. and Viruru, R. (2004) *Childhood and Postcolonization: Power, Education and Contemporary Practice*, New York: RoutledgeFalmer.

Cavanagh, S. (2007) *Sexing the Teacher: School Sex Scandals and Queer Pedagogies*, Vancouver BC: University of British Columbia Press.

Chase, S. (2005) 'Narrative Inquiry: Multiple Lenses, Approaches, Voices', in Denzin, N. and Lincoln, Y. (eds) *The Handbook of Qualitative Research Third Edition*, Thousand Oaks: Sage: 651–79.

Children, Families and Schools Select Committee Inquiry (2009) *Allegations Against School Staff*, available at http://www.parliament.uk/parliamentary_committees/csf/csfpn010409.cfm (accessed 1 May 2009).

Clandinin, D. and Connelly, F. (1994) 'Personal Experience Methods' Inquiry', in Denzin, N. and Lincoln, Y. (eds) *The Handbook of Qualitative Research*, Thousand Oaks: Sage: 413–27.

Clough, Patricia (1992) *The Ends of Ethnography*, London: Sage.

Clough, Peter (2002) *Narratives and Fictions in Educational Research*, Maidenhead: Open University Press.

Cohen, S. (1972) *Folk Devils and Moral Panics: The Creation of the Mods and Rockers*, Oxford: Blackwell.

Corbin, J. and Holt, N. (2005) 'Grounded Theory', in Somekh, B. and Lewin, C. (eds) *Research Methods in the Social Sciences*, London: Sage: 49–55.

Cowburn, M. and Dominelli, L. (2001) 'Masking Hegemonic Masculinity: Reconstructing the Paedophile as the Dangerous Stranger', *British Journal of Social Work*, 31: 399–415.

Cummings, D. (2006) 'A Full Stop to Moral Panic', *Spiked online*, available at http://www.spiked-online.com/index.php?/site/article/154/ (accessed 20 February 2009).

Dawson, A. (1994) 'Professional codes of practice and ethical conduct', *Journal of Applied Philosophy*, 11(2): 145–53.

Denzin, N. (1997) *Interpretative Ethnography: Ethnographic Practices for the 21st Century*, Thousand Oaks: Sage.

Denzin, N. (2003) *Performance Ethnography, Critical Pedagogy and the Cultural Politics of Change*, Thousand Oaks: Sage.

Denzin, N. and Lincoln, Y. (2005) 'Introduction: The Discipline and Practice of Qualitative Research', in Denzin, N. and Lincoln, Y. (eds) *The Sage Handbook of Qualitative Research: Third Edition*, Thousand Oaks: Sage: 1–32.

DfES (2004a) *Proposals for Dealing with Allegations against Teachers and Other Staff: A Consultation*, London: DfES.

DfES (2004b) *Definitions and Thresholds for Managing Allegations Against Education Staff*, London: DfES.

DfES (2004c) *Thresholds for and Alternatives to Suspension*, London: DfES.

DfES (2004d) *'Walking Tall'* – *More Support For Schools to Tackle Bad Behaviour*, available at http://www.dfes.gov.uk/pns/DisplayPN.cgi?pn_=2004_0196 (accessed 9 August 2007).

Donal MacIntyre Show 14 September 2008, available at http://www.bbc.co.uk/programmes/b00df56q (accessed 20 March 2009).

Drum, K. (2009) Sex offenders in our schools. *Mother Jones*, Available at http://www.motherjones.com/kevin-drum/2009/05/sex-offenders-our-schools (accessed 20 May 2009).

Ecclestone, K. and Hayes, D. (2009) *The Dangerous Rise of Therapeutic Education*, Oxon: Routledge.

Edemariam, A. (2009) 'In her first interview since being dismissed as head of Haringey's children's services over the Baby P case, Sharon Shoesmith tells her side of the story', *The Guardian*, 7 February 2009: 4–6.

Ellis, C. and Bochner, A. (2000) 'Autoethnography, Personal Narrative, Reflexivity', in Denzin, N. and Lincoln, Y. (eds) *The Handbook of Qualitative Research: Second Edition*, Thousand Oaks: Sage: 733–65.

England and Wales Court of Appeal (Civil Division) (2007) Case of 'Mezey vs South West London and St George's Mental Health NHS Trust', available at http://www.bailii.org/ew/cases/EWCA/Civ/2007/106.html (accessed 20 March 2009).

ESRC (2005) *Research Ethics Framework*, available at http://www.esrc.ac.uk/ESRCInfoCentre/Images/ESRC_Re_Ethics_Frame_tcm6-11291.pdf (accessed 29 January 2009).

Every Child Matters website, available at http://www.everychildmatters.gov.uk/ (accessed 23 March 2009).

F.A.C.T. *About Us*, available at http://www.factuk.org/Page3.aspx (accessed 12 January 2009).

Feldman, S. and Marks, V. (2005) *Panic Nation*, London: John Blake.

File on 4, 3 March 2009, available at http://news.bbc.co.uk/1/hi/education/7919663.stm (accessed 21 March 2009).

Fine, M., Weiss, L., Wesen, S. and Wong, L. (2000) 'For Whom? Qualitative Research, Representations and Social Responsibilities', in Denzin, N. and Lincoln, Y. (eds) *Handbook of Qualitative Research: Second Edition*, Thousand Oaks: Sage: 107–31.

Frith, H. (2000) 'Focusing on Sex: Using Focus Groups in Sex Research', *Sexualities*, 3(3): 275–97.

Furedi, F. (1994) 'A Plague of Moral Panics', *Living Marxism*, 73, November, available at www.informin.co.uk/LM/LM73?LM73_Franf.html (accessed 6 March 2008).

Furedi, F. and Bristow, J. (2008) *Licensed to Hug: How Child Protection Policies are Poisoning the Relationships Between the Generations and Damaging the Voluntary Sector*, London: Civitas.

Gatto, C. (2009) Fitzgerald v. Barnstable School Committee: Parallel discrimination claims under Title IX & Section 1983. *The Suffolk Lawyer*, 25(8), 6+.

Giddens, A. (1991) *Modernity and Self-Identity*, Cambridge: Polity Press.

Gilbert, R., Kemp, A., Thoburn, J., Sidebotham, P., Radford, L., Glaser, D. and MacMillan, H. (2009) 'Recognising and Responding to Child Maltreatment', *The Lancet*, 373 (9658): 167–80.

Gill, T. (2007) *No Fear: Growing Up In A Risk Averse Society*, London: Calouste Gulbenkian Foundation.

Goodchild, S. and Barrett, C. (2004) 'Innocent Families Hit By Anti-Paedophile Vigilante Mobs', *Independent OnLine*, available at http://www.independent.co.uk/news/uk/crime/innocent-families-hit-by-antipaedophile-vigilante-mobs-535406.html (accessed 4 April 2009).

Goode, E. (2000) 'Moral panic: changing concepts of the child molester in modern America', *Sociological Forum*, 15: 543–52.

Goode, E. and Ben-Yehuda, B. (1994) *Moral Panics: The Social Construction of Deviance*, Oxford: Blackwell.

Goodson, I. (1997) 'The educational researcher as a public intellectual', The Lawrence Stenhouse Memorial Lecture, British Educational Research Association, University of York.

Goodson, I. and Sikes, P. (2001) *Life History Research in Educational Settings*, Buckingham: Open University Press.

Guardian (2009) *Leader Comment, Punishing Times*, 7 February 2009: 40.

Hall, S. and Jefferson, T. (1976) (eds) *Resistance Through Rituals*, London: Hutchinson.

Hall, S., Critcher, C., Jefferson, T. and Roberts, B. (1978) *Policing the Crisis: Mugging, the State and Law and Order*, London: Macmillan.

Halse, C. and Honey, A. (2007) 'Rethinking Ethics Review as Institutional Discourse', *Qualitative Inquiry*, 13(3): 336–52.

Hammersley, M. (2008) 'Against the Ethicists: On the Evils of Ethical Regulation', *International Journal of Social Research Methodology*, 1–14, first article available at http://www.informaworld.com.libezproxy.open.ac.uk/smpp/content~content=a901809266~db=all~order=pubdate (accessed 15 January 2009).

Hansard (1 April 2009) Column 1015 Debate about Nick Cousins instigated by Paul Goodman, available at http://www.publications.parliament.uk/pa/cm200809/cmhansrd/cm090401/debtext/90401-0019.htm (accessed 20 April 2009).

Hatty, S.E. (2000) *Masculinities, Violence, and Culture*, London: Sage.

Herring, D. (2008) *Major Enquiry (East Riding Schools) 2006/07*, available at www.erscb.org.uk (accessed 24 December 2008).

Hier, S.P. (2003) 'Risk and Panic in Late Modernity: Implications of the Converging Sites of Social Anxiety', *British Journal of Sociology*, 54(1): 3–20.

HM Government (1989) *The Children Act*, London: TSO.

HM Government (2003) *Every Child Matters*, London: TSO.

HM Government (2006) *Working Together to Safeguard Children: A guide to inter-agency working to safeguard and promote the welfare of children*, London: TSO.

Hobbs, C. and Wynne, J. (1986) 'Buggery in Childhood: A Common Syndrome of Child Abuse', *Lancet*, 2: 792–6.

Homan, R. (1991) *The Ethics of Social Research*, London: Longman.

Home Affairs Select Committee (2002) 'Investigations into Past Abuse in Children's Homes', available at http://www.publications.parliament.uk/pa/cm200102/cmselect/cmhaff/836/83602.htm (accessed 14 January 2009).

Hume, M. (2006) 'Who will vet the vetters and protect my children from fear and mistrust?', *Times Online*, 20.01.06., available at http://www.timesonline.co.uk/tol/comment/columnists/mick_hume/article715875.ece (accessed 24 February 2009).

Humphries, L. (1970) *Tearoom Trade: A Study of Homosexual Encounters in Public Places*, London: Duckworth.

Hyvarinen, M. (2007) 'Revisiting the Narrative Turns', paper presented at ESRC Seminar *Narrative Turn: Revisioning Theory*, University of Edinburgh, 23 March 2008.

Independent Safeguarding Authority (2009), available at http://www.isa-gov.org.uk/Default.aspx?page=385 (accessed 21 April 2009).

Innocence Network UK, available at http://www.innocencenetwork.org.uk/index.htm (accessed 27 April 2009).

James, M. (1999) *'That'll Teach You!'*, East Molesey: Recognition Publishing.

Johnson, T.S. (2008a) *From Teacher to Lover: Sex Scandals in the Classroom*, New York: Peter Lang.

Johnson, T.S. (2008b) 'Qualitative Research in Question: A Narrative of Disciplinary Power With/in the IRB', *Qualitative Inquiry*, 14(2): 212–32.

Jones, A. (ed.) (2001) *Touchy Subject: Teachers Touching Children*, Dunedin, New Zealand: Otago University Press.

Jones, A. (2004) 'Social Anxiety, Sex, Surveillance and the "Safe" Teacher', *British Journal of Sociology of Education*, 25(1): 153–166.

Jones, J. (1981) *Bad Blood: The Tuskegee Syphilis Experiment*, New York: Free Press.

Kincaid, J. (1992) *Child Loving: The Erotic Child and Victorian Culture*, New York and London: Routledge.

Kincaid, J. (1998) *Erotic Innocence: The Culture of Child Molesting*, Durham and London: Duke University Press.

Kushner, S. (2006) 'A Lament for the ESRC', *Research Intelligence*, 94, February: 9–11.

Kvale, S. (2008) *Interviews: Second Edition: Learning the Craft of Qualitative Research Interviewing*, Thousand Oaks: Sage.

La Fontaine, J.S. (1994) *The Extent and Nature of Organised and Ritual Abuse: Research Findings*, United Kingdom Department of Health Report. London: HMSO Publications.

La Fontaine, J.S. (1998) *Speak of the Devil: Tales of Satanic Abuse in Contemporary England*, Cambridge: Cambridge University Press.

Lather, P. (2004) 'This *IS* Your Father's Paradigm: Government Intrusion and the Case of Qualitative Research in Education', in Satterthwaite, J., Atkinson, W. and Martin, W. (eds) (2004) *The Disciplining of Education: New Languages of Power and Resistance*, Stoke on Trent: Trentham Books: 21–36.

Leader, D. (2009) 'Talking Therapy', *The Guardian*, 9 April 2009: 32.

Lee, R. (1993) *Doing Research on Sensitive Topics*, London: Sage.

Lepkowska, D., Smith, N. and Stewart, W. (2003) 'Colleagues Stress Us Out, Say Staff', *Times Educational Supplement 5*, December: 3.

Lewis, A. (2008) 'Man Killed "Was Mistaken For A Paedophile"', *St Albans and Harpenden Review*, available at http://www.stalbansreview.co.uk/news/2284851 (accessed 7 January 2009).

Lewis, J. (1987) 'Judge Unites Two Cleveland Families', *The Guardian*, 31 July 2009.

Lincoln, Y. (2005) 'Institutional Review Boards and Methodological Conservatism: The Challenge to and from Phenomenological Paradigms', in Denzin, N. and Lincoln, Y. (eds) *The Sage Handbook of Qualitative Research: Third Edition*, Thousand Oaks: Sage: 165–181.

Lincoln, Y. and Denzin, N. (1994) 'The Fifth Moment', in Denzin, N. and Lincoln, Y. (eds) *The Handbook of Qualitative Inquiry*, Thousand Oaks: Sage: 575–86.

Lynd, R.S. and Lynd, H.M. (1929) *Middletown: A Study in Contemporary American Culture*, New York: Harcourt, Brace, and Company.

Lynd, R.S. and Lynd, H.M. (1937) *Middletown in Transition: A Study in Cultural Conflicts*, New York: Harcourt, Brace, and Company.

MacLure, M. (2003) *Discourse in Educational and Social Research*, Buckingham: Open University.

Marshall, K. (2004) *'Names Can Never Hurt Me': Does Naming Suspects Help Children?* McLintock Lecture, available at http://www.sccyp.org.uk/webpages/speeches.php (accessed 23 March 2009).

Marshall, K. (2005) *The Power to Abuse and the Power to Accuse: Implications of Shifts in the Balance of Fear*, Annual Research Collections Lecture, Glasgow Caledonian University, 29 November 2009, available at http://www.sccyp.org.uk/webpages/speeches.php (accessed 23 March 2009).

McRobbie, A. (1995) *Post Modernism and Popular Culture*, London: Routledge.

Mertens, P. and Ginsberg, P. (eds) (2008) *The Handbook of Social Research Ethics*, Thousand Oaks: Sage.

Midgely, C. (2006) 'Our Stolen Childhood', *Times Online*, 10 January 2006. available at http://www.timesonline.co.uk/tol/life_and_style/article786662.ece (accessed 3 February 2009).

Mills, C.W. (1970) *The Sociological Imagination*, Penguin: Harmondsworth (first published in 1959 by Oxford University Press).

Mills, M., Martino, W. and Lingard, B. (2004) 'Attracting, Recruiting and Retaining Male Teachers: Policy Issues in the Male Teacher Debate', *British Journal of Sociology of Education*, 25(3): 355–69.

Moustakis, C. (1990) *Heuristic Research: Design, Methodology and Applications*, Newbury Park: Sage.

Murray, J. (2009) 'Jobs for the Boys', *Guardian Online*, available at http://guardian.co.uk/education/2009/mar/31/primary-school-teachers (accessed 19 April 2009).

Myers, K. with Clayton, G., James, D. and O'Brien, J. (2005) *Teachers Behaving Badly: Dilemmas for School Leaders*, London: RoutledgeFalmer.

NASUWT (24 April 2003) 'Campaign to Protect Teachers from Malicious Allegations' available at http://www.teachersunion.org.uk/Templates/internal.asp?NodeID=69333 (accessed 16 July 2006).

NASUWT (9 June 2004) 'Petition for Anonymity for Teachers facing Malicious Allegations to be presented to House of Commons' available at http://www.teachersunion.org.uk/Templates/internal.asp?NodeID=70839 (accessed 16 July 2006).

NASUWT (19 February 2009) 'Malicious Allegations' available at http://209.85.229.132/search?q=cache:VdmgnP4SmOUJ:www.teachersunion.org.uk/Templates/Internal.asp%3FNodeID%3D70201%26ParentNodeID%3D43074+nasuwt+malicious+allegationsandcd=1andhl=enandct=clnkandgl=uk (accessed 23 March 2009).

Nathan, D. and Snedeker, M. (1995) *Satan's Silence*, New York: Basic Books.

Naughton, M. (2007) 'Confronting An Uncomfortable Truth: Not All Victims of Alleged False Accusations Will Be Innocent!' *Faction*, 3(10): 8–11.

Nind, M., Rix, J., Sheehy, K. and Simmons, K. (eds) (2005) *Ethics and Research in Inclusive Education*, London: RoutledgeFalmer.

Oakley, A. (1981) 'Interviewing Women: A Contradiction in Terms', in Roberts, H. (ed.) *Doing Feminist Research*, London: Routledge and Kegan Paul: 30–61.

O'Neill, B. (2008) 'Paedophile scares are always driven by the elite', *Spiked-online*, available at http://www.spiked-online.com/index.php?/site/article/5168/ (accessed 7 May 2009).

Pazder, L. and Smith, M. (1980) *Michelle Remembers*, US: Pocket Books.

Pelias, R. (2004) *A Methodology of the Heart*, Walnut Creek: AltaMira.

Phoenix, A. (2009) 'Enabling Research? Silencing and Recognition in Social Research', in Satterthwaite, J., Piper, H. and Sikes, P. (eds) *Power in the Academy*, Stoke on Trent: Trentham Books: 61–78.

Piper, H. (2003) 'The Linkage of Animal Abuse With Interpersonal Violence: A Sheep in Wolf's Clothing?', *Journal of Social Work*, 3, 2: 161–77.

Piper, H. and Smith, H. (2003) 'Touch in educational and child care settings: dilemmas and responses', *British Educational Research Journal*, 29(6): 879–94.

Piper, H. and Stronach, I. (2008) *Don't Touch: The Educational Story of a Panic*, Oxon: Routledge.

Piper, H., MacLure, M. and Stronach, I. (2006) *Touchlines: The Problematics of Touching between Children and Professionals,* ESRC funded project RES-000-22-0815. available at http://www.esrcsocietytoday.ac.uk/ESRCInfoCentre/ViewAwardPage.aspx?AwardId=3451 (accessed 10 May 2009).

Piper, H., Powell, J. and Smith, H. (2005) 'Parents, Professionals and Paranoia: The Touching of Children in a Culture of Fear', *Journal of Social Work*, 34(2): 151–67.

Piper, H. and Scott, C. (2006) *Battle in Print: 'Does Every Child really Matter – has the abuse panic gone too far?*, available at http://www.battleofideas.co.uk/C2B/document_tree/ViewADocument.asp?ID=274andCatID=42 (accessed 29 April 2909).

Plummer, K. (1995) *Telling Sexual Stories: Power, Change and Social Worlds*, London: Routledge.

Plummer, K. (2000) *Documents of Life 2: An Invitation to a Critical Humanism*, London: Sage.

Polkinghorne, D.E. (1988) *Narrative Knowing and the Human Sciences*, Albany: SUNY Press.

Porter Abbott, H. (2002) *The Cambridge Introduction to Narrative*, Cambridge: Cambridge University Press.

Porter Abbott, H. (2005) *The Cambridge Introduction to Narrative: Second Edition*, Cambridge: Cambridge University Press.

Pring, R. (2000) *Philosophy of Educational Research*, London: Continuum.

Prison Rules/YOI Rules Relating to Segregation, available at http://pso.hmprisonservice.gov.uk/pso1700/Prison%20Rules.htm (accessed 14 January 2009).

Punch, M. (1986) *The Politics and Ethics of Fieldwork*, Beverley Hills: Sage.

Rachel Nickell available at http://en.wikipedia.org/wiki/Rachel_Nickell (accessed 26 December 2008).

Rambo, C. (2007) 'Handing IRB an Unloaded Gun', *Qualitative Inquiry*, 13, 3: 353–67.

Reavey, P. and Warner, S. (eds) (2003) *New Feminist Stories of Child Sexual Abuse: Sexual Scripts and Dangerous Dialogues*, London and New York: Routledge.

Redfern, M. (2001) *The Royal Liverpool Children's Inquiry Report*, London: TSO.

Redwood, S. (2008) 'Practitioner Enquiry, Ethics and the Postmodern Detective' (unpublished paper given at DPR Conference, 2007, Manchester. Abstract available at http://www.esri.mmu.ac.uk/dpr_08/abstracts_08/abstract_profile.php?id=105) (accessed 5 February 2009).

Revell, P. (2007) *Guilty by Accusation: a research paper presented for discussion at the NAHT Conference*, paper presented at the NAHT Conference, Bournemouth.

Ricoeur, P. (1980) 'Narrative Time', *Critical Enquiry*, 7: 160–80.

Richardson, L. (1990) *Writing Strategies: Reaching Diverse Audiences*, Thousand Oaks: Sage.

Richardson, L. (1994) 'Writing: A Method of Inquiry', in Denzin, N. and Lincoln, Y. (eds) *The Handbook of Qualitative Research*, Thousand Oaks: Sage: 516–29.

Richardson, L. (2000) 'Writing: A Method of Inquiry', in Denzin, N. and Lincoln, Y. (eds) *The Handbook of Qualitative Research: Second Edition*, Thousand Oaks: Sage: 923–48.

Richardson, L. (2003) 'Poetic Representations of Interviews', in Gubrium, J. and Holstein, J. (eds) *Postmodern Interviewing*, London: Sage: 187–201.

Riessman, C. (1993) *Narrative Analysis*, London: Sage.

Riessman, C. (2003) *Narrative Analysis*, Thousand Oaks: Sage.

Riessman, C. (2008) *Narrative Methods for the Human Sciences*, Thousand Oaks: Sage.

Roseman, S. (1998) (ed) *The Public Papers of Franklin D. Roosevelt, Volume Two: The year of Crisis, 1933*, New York: Random House: 11–16.

Rudrum, D. (2005) 'From Narrative Representation to Narrative Use: Towards the Limits of Definition', *Narrative*, 13(2): 195–204.

Said, E. (1995) *Orientalism: Western Conceptions of the Orient*, London: Penguin.

Satterthwaite, J., Watts, M. and Piper, H. (eds) (2008) *Talking Truth Confronting Power*, Stoke on Trent: Trentham.

Saunders, T. (2008) *Paying for Pleasure: Men Who Buy Sex*, Cullompton: Willan.

Scott, C. (2003) 'Ethics and Knowledge in the Contemporary University', *Critical Reviews in International Social and Political Philosophy*, 6(4): 93–107.

Scott, C. (2006) 'A little knowledge is a dangerous thing', *Spiked! online*, 02.03.06, available at http://www.spiked-online.com/index.php?/site/article/224/ (accessed 20 June 2008).

Shakeshaft, C. (2004) *Educator Sexual Misconduct: A Synthesis of Existing Literature*, (ED-02-PO-3281) Washington, DC: US Department of Education.

Shweder, R. A. (2004) 'Tuskegee re-examined', *Spiked*, available at http://www.spiked-online.com/Articles/0000000CA34A.htm (accessed 19 January 2009).

Sikes, P. (2000) '"Truth" and "Lies" Revisited', *British Educational Research Journal*, 26(2): 257–70.

Sikes, P. (2006a) 'Scandalous Stories and Dangerous Liaisons: When Male Teachers and Female Pupils Fall in Love', *Sex Education*, 6(3): 265–80.

Sikes, P. (2006b) 'On Dodgy Ground? Problematics and Ethics in Educational Research', *International Journal of Research and Method in Education*, 29, 1: 105–17.

Sikes, P. (2006c) 'A Cautionary Tale Concerning Journalists and Moral Panic', *Research Intelligence*, 95: 4–6.

Sikes, P. (2008) 'At the Eye of the Storm: An Academic(s) Experience of Moral Panic', *Qualitative Inquiry*, 14(2): 235–53.

Sikes, P. (2009) 'Will the Real Author Come Forward? Questions of Ethics, Plagiarism, Theft and Collusion in Academic Research', *International Journal of Research and Method in Education*, 32(1): 13–24.

Sikes, P. and Piper, H. (2008) 'Risky Research or Researching Risk? The Real Role of Ethics Review', in Satterthwaite, J., Watts, M. and Piper, H. (eds) *Talking Truth Confronting Power*, Stoke on Trent: Trentham: 51–65.

Silverman, D. (1998) *Qualitative Research: Theory, Method and Practice*, London: Sage.

Simons, H. and Usher, R. (eds) (2000) *Situated Ethics in Educational Research*, London: Routledge/Falmer.

Simpson, A. (2009) 'More Than a Quarter of England's Primary Schools Have No Male Teachers', *Telegraph Online*, available at http://www.telegraph.co.uk/education/educationnews/5033012/more-than-a quarter-of Englands-primary-schools-have-no-male-teachers.html (accessed 10 May 2009).

Simpson, Mike, available at http://en.wikipedia.org/wiki/Mike_Simpson_(writer) (accessed 21 January 2009).

Skelton, C. (2003) 'Male Primary Teachers and Perceptions of Masculinity', *Educational Review*, 55(2): 195–209.

Smith, B. (2002) 'The (In)visible Wound: Body Stories and Concentric Circles of Witness', *Auto/Biography*, 10(1): 113–21.

Smith, J. and Hodkinson, P. (2005) 'Relativism, Criteria and Politics', in Denzin, N. and Lincoln, Y. (eds) *The Sage Handbook of Qualitative Research: Third Edition*, Thousand Oaks: Sage: 915–32.

Song, J. (2009) Accused of sexual abuse, but back in the classroom. *Los Angeles Times*. Retrieved Available at http://www.latimes.com/news/local/la-me-teachers10-2009may10,0,1620156, full.story (accessed 20 May 2009).

Sparkes, A. (1995) 'Physical Education Teachers and the Search for Self: Two Cases of Structured Denial, in Armstrong, N. (ed.) *New Directions in Physical Education: 3*, London: Cassell: 157–78.

Sparkes, A. (2003) 'Men, Sport, Spinal Cord Injury and Narrative Time', *Qualitative Research*, 3, 3: 295–320.

Sparkes, A. (2007) 'Embodiment, Academics and the Audit Culture', *Qualitative Research*, 7(4): 521–50.

Staines, R. (2009) 'Nurses' human rights were breached under POVA scheme, Law Lords rule,' *Nursing Times*, 27.1.09, available at http://www.nursingtimes.net/whats-new-in-nursing/nurses%E2%80%99-human-rights-were-breached-under-pova-scheme-law-lords-rule/1975700.article (accessed 6 May 2009).

Stanley, E. (1992) *The Auto/biographical I: Theory and Practice of Feminist Auto/biography*, Manchester: Manchester University Press.

Teacher Support Network (2008) *Support Through False Allegations*, available at http://www.teachersupport.info/support-this-work/testimonials/john.php (accessed 19 March 2009).

Tierney, W. and Blumberg Corwin, Z. (2007) 'The tensions between academic freedom and institutional review boards', *Qualitative Inquiry*, 13(3): 388–98.

Todorov, T. (1977) *The Poetics of Prose*, New York: Cornell University Press.

Troyna, B. (1994) 'Blind Faith? Empowerment and Educational Research', *International Studies in the Sociology of Education*, 4(1): 3–24.

Tuhiwai Smith, L. (1999) *Decolonizing Methodologies: Research and Indigenous Peoples*, London: Zed Books.

Ungar, S. (2001) 'Moral Panic Versus the Risk Society: The Implications of the Changing Sites of Social Anxiety', *British Journal of Sociology*, 52(2): 271–91.

Van Hasselt, V.B. and Hersen, M. (1999) (eds) *Handbook of Psychological Approaches with Violent Offenders: Contemporary Strategies and Issues*, New York: Plenum.

Van Maanen, J. (1988) *Tales of the Field*, Chicago: University of Chicago Press.

Victor, J.S. (1993) *Satanic Panic: The Creation of a Contemporary Legend*, Illinois: Open Court Press.

Wachter, C. A., and Lee, R. (2009) 'Sexual assault and sexual abuse', in Jackson Cherry, L. and Erford, B. (eds.). *Crisis Intervention*, Pearson/Merrill Prentice Hall.

Waller, W. (1932) 'Preface' in *The Sociology of the Teacher*, New York: John Wiley.

Waterhouse, R. (1990) 'The making of a satanic myth', *Independent on Sunday*, 12 August 1990: 8–9.

Webster, R. (1998) 'Satanic Abuse and McMartin: A Global Village Rumour', *New Statesman*, 27 February 1998.

Webster, R. (2005) *Bryn Estyn: The Making of a Modern Witchhunt*, Oxford: Orwell Press.

Williams, E. (2004) 'False Accusations', *Times Educational Supplement*, 20 February: 11–14.

Woolf, V. (1992) 'Mr Bennett and Mrs Brown', in Woolf, V. and Bowlby, R. (eds) *A Woman's Essays*, London: Penguin.

Young, J. (1971) *The Drugtakers: The Social Meaning of Drug Use*, London: Paladin.

Zero Tolerance, available at http://www.factuk.org/about-us/zero-tolerance/ (accessed 27 April 2009).

Index